ROME

Contents

the magazine 5

Finding Your Feet 27

The Ancient City 43

The Heart of Rome 75

Written by Tim Jepson
Additional research by Sara Liney

Updated by Tim Jepson

American editor Tracy Larson

Edited, designed and produced by AA Publishing
© Automobile Association Developments Limited 2006, 2008
Maps © Automobile Association Developments Limited 2006, 2008

Published in the United States by AAA Publishing,
1000 AAA Drive, Heathrow, Florida 32746-5063
Published in the United Kingdom by AA Publishing

ISBN-13: 978-1-59508-243-5

Cover design and binding style by permission of AA Publishing
Color separation by Keenes, Andover
Printed and bound in China by Leo Paper Products

10 9 8 7 6 5 4 3 2 1

A03183

the magazine

Rome is over 3,000 years old: that's a lot of history and a lot of myth. Intimidating? Not really – you probably know more about both than you think. Do Spartacus, crossing the Rubicon, the rape of Lucretia, or Romulus and Remus mean anything? And what about Rome's Seven Hills, Antony and Cleopatra, the Ides of March? The chances are you know the names but can't quite place the story, so here is a checklist of myths and well-known historical incidents that Rome has given the world.

Myth & History

The Seven Hills

Nothing mythical here: Rome's celebrated hills exist to this day, although they're smaller than you might expect and have been all but obliterated by modern building. Rome probably began life as a farming village on one of the hills, the Capitolino (Capitoline), which provided a safe refuge above the marshes of the River Tiber. By the 9th century BC, there were probably villages on all the remaining hills: the Aventino, Caelio, Esquilino, Palatino, Quirinale and Viminale.

The Rape of Lucretia

Rome was probably ruled in its earliest days by Etruscan kings, as part of a civilisation that prospered across much of central Italy from about the 8th century BC. According to the historian Livy (59 BC–AD 17), the event that precipitated the overthrow of the

The Colosseu seen from the Aventino, the most souther of Rome's original Seve Hills

ruscan dynasty and the
establishment of Roman inde-
pendence occurred in 507 BC,
when Lucretia, a respectable
Roman matron, was raped by
Sextus, son of Tarquinius, the
Etruscan ruler. Racked with
shame, Lucretia committed
public suicide, prompting a
mob of outraged Romans to
chase Tarquinius from the
city. The Roman republic was
proclaimed the same day.

Spartacus

In 82 BC, a conservative army
general, Sulla, gained control
of Rome during a period of
political instability. He sub-
jected the city to a brutal
dictatorship that led – among
other things – to an uprising
of some 70,000 slaves and
dispossessed farmers under
the command of a gladiator,
Spartacus. The revolt was put
down, Spartacus died in battle

Below: Symbol
of the city –
the she-wolf
suckling
Romulus and
Remus, Rome's
legendary
founders

Romulus and Remus

Rome probably began life as a hilltop village some 1,200 years before the birth of
Christ, but for most people the myth of its origins – the story of Romulus and
Remus – is far more interesting.

The way the Roman historian Livy tells it, the story begins in a place called Alba
Longa, the capital of a tribe known as the Latins. Its ruler, Numitor, had been
usurped by his brother, Amulius who, to prevent any rival claimants to his throne,
forced Numitor's only daughter, Rhea Silvia, to become a Vestal Virgin (► 54).

Rhea, however, became pregnant through the attentions of the god Mars, and
gave birth to twins, Romulus and Remus. Amulius had the twins cast adrift in a
basket, only for the gods to guide them to the safety of the Velabrum, a marshy area
on the banks of the Tiber. Here they were found and suckled by a she-wolf – you'll
see statues recording the event across the city – before being adopted by a shepherd. In later life, Mars appeared to the twins and told them it was their destiny to
found a city, which – in 753 BC, according to legend – they duly did.

Unfortunately, both Romulus and Remus wished to rule the new city. Worse,
neither could agree on a name for their domain: Remus wanted Rema,
Romulus preferred Roma. They

decided to invoke
the gods to help settle
the dispute. Remus saw
six vultures over his
chosen hill, but
Romulus saw twelve of
the same birds over his
refuge, and he marked
a line around it using a
plough. Remus,
incensed, jumped over
the line and was
killed by his
brother – not
an auspicious
start.

at Lucania and 6,000 of his followers were crucified on the Via Appia Antica, the Roman road that leads south from the city to this day.

Crossing the Rubicon

Julius Caesar, then just an army general, brought his troops back to Italy from campaigns in northern Europe in 49 BC. En route he crossed the Rubicon, a river in northern Italy. In doing so, he deliberately broke a law that forbade returning armies to travel beyond the river without permission from the Senate, the body that ruled the Roman republic. Faced with Caesar's challenge to its authority, the Senate's power crumbled and its members fled on his return to Rome. A year later Caesar became the absolute ruler of Rome.

"Beware the Ides of March"

Why? Because the Ides, the 15th day of the month in the Roman calendar, was the day in March 44 BC that a jealous clique in the Roman Senate murdered Julius Caesar. The conspirators included Brutus, Caesar's adopted son.

Beware *the Ides of March*

Julius Caesar was murdered by a jealous clique in the Senate

Antony and Cleopatra

Famous names, but who were they? After Julius Caesar's murder, control of the Roman Empire was divided among three leaders: Lepidus, Mark Antony and Octavius (Caesar's grand nephew). Antony and Octavius became the dominant players, but Antony compromised his chances of total power by repeated absence from Rome in the arms of Cleopatra, the queen of Egypt. Octavius concentrated on building up his military strength, and defeated Antony in 31 BC. Antony and Cleopatra both committed suicide; Octavius changed his named to Augustus Caesar and became the first true Roman emperor.

Antony and Cleopatra's love affair was infamously played out by Richard Burton and Elizabeth Taylor

What's in a Word

Rome has given the English-speaking world a host of words and phrases which are still in common use.

Asylum The word comes from an area of sanctuary in the early days of Rome, between the twin peaks of the Capitoline Hill.

Bread and circuses Coined by the Roman satirist Juvenal (CAD 55–140) to mock the indolence of a Roman populace who had sold their freedoms for the trivial entertainments of the Colosseum.

Caesarean Legend claims Julius Caesar was the first person to be born by "caesarean" section, hence the present-day name for this operation.

Capitol Capitol Hill and the Capitol Building derive from the Capitolino, one of Rome's seven Hills and the site of the city's earliest citadel.

Forum The Roman Forum gave us forum, but also – directly or indirectly – words such as censor, census, civic, committee, dictator, forensic, plebiscite, pontiff, pontificate, suffrage, and many more.

Money Comes from the Latin moneta, which in turn comes from the Temple of Juno Moneta on the Capitoline Hill, where some of the first Roman coins were minted.

Nepotism From the Italian nipote, meaning nephew, because medieval popes often gave favoured positions to their "nephews" (many of whom were actually their sons).

Palace Derives from "Palatino", after the large houses built by Roman emperors and others on the Roman hill of the same name.

Republic Comes from res publica, used after the 5th century BC to describe Rome, where in theory the state was literally the thing (res) or concern of the "public" (publica).

Rostrum From the bronze prows of ships (rostra) captured by the Romans and used to adorn the platforms of orators in the Roman Forum.

Rome's streets are its curse and its salvation. Many were built for horses and carts, and prove horribly ill suited to the demands of a modern city. Some are grand papal thoroughfares, others – like Via dei Fori Imperiali – the result of Fascist megalomania.

The 64 Bus

One of the best ways to explore Rome's tight labyrinth of central streets is to walk (▶ 180–182). Another is to take a bus, and one bus in particular – the infamous number 64. Rome's bus numbers change all the time: one year the number 27 takes you to the Colosseum, the next it's the 81. But the 64 – for now at least – seems immune to bureaucratic meddling; the 64 is a way of life.

Jump aboard and you'll be following in the footsteps of millions before you. Why? Because the 64 plies one of Rome's seminal routes, starting in the sprawl of buses outside Termini, Rome's central railway station, and then struggling through the heart of the city before arriving at the most majestic destination any bus could hope for – St Peter's Basilica.

The route is a battle for bus and passenger alike. The confrontation starts at Termini, where the arrival of each new bus is the cue for an assault by Romans and tourists on three fronts – the bus's trio of doors. No quarter is given, and no such thing as a queue has ever been known to form. Give as good as you get – shove, push and jostle with elbows to the fore if you want to get aboard, never mind find a seat. Hold back for just a short time and you'll be left standing – probably on the pavement.

Once aboard, you become part of a close-knit band. Often too close-knit, for

Rome's police officers (left) often fight a losing battle against the city's traffic Right: Via Condotti

Crossing a Roman Street

Crossing the street in Rome is no easy matter unless you know one salient fact: cars are supposed to stop or slow down to let you cross. The secrets of success are never to dither – stride purposefully through gaps in the traffic – and never to look as if you might blink first or back down in that decisive encounter between you and the leading car. If in doubt, walk in the slipstream of a Roman crossing ahead of you.

Bus Tour

The number "110 Open" open-top bus tour lasts 2 hours (daily every 20 minutes 8:40am–8:20pm) from outside Stazione Termini. There are ten other pick-up and drop-off points. It visits over 80 sites of historic and artistic interest, stopping at sights such as the Colosseum and St Peter's. Tickets are available from the ATAC kiosk in Piazza dei Cinquecento (Marciapiede C)or on the bus. Stop & Go tickets (currently €13) allow you to get on and off. For information and bookings, tel: 041 4695 2252 or toll-free in Italy 800 281 281 (daily 9–8) or visit www.trambusopen.com

Piazza Venezia, where you should look out for the police officer directing traffic with almost balletic poise. Then it's a stop-start shunt down the busy Corso Vittorio Emanuele II, with hordes of passengers trying to board what is invariably an already full bus at Torre di Largo Argentina and points west. When you cross the river you know that St Peter's – and relief – is almost at hand.

the 64 is notorious for the occasional stray hand; Roman women won't stand for this, turning round to hurl a well-aimed insult at the presumed perpetrator. Hands can also find their way elsewhere – watch out for pickpockets and keep an eye on your valuables.

Forewarned, you can then enjoy the fray. Look at the bus windows. Are they open or shut? If they are shut, that means it's not yet summer – whatever you might think and whatever the weather. Some of the locals who often guard the windows seem to have some mysterious and unspoken sense of when the season turns: one day the windows are shut, the next they are open. And they will stay that way – summer showers aside – until the collective decides autumn has come. Don't dare open or close them on your own account.

Stay aboard to the bitter end and you will rumble down Via Nazionale and into

Below: A good trick in a tight squeeze – parking in Rome is legendary

Bottom: Via Appia Antica, an old Roman highway

BAROQUE

Pearls

you knew little about baroque architecture before you visited Rome, there is no doubt you will know, or have seen, a great deal more by the time you leave. Countless buildings across the city are arrayed in this most extravagant of architectural styles, the result – in the main – of papal munificence and the work of two larger-than-life architects.

No one has been able to come up with a decent definition of baroque, or a totally convincing explanation of where the word might come from. The person who has perhaps come closest was the Italian writer and journalist Luigi Barzini. Noting that the word may derive from large, irregularly shaped pearls – still known as *perle baroche* in Italian – Barzini observed that the word came to be

At San Carlo alle Quattro Fontane baroque master Francesco Borromini showed his disregard for convention

used metaphorically to describe "anything pointlessly complicated, otiose, capricious and eccentric".

This goes some way to describing the architectural style that succeeded the Romanesque (simple lines and rounded arches) and Gothic (soaring spaces and pointed arches). So fully did the style sweep all before it in Rome that there is barely a building that escaped its transforming touch.

One reason for the transformation was money, for the popes were rich and keen to spend lavishly; another was the buoyant spirit of the times, and the air of self-confidence engendered by the success of the Counter-Reformation, the Roman Catholic response to the rise of Protestantism across northern Europe.

Two architects of contrasting outlook dominated Rome's baroque heyday – Gian Lorenzo Bernini and Francesco Borromini – and both owe their fame and success to the largesse of three prominent popes: Urban VIII (pope from 1623 to 1644), Innocent X (1644–55) and Alexander VII (1655–67).

Bernini and Borromini

Bernini (1598–1680) was born in Naples but settled with his family in Rome at the age of seven. He would live and work in the city for the rest of his life. A youthful prodigy and near universal genius, he was an accomplished painter and poet as well as an architect and sculptor. His fame as a sculptor was already secure by his early twenties, thanks to virtuoso works such as *David*

and *Apollo and Daphne* (► 113 and 129), the first major sculptures executed in Italy since the days of Michelangelo almost a century earlier. He went on to take charge of work on St Peter's and designed countless major Roman monuments, notably Piazza Navona's Fontana dei Quattro Fiumi (► 15 and 83), and Piazza San Pietro; smaller masterpieces such as the church of Sant'Andrea al Quirinale are also scattered across the city.

Borromini (1599–1667) was born near Lake Lugano in

northern Italy. He came to Rome in 1619, where he obtained work as a stone-carver on the new St Peter's. In time, he became Bernini's chief assistant at St Peter's, but the two shared an uneasy relationship. Borromini – who was a consummate craftsman – despised what he saw as Bernini's

Detail from Sant'Andrea della Valle

Left: Gian Lorenzo Berni

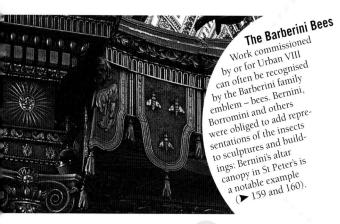

The Barberini Bees

Work commissioned by or for Urban VIII can often be recognised by the Barberini family emblem – bees. Bernini, Borromini and others were obliged to add representations of the insects to sculptures and buildings: Bernini's altar canopy in St Peter's is a notable example (► 159 and 160).

Five Great Works of Art

Apollo and Daphne One of several Bernini statues in which marble is almost made flesh; this is arguably the artist's masterpiece ► 113 and 129.

Baldacchino You may not like Bernini's altar canopy in St Peter's basilica, but you can't help but be impressed by its colossal scale ► 159 and 160.

Cappella Cornaro Bernini's chapel in Santa Maria della Vittoria is a triumph of colour, illusion, lighting, perspective and sublime sculpture ► 132.

Fontana dei Quattro Fiumi Bernini's grandiose fountain occupies pride of place in Piazza Navona, one of the grandest stages in the city ► 83.

Fontana di Trevi No one is sure who dreamt up Rome's loveliest fountain – Bernini may have been involved – but the result is a triumph ► 124–125.

technical shortcomings. The two parted company for good in 1634.

Where Bernini was joyous, outgoing and self-confident, his chief and most jealous rival was a lonely, neurotic and tortured individual who may have suffered from schizophrenia. Introspective and frustrated, Borromini was eventually driven to suicide – possibly by what he saw as his failure to secure the commissions he deserved. At the same time, he was the more innovative and iconoclastic architect. In churches such as Sant'Ivo alla Sapienza and San Carlo alle Quattro Fontane he produced buildings in which strangeness and skill combine to dazzle architects to this day.

Builders and Barbarians

Pope Urban VIII, one of the baroque's chief patrons, belonged to the Barberini, an important Roman family who razed or altered so many of the city's buildings to make way for their own creations that the Romans coined a famous pun: *Quod non fecerunt barbari, fecerunt Barberini* – "What was not done by the barbarians was done by the Barberini."

Secrets and Oddities

Macabre decoration in Santa Maria della Concezione

Rome is a city fuller than most of the weird and wonderful. Many of its more unusual sights are connected with death – notably the catacombs – or are the sometimes strange consequences of religion. Others are not so much bizarre as secret, unusual places seen by few visitors: here are some of the best to whet your appetite.

A Way With Bones

One of the city's most bizarre sights lurks inside the 17th-century church of Santa Maria della Concezione. In its crypt lie the skeletons and loose bones of some 4,000 Capuchin monks, strange enough on their own; stranger still is the way many of the bones have been used to create chandeliers and beautifully crafted decorative patterns. Monks were originally buried here in soil brought from Jerusalem. When this ran out, they were left in the open, a practice that continued until as recently as 1870. *Santa Maria della Concezione, Via Vittorio Veneto 27 (tel: 06 487 1185). Crypt open daily 9–noon, 3–6. Donation*

Secret Keyhole

Rome's most charming view can be enjoyed from Piazza dei Cavalieri di Malta – a square designed by Giovanni Piranesi – on the Aventine Hill southwest of the Colosseum. To find it, walk to the left of the church of Santa Sabina as you face it (the church and the gardens to its right are lovely places in their own right). Continue to the end of the piazza and look through the keyhole of the huge door of the Priory of the Knights of Malta (No 3). Through the tiny hole you see a secret garden and an avenue of trees cleverly framing…but let's not spoil the surprise: see for yourself.

Wall of Horrors

Here's a departure from the mosaics and refined paintings of many of Rome's churches.

Above: The frescoes decorating the circular walls the 5th-century church of Santo Stefano Rotondo portray many grisly martyrdoms

Frescoes in the church of Santo Stefano Rotondo portray all manner of grisly martyrdoms, their subjects described by an enthralled Charles Dickens during a visit in the 19th century: "Grey-bearded men being boiled, fried, grilled, crimped, singed, eaten by wild beasts, worried by dogs, buried alive, torn asunder by horses, chopped up with small hatchets: women having their breasts torn off with iron pincers, their tongues cut out, their ears screwed off, their jaws broken, their bodies stretched on the rack, or skinned on the stake, or crackled up and melted in the fire – these are among the mildest subjects."

Santo Stefano Rotondo, Via di Santo Stefano Rotondo 7 (tel: 06 421199 for information). Currently closed for restoration.

Going Underground

Burial within the city limits was forbidden to all but emperors in ancient Rome. As a result the city has some 300km (186 miles) of catacombs, the burial place of pagans, Jews and – above all – early Christians. Most date from between the 4th century BC and 1st century AD, and consist of long passages and chambers filled with niches used to inter the linen-wrapped bodies. Some have larger chambers, often the resting places of saints or martyrs. Many were cleared when the long-forgotten catacombs were rediscovered in the 9th century. Many relics were removed to St Peter's and other churches, but it was not until the 16th century that the catacombs' full extent was realised.

The most visited catacombs lie close together near the Via Appia Antica. These are the catacombs of Domitilla, San Sebastiano and San Callisto. Other catacombs are less well known but often even more atmospheric: try

the Catacombe di Priscilla on the city's northern fringes, or the smaller catacombs below the church of Sant'Agnese fuori le Mura, a short way southeast of the Catacombe di Priscilla. The church and its near neighbour, Santa Costanza, are worth a visit for their superb early mosaics. Note that a moderate admission fee is charged to all the catacombs below.

Catacombe di Domitilla, Via delle Sette Chiese 282 (tel: 06 511 0342, www. catacombe.domitilla.it). Mon, Wed–Sun 8:30–noon, 2:30–5:30 (5, in winter). Closed Jan

Catacombe di San Sebastiano, Via Appia Antica 136 (tel: 06 785 0350). Mon–Sat 8:30–noon, 2:30–5:30. Closed mid-Nov to Feb

Catacombe di San Callisto, Via Appia Antica 110 (tel: 06 5130 1580, www.catacombe.roma.it). Thu–Tue 8:30–noon, 2:30–5:30 (5, in winter). Closed Feb

Catacombe di Priscilla, Via Salaria 430 (tel: 06 8620 6272, www.catacombedipriscilla.com). Tue–Sun 8:30–noon, 2:30–5. Closed Jan

Catacombe di Sant'Agnese, Via Nomentana 349 (tel: 06 861 0840, www.santagnese.org). Tue–Sat 9–noon, 4–6, Mon 9–noon

ow: The acombs at Callisto are largest in city with e 20km miles) of eries and 0,000 burial ces

ht: Ancient oration in Catacombe Jomitilla

The image is a familiar one: trattoria tables scattered outdoor children running riot between courses, and heaped plates of spaghetti arriving to appreciative exclamations. Trams rumb in the background and Papà talks women and football, while Mamma keeps a steady eye on proceedings.

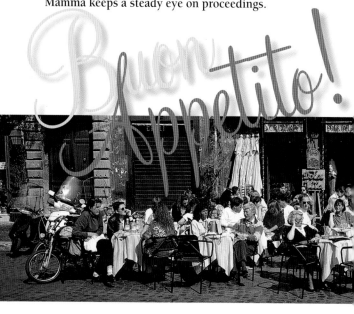

Buon appetito!

At least, this is how we think it is done, and it's the image Federico Fellini gave us in films such as *Roma*. Yet these days the old image is not always the reality of eating in Rome. True, you can still find the odd humble trattoria of popular imagination, and on a summer Sunday Campo de' Fiori and similar delightful outdoor locations around the city still play host to families tucking into their ritual lunchtime feasts.

The old Felliniesque vignettes are increasingly a fading memory, however – restaurants and eating out in Rome have moved on as they have in many European and other culinary capitals. But if the traditional atmosphere of eating out has changed, then the quality and variety of the food on offer, not to mention

the types of places to dine out, have improved beyond recognition.

Once, eating out in Rome was almost cheaper than cooking for yourself at home. A rickety chair, a rough wooden table and a plate of fresh pasta – plus a flask of Frascati – was all a Roman wanted and all a visitor could get. Then came the 1980s and rampant expense accounts, resulting in a rash of luxurious and ludicrously over-priced restaurants.

Between the extremes of traditional trattoria and top-price restaurant, Rome has recently seen the emergence of predominantly young, stylish eating places where the food – often lighter and more innovative than in the past – takes centre stage. Furthermore, restaurant

Dining alfres is one of the greatest pleasures of summer in Rome

Snails are eaten on the festival of San Giovanni

interiors now increasingly eschew the unsophisticated paintings and wicker-wrapped wine bottles of traditional

Awful Offal

The most traditional Roman specialities include tripe (*trippa*), oxtail braised in celery broth (*coda alla vaccinara*), strips of cartilage (*nervetti*), brain (*cervello*) – delicious with peas – the pancreas and thyroid glands (*animelle*), and *pajata*: baby veal's intestines with the mother's milk still inside (cooked in lard for added effect). And how about *lingua* (tongue), *guanciale* (pig's cheek) and *insalata di zampa* (hoof jelly salad)? You'll need a strong stomach!

trattoria decor in favour of light, airy dining rooms and decorative grace notes of stone, glass and steel.

If the notion of modernisation fills you with dread, if you want to eat in Rome as you imagine the Romans eat, all is not lost. There are still old places, still pizzerias and authentic bars for stand-up

snacks. And eating in Rome will always have an atmosphere that is all its own, if only because the surroundings, especially outdoors on a balmy summer's evening, are so magical.

As with almost any Italian city or region, Rome has a plethora of culinary specialities that set it apart from the gastronomic mainstream. Among these are the widely available *saltimbocca alla Romana* (veal with ham and sage) and *bucatini all'Amatriciana* (pasta with a hot tomato and pancetta sauce). Other culinary influences include those introduced over the centuries by the city's Jewish population – restaurants in the old Ghetto and elsewhere serve wonderful and otherwise little known dishes such as deep-fried artichokes, pasta and chickpea broth, and *minestra d'arzilla* (ray fish soup).

Rome has other specialities that you will not necessarily want to try. Traditional Roman cooking is based on the *quinto quarto* – the so-called "fifth quarter", or what is left of an animal when everything that would normally be considered edible has been stripped from the carcass. This penchant for the obscure originally had little to do with taste, and everything to do with the huge old slaughterhouse in the Testaccio district – where offcuts went to workers and led to recipes that made use of the "perk" – and to poverty, long the culinary mother of invention in what for centuries was a mostly impoverished city. In practice this meant – and still means – menus filled with items that might startle even the most adventurous diner.

Buon Appetito!

A SNAPSHOT OF ROME

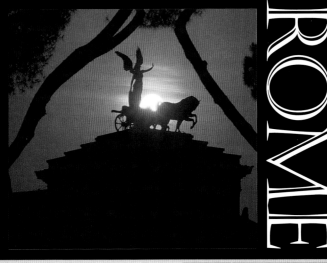

One of the greatest pleasures of exploring Rome is the number of times you stumble across hidden corners, wonderful viewpoints, evocative street scenes and telling vignettes of daily life.

Rome's Best

Best Views

Some of Rome's best views are obvious – the panorama from the dome of St Peter's (► 161), the view of the Forum from behind Piazza del Campidoglio (► 55) and the view of the city from Viale Trinità dei Monti (► 183–184). Others are the views from the Gianicolo Hill above Trastevere or the ramparts of Castel Sant'Angelo (► 165). Best of all is the "secret" view through the keyhole in Piazza dei Cavalieri di Malta (► 16).

Above: Campo de' Fiori

Best Ice-cream

No dispute here: the **Gelateria di San Crispino** is currently Rome's best source of ice-cream (► 138). An honourable mention goes to the chocolate chip *tartufo* of the **I Tre Scalini** (► 108).

Best Bus Rides

The **64 bus** between Termini and St Peter's will give you one of Rome's most distinctive rides (► 10–12). Otherwise, step aboard the **110 Open bus** for a special sightseeing tour of the city (► 11).

Right: Rome's most macabre altar lies in the church of Santa Maria della Concezione

est of the Bizarre

he decoration using human ones in the church of **Santa aria della Concezione** ► 16) is pretty memorable, are the shops selling church stments and other religious hemera on Via dei Sediari.

est Cakes and Coffee

ost Romans think **Tazza Oro** near the Pantheon pro-uces the city's best cup of offee (► 94). For great cakes d pastries, visit **Bernasconi** iazza Benedetto Cairoli 16, l: 06 6880 6264) just off Via renula, or **Dagnino** (Galleria sedra, Via Vittorio E rlando 75, tel: 06 481 8660), a old-fashioned Sicilian atisserie with wonderful 950s decor.

Best Markets

For local colour, nothing beats **Campo de' Fiori** (► 80–81), but for serious shopping Romans head to the covered market near **Piazza Vittorio Emanuele** (► 139–141). **Porta Portese** is the best flea market (► 41).

Best Green Spaces

The **Colle Oppio** park northeast of the Colosseum is a pleas-ant place to sit, stroll or snooze (but avoid at night), and is more central than the bigger **Villa Borghese.** The Palatine Hill also has lovely gardens, but you need to pay to enjoy them (► 51). Lesser-known oases include the small gardens off Via del Quirinale towards Via Piacenza, Villa Celimontana (► 70) and the Orto Botanico in Trastevere (► 98).

Spoiled for choice in Piazza Vittorio Emanuele market

One of the statues on the approaches to Castel Sant'Angelo

Did You Know?

Proclaiming a Pope

There used to be three ways the cardinals convened in the Sistine Chapel to elect a pope: acclamation, in which divine intervention caused all the cardinals to call a single name; by majority vote, where votes are cast four times daily until a candidate secures a two-thirds majority (the method still used); and by compromise, where the recommendation of a committee is accepted.

Devil's Advocate

The Vatican still has an office for what used to be called the "Avvocato del Diavolo", or Devil's Advocate, from which the expression in general use originally derives. Its purpose is to investigate the lives of individuals who are being considered for sainthood to discover reasons why he or she should not be canonised.

Population

Rome's population in the middle of the 2nd century was probably around 1.25 million, the greatest of any city until the 19th century. The Roman Empire as a whole numbered about 65 million, or 20 per cent of the world's then population. At the last count (2001), the population was 2,546,804, including 65,000 more men than women.

Mystery Tomb

The right-hand wall of the portico to the church of San Marco off Piazza Venezia (▶ 66) contains the tomb of Vannozza Cattenei, mistress of the infamous Borgia pope, Alexander VI, and mother of Lucrezia and Cesare Borgia. The tomb used to be in Santa Maria del Popolo, but was moved here in complete secrecy – no one knows when, why or by whom.

The Swiss Guard

The Swiss Guard are the pope's official bodyguards. They are traditionally recruited from Switzerland's four predominantly Catholic cantons. Each must be between 19 and 25, at least 1.75m (5 feet 9 inches) tall, and unmarried during his tour of duty. Their distinctive uniforms were designed by Michelangelo in the colours of the Medici popes – red, yellow and blue.

Humble Reminder

Emperors and generals, returning to Rome after military victories, were followed in their triumphal procession to offer thanks to the Capitol's deities by a slave who whispered: *respice post te! Hominem esse te memento* – "remember that you are but a man."

Deathly Portents

A monument to Pope Sylvester II in San Giovanni in Laterano (▶ 64) is said to sweat and make the sound of rattling bones before the death of a pope.

End of the World?

The church of San Paolo fuori le Mura contains a nave mosaic with portraits of all the popes from St Peter onwards. According to Roman legend, the world will end when there is no room for another portrait; there are just seven spaces left after Benedict XVI.

Finding Your Feet

First Two Hours

Arriving at Fiumicino Airport

Scheduled international and internal flights land at Rome's main airport, Leonardo da Vinci (central line: 06 65951; international flight information 06 6563 4956; www.adr.it), more usually known as Fiumicino after its nearest village. The airport lies 36km (22 miles) southwest of the city centre.

- The airport (open 24 hours daily) has two main **terminal complexes**: international departures (*Partenze Internazionali*) and international arrivals (*Arrivi Internazionali*), and linked domestic departures (*Partenze Nazionali*) and domestic arrivals (*Arrivi Nazionali*). The international terminal is divided into two: arrivals is on the lower floor, departures on the floor above: stairs, lifts and escalators link the two.
- Facilities in arrivals include foreign exchange desks (*cambio*), automated exchange and cash machines, a small bar and a branch of the EPT, or Rome tourist board (daily 8:15–7).
- Avoid all taxi and hotel touts who approach you in the airport, even those who appear simply to be offering general help. Keep a close watch on your luggage at all times.

Getting to Central Rome by Public Transport

- The best way to get from the airport to the city centre is the **express rail service** to Rome's main railway station, Stazione Centrale Giovanni Paolo II more commonly known by it's previous name "Termini". For information or onward travel from Termini ► 31–33. Trains depart from a dedicated rail terminal situated close to the main international terminal – look for the raised covered walkway from the main terminal building. It can also be reached via an underpass from the arrivals hall or by walking across the road and coach parking area from outside the arrivals terminal.
- **Tickets** (€€€) for the express rail service can be bought from automatic machines in the arrivals terminal and on the station concourse, or from a small ticket office (daily 7:48–2:30, 2:48–9:30) and adjoining "Tabacchi & Giornali" newsagents on the right of the station as you face the platforms. Consider buying a second ticket for your return journey, as there can be long queues at Stazione Termini.
- Tickets **must be validated** at Fiumicino in the small machines at the entrance to the platforms before boarding the train. On your return from Rome you must stamp your ticket in the small yellow or gold machines on each platform immediately before travelling. Failure to do so results in a heavy fine.
- **Express trains depart** between 6:37am and 11:37pm with departures at 7 and 37 minutes past the hour. Journey time to Termini is just over 30 minutes. Be sure to board the right train, as departures from the airport station also link (roughly every 20 minutes) to four other Rome stations: Ostiense, Tuscolana, Tiburtina and Trastevere. The journey time is longer, around 50 minutes, but costs about half the price of the express train. Tickets (€€) can be bought from the same sources as tickets for the express trains (see above).
- During and outside express train hours, a **bus service** runs approximately every two hours (8:30–8:30) from outside the arrivals hall to Tiburtina station and Termini, including four services between 1:15am and 5am. Journey time is about 70 minutes with four stops. Tickets (€€€) can be bought on board or online (www.terravision.it).

blic transport and taxi fares
e following categories have been used to denote prices for transport.
€ under €2 €€ €2–6 €€€ over €6

etting to Central Rome by Taxi
xis from the airport to the city centre are expensive, costing in the region of
0–€50. Journey times to the centre are around 40 minutes, but often take
nsiderably longer because of heavy traffic.

Check the **meter** is set and running before you depart, and note that special
supplements are payable for taxis between Fiumicino and Rome (higher
from Rome to the airport), as well as for items of luggage placed in the
boot, journeys on Sunday, and journeys at night. By law, all surcharges
must be clearly displayed inside the taxi.
Only take rides in **licensed cabs** (generally white or yellow), which wait in a
line just outside the arrivals hall. Never accept the offer of a taxi from
touts, even those who seem to have an "official" badge and uniform.
Prepaid taxis and limousine services can be booked at dedicated desks in
the arrivals hall. These cost about the same or a little more than taxis that
wait outside, and have the advantage that you know exactly how much
you're paying before setting off. They are also usually more comfortable.

r Rental
iving into the city centre is not advised as traffic and parking present enor-
ous problems. The car rental desks at Fiumicino are not in the main arrivals
ll, but are located in the same complex as the airport train station (➤ 28).

rriving at Ciampino Airport
any charter flights and a few European low-cost scheduled flights use
ampino, Rome's second airport (tel: 06 794 941; www.adr.it), which lies
out 15km (9 miles) southeast of the city centre. There are few facilities at
e airport, so it is a good idea to get some euros before you arrive.

etting to the City Centre
Links between Ciampino and the centre by public transport are more
complicated than those from Fiumicino. The easiest approach is by **taxi**,
which costs from about €40.
By public transport, you need to take a COTRAL **bus** (➤ 31) from the
airport forecourt to the Anagnina *Metropolitana* (Metro) station on the Metro
system's Line A (➤ 32). The journey takes approximately 25 minutes.
From here, subway trains link to Termini in about 20 minutes. COTRAL
buses leave from outside the arrivals hall every 30–60 minutes from about
7am to 11pm. Tickets (€€) can be bought from an automated machine in
arrivals or the newspaper stand (*edicola*) in departures.
Easyjet and Ryanair operate their own **shuttle service** from Ciampino to
Termini. Passengers can buy return tickets (€€€) for this coach service at
the exit from arrivals (tel: 06 7949 4572; www.terravision.it).

rriving by Train
Most national and international train services arrive at **Stazione Centrale
Giovanni Paolo II (Termini)** railway station (5am–midnight. Information, tel:
06 6880 4807; www.trenitalia.com).
Some long-distance services, and services arriving at night, terminate at
Ostiense or **Tiburtina** stations, from where the best way into the city centre
at night is by taxi (➤ 33). During the day, you can take a Metro train from
Piramide station close to Ostiense station.

From the Station to Your Hotel

Termini lies on the eastern side of central Rome and it is too far to walk wit
luggage from here to the heart of the old city or to most central hotels. Mon
lavished on a taxi at this point will be well spent.

The station is a haven for pickpockets, so it is vital to keep a close watch
on your luggage and valuables at all times. Never accept offers from any
hotel, taxi or other touts who approach you.

- **Taxis** depart from immediately outside the front of the station building –
  not exit using the side entrances off the central concourse and walkway.
  aware that queues for taxis are often long.
- The open area that serves as central Rome's main **bus terminal** spreads out
  beyond the taxis. Finding your bus in the big and busy area can be an intim
  dating prospect on a first visit. If you do decide to take a bus, however, note
  that you must buy tickets before boarding (➤ 32). You will also have to pay
  supplement for pieces of luggage over a certain (small) size; taking cumber-
  some luggage on buses is frowned upon and difficult as they get very crowde
- Depending on where in the city your hotel is situated, you may be able to
  take advantage of the two **Metro** lines from Termini (➤ 32). These presen
  a less intimidating prospect than the buses. Follow signs from the main
  station concourse for the relevant platforms. The Metro is especially usef
  for hotels north of the Vatican or in the area around Piazza di Spagna.

Tourist Information

- Rome's **main visitor centre** is close to Piazza della Repubblica at Via
  Parigi 5 (tel: 06 3600 4399; www.romaturismo.it). It is open Monday to
  Saturday 8–7. There is also a general "info-tourist" line (tel: 06 8205
  9127, daily 9–7).
- There are also 11 **Tourist Information Points** (PIT) at key tourist locations
  around the city. All are open daily 9–6 (except Termini, which may open
  longer hours). The locations are as follows:

  Via del Corso, Largo Goldoni (tel: 06 6813 6061)
  Castel Sant'Angelo, Piazza Pia (tel: 06 6880 9707)
  Fori Imperiali, Piazza Tempio della Pace (tel: 06 6992 4307)
  Piazza Navona, Piazza delle Cinque Lune (tel: 06 6880 9240)
  Via Nazionale, Palazzo delle Esposizioni (tel: 06 4782 4525)
  Trastevere, Piazza S Sonnino (tel: 06 5833 3457)
  San Giovanni in Laterano, Piazza San Giovanni (tel: 06 7720 3535)
  Santa Maria Maggiore, Via dell'Olmata (tel: 06 474 0995)
  Termini (main hall), Piazza dei Cinquecento (tel: 06 4782 5194)
  Termini, Galleria Gommata, Platform 4 (tel: 06 4890 6300)
  Fontana di Trevi, Via Marco, Minghetti (tel: 06 678 2988)

- For information on **gay and lesbian matters** contact Arci-Lesbica Roma at
  Viale G Stefanini 15 (tel: 06 418 0211; www.arcilesbicaroma.org or
  www.women.it) or Circolo Mario Mieli at Via Efeso 29 (tel: 06 541 3985
  www.mariomieli.org).

Websites

The following websites are useful sources of general information:

- **www.romaturismo.it**
- **www.vatican.va** is the official site of the Vatican
- **www.romeguide.it** provides a general guide to the city's principal
  monuments and most famous sights
- **www.capitolium.org** is the official site of the Forums

Getting Around

Much of central Rome is small enough to explore on foot, but you will probably need to use taxis or public transport at some point during your visit, especially to reach the more outlying sights and for excursions from the city.

The city's transport system has three basic components: **ATAC**, which runs Rome's distinctive buses and trams; **COTRAL**, which operates longer distance (regional) blue buses and the city's two *Metropolitana* underground lines; and **Trenitalia** (or FS, Ferrovie dello Stato), which runs the state railways. Note that COTRAL may also be referred to as Linee Laziali or LiLa.

The network is generally safe, reliable and inexpensive, although Rome's heavy traffic can make travel by bus frustratingly slow. Buses and Metro trains are often crowded, especially at **peak times** – roughly 7:30–9am, 12:30–1:45pm and 7:30–8:30pm. Trains and buses are also uncomfortably hot in high summer.

It is essential to be on your guard against pickpockets on crowded buses. The popular 64 bus between Termini and St Peter's is notorious in this regard.

Public transport and taxi fares
The following categories have been used in this section to denote approximate prices for transport:

€ under €2   €€ €2–6   €€€ over €6

Buses and Trams
ATAC's red-grey, orange or green buses and trams run on a web of routes across the city. The main terminus is outside Termini railway station, which is where you'll find the main **ATAC information kiosk** (open daily 8–6; www.atac.roma.it). Kiosk staff speak English. The main ATAC office is at Via Ostiense 131L (1st floor, tel: 06 4695 2057, Mon–Fri 9–5).

Bus Routes
Relevant bus and tram **route numbers** are given alongside individual sights throughout the book but these may be subject to change. The free *Charta Roma: The Official City-Map* contains up-to-date bus-tram-Metro information for key sights. It is available from visitor centres and tourist information points throughout the city (➤ 30). Alternatively, buy a *Lozzi* transport map (€€€), available from most newspaper stands.

Useful bus services in the city include:

23 San Paolo–Ostiense–Piazza Risorgimento (for the Vatican Museums)
40 Termini–St Peter's. Express with fewer stops than 64
64 Termini–Piazza Venezia–Corso Vittorio Emanuele II–St Peter's
75 Termini–Roman Forum–Colosseum
81 Piazza Venezia–St Peter's–Piazza Risorgimento (for Vatican Museums)
116 Via Veneto–Campo de' Fiori–Piazza Navona
117 San Giovanni in Laterano–Colosseum–Piazza di Spagna–Piazza del Popolo
119 Circular minibus service in the historic centre: Piazza Augusto Imperatore–Piazza della Rotonda (Pantheon–Via del Corso–Piazza di Spagna)

Bus Essentials

- Tickets must be bought before boarding a bus or tram (► Tickets, below).
- You should always **board a bus** by the rear doors (Salita) and exit by the central doors (Uscita). If you have a validated ticket, you may enter at the front doors by the driver. Often buses are too crowded to reach the central doors, in which case it is acceptable – if sometimes difficult – to leave by front or rear doors.
- Route numbers, headstops (capolinea) and main intermediate stops are listed at each bus stop (una fermata) for the direction of travel. Note that the city's one-way system means that outward and return routes may differ
- **Night buses** operate after the main bus, Metro and tram services cease afte about midnight. Most have conductors, and here you are permitted to buy tickets on board.

Tickets

- A ticket (un biglietto) for buses and trams must always be bought in advance of your journey. Inspectors board buses frequently and at random; travelling without a valid ticket incurs a heavy automatic fine. Tickets are sold from automated ATAC machines around the city, and from shops, news-stands, tobacconists (tabacchi) and bars displaying an ATAC sticker.
- Tickets must be **validated** immediately you enter the bus by stamping then in the small orange or yellow boxes at the rear of buses.
- The basic ticket (€) is a timed ticket known as the **Biglietto Integrato a Tempo** (BIT). Ask for "un biglietto per l'autobus per favore" (a ticket for th bus please) and this is what you will be given. It is valid for 75 minutes from the time of validation for any number of bus journeys and one Metro journey. A five-ticket 5BIT-MULTIBIT pass (€€) is also available. It must be validated on each journey.
- The integrated ticket (€€), the **Biglietto Integrato Giornaliero** (BIG), is valid until midnight on the day of first validation across the ATAC and COTRAL network and FS suburban services, except the Fiumicino airport express train. It need only be validated once, on your first journey.
- Also available are integrated three-day (€€€) tickets (BTI) and weekly (CIS and monthly (**Abbonamento Mensile**) tickets (both €€€), but these last two are unlikely to be useful for most casual visitors.

Metro

Rome's simple underground system, known as la Metropolitana, or Metro for short, consists of just two lines, A and B, which intersect at Stazione di Papa Giovanni (Termini). The primarily commuter service serves several key sites in the city centre and provides fast trans-city journeys. Extensions to the system are under construction – though the wealth of archaeological treasure that lie beneath the city's streets inevitably make the process slow.

- Station entrances are marked by a white M on a red background.
- Services run daily about every five to ten minutes from 5:30am to 11:30pm, except Saturday when they stop at 12:30am.
- Buy standard **BIT tickets** from the usual sources (see above) for use on the Metro. Tickets (€) valid for a single Metro journey are also available from machines at Metro stations.
- **Line A** is the most useful for the majority of visitors, linking Termini with stations near Piazza Barberini (Barberini), Piazza di Spagna (Spagna), Piazza del Popolo (Flaminio), the Vatican Museums (Ottaviano–San Pietro and San Giovanni in Laterano (San Giovanni).
- **Line B**, which also runs through Termini, has a useful station (Colosseo) immediately opposite the Colosseum.

axis

licensed Roman taxis generally are white (or very occasionally yellow) and are
identified by a name and number, usually on the outside of the rear door
and/or a plaque inside the car.

Cabs are generally difficult to hail on the street. Instead you should go
to a **taxi stand**, indicated by blue signs with "TAXI" written in white: key
central stands can be found at Termini, Piazza Venezia, Largo di Torre
Argentina, Piazza San Silvestro, Piazza di Spagna and Piazza Sonnino
(in Trastevere).
When you pick up a cab, check that the **meter** is set at zero. As you
set off it will jump to the current minimum fare (€€) for the first 200m
(220 yards) and then rise quickly.
Supplements are charged on Sundays, public holidays, for journeys between
10pm and 7am, for trips to and from Fiumicino, and for each individual
item of luggage larger than 35 by 25 by 50cm (14 by 10 by 20 inches).
All current supplements should be clearly posted on a list inside the cab.
If you suspect the driver has been dishonest, take the cab's name and
number – making it clear to the driver that you are doing this is often
enough to set matters right. Register any complaint with the drivers'
co-operative – the number is displayed in cabs – or, in serious cases, with
the police (► 189).
The best way to be sure of a taxi is to call a **phone cab**. Most operators
speak a little English; or you can ask your hotel to call for you. When you
call, give the address of where you wish to be picked up. The operator will
then give you a taxi-code number (always a geographical location followed
by a number), plus the time you will have to wait: for example, "*Londra
dodici in cinque minuti*" (London 12 in five minutes). Meters run from the
moment a taxi sets off to pick you up.

Phone cab numbers include:
199 106 601 (central line – look for free-phone green "columns" on the
streets)
06 3570
06 4994
06 6645
06 8822

ikes and Scooters

everal outlets rent bicycles and scooters, but it is vital to realise that traffic
 busy and potentially extremely dangerous. However, bicycles are good for
xploring the quieter streets, and the open spaces of the Villa Borghese park.

To rent a **moped** (*motorino*) you must be over 21. Rental requires a credit
card, ID and/or a cash deposit. Helmets are compulsory.
When you rent a **bicycle** it is usual to leave your passport or other ID such
as driver's licence as a deposit.

dmission Charges

he cost of admission for museums and places of interest mentioned in the
xt is indicated by the following price categories.

expensive under €4
oderate €4–7
xpensive over €7

Accommodation

Rome has hundreds of hotels in all price categories. Prices are often rather high for the facilities on offer, however, and good hotels in the mid-range bracket are in short supply. Rooms may be small, even in grand hotels, and noise is a problem just about everywhere. Central options are best, but you need to reserve early to be sure of securing a room.

Grading
Hotels are officially graded from one-star, the simplest accommodation, to five-star (luxury). Grading criteria are complex, but in a three-, four- or five-star hotel, all rooms should have en-suite bathroom, a telephone and a TV. Most two-star establishments also have private bathrooms. Even in the smartest hotels, however, bathrooms may have only a shower (*una doccia*) an no bath (*una vasca*). Always ask to see a selection of rooms – you may be shown the worst first. All-day room service and air-conditioning are rare in all but four- or five-star hotels. Set prices for each room must by law be posted i individual rooms.

Location
In Rome it pays to be in the centre, despite the fact that traffic and other street noise may be worse here. The areas around Piazza Navona or Piazza di Spagna are best. Trastevere is pleasant, but has relatively few hotels. Via Vittorio Veneto (Via Veneto) is also a good, if slightly peripheral, place to stay but has mostly larger and grander hotels. The area around Stazione Termini has the biggest selection of inexpensive hotels, but this is not a pleasant area especially at night, and is some distance from most of the key sights. Hotels north of St Peter's are also inconvenient, but this area is quieter and generall more pleasant than Termini. To reduce noise problems, try to choose a hotel away from main streets, or request a room at the rear or overlooking an internal courtyard.

Reservations
It is advisable to reserve all hotels in advance, especially in high season (Easter and May–September). Reservations should be made by phone and followed by a faxed confirmation. It is also a good idea to reconfirm reservations a couple of days before arrival. Hoteliers are obliged to register every guest, so on checking in you have to hand in your passport. Usually it is returned within a few hours, or on the day of departure. Check-out times range from around 10am to noon, but you should be able to leave luggage at reception for collection later in the day.

Prices
All prices are officially set, and room rates must by law be displayed in the reception area and in each room. Prices for different rooms can vary within a hotel, but all taxes and services should be included in the rate. Hotels often levy additional charges for air-conditioning and garage facilities, while laundry drinks from mini-bars and phone calls made from rooms invariably carry surcharges.

Room rates usually include breakfast (*colazione*), but where breakfast is optional (see rate cards in rooms), it always costs less to eat at the nearest bar. Breakfasts in better hotels are improving – buffets are now more commo – but for the most part *colazione* just means a "continental" breakfast: coffe roll and jam.

Reservation Agencies

If you haven't reserved a room, then *on no account* accept offers of rooms from touts at Fiumicino airport or Termini railway station. Instead, contact **Enjoy Rome**, Via Marghera 8A (tel: 06 445 1843; www.enjoyrome.com), which operates a free room-finding service. Or try the free **Hotel Reservation Service** (tel: 06 699 1000; www.hotelreservation.it; daily 7am–10pm), which has desks at Fiumicino, Ciampino and Termini – the latter is often busy.

Budget Accommodation

Youth Hostel: Ostello del Foro Olimpico (Viale delle Olimpiadi 61, tel: 06 323 6267; www.ostellionline.org)

YWCA (Via Cesare Balbo 4, tel: 06 488 0460; www.ywca-ucdg.it). All welcome.

Sandy (Via Cavour 136, tel: 06 488 4585; www.sandyhostel.com). Dorm hostel-type accommodation.

Suore Pie Operaie (Via di Torre Argentina 76, tel: 06 686 1254). Centrally located, women only. Booking essential.

Price Categories

Price categories below are for double (*una matrimoniale*) or twin (*una camera doppia*) rooms, and are given for guidance only. Seasonal variations may apply, with more reasonable low-season (winter) rates.

€ under €125   **€€** €125–225   **€€€** over €225

Campo de' Fiori €€

This recently renovated hotel could not have a better location, housed as it is in an ochre-coloured *palazzo* close to the central Campo de' Fiori, one of Rome's most colourful and pleasant squares (➤ 80–81). The 27 rooms vary considerably in size and in decoration – most are rather small – but all are clean and appealing. The hotel has a bar but no restaurant, and no lift or air-conditioning. From the roof terrace there are fine views over the city centre.

➕ 194 C2   ✉ Via del Biscione 6
☎ 06 6880 6865; fax: 06 687 6003;
www.hotelcampofiori.com

Celio €€

The three-star Celio appeals on several counts; its intimacy (it has just 19 rooms); its location, which is in a reasonably quiet street close to the Colosseum; and its comfort and aesthetics. All the rooms are tastefully appointed and frescoed with scenes inspired by Renaissance painters.

➕ 202 A4   ✉ Via SS Quattro 35c
☎ 06 7049 5333; fax: 06 7096 6377;
www.hotelcelio.com

Cesari €€–€€€

Opened in 1787, the three-star Cesari has been in the hotel business long enough to get things right, and latterly has maintained its standards through the pleasant efficiency of its staff and regular renovation – the last major overhaul was in 1999. It also has the bonus of a quiet and central position in a hard-to-find little street between the Pantheon and Via del Corso. The 47 rooms are comfortable and have modern decorative touches, as well as TVs and air-conditioning. Prices are mostly at the lowest end of the expensive category.

➕ 195 E4   ✉ Via di Pietra 89/a
☎ 06 674 9701; fax: 06 6749 7030;
www.albergocesari.it

Eden €€€

The five-star Eden ranks among Rome's three or so top hotels for its style, old-fashioned luxury, and a more relaxed atmosphere than many of its stuffier rivals on nearby Via Veneto. It's been an exclusive favourite among celebrities for more than a century, attracting European royalty, and stars of film and stage. Renovation of the 110 rooms and 11 suites in 1994 ensured it reinforced its position as one of the world's great hotels. At the same time it retained its distinctive and sumptuous decoration, enormous rooms (most of them different), antique furniture and marble bathrooms. The Terrazza (➤ 137) restaurant is superb, and there are spectacular views from the roof terrace.

🚪 198 C3 ✉ Via Ludovisi 49
☎ 06 478 121, toll free in Italy 800 820 088; fax: 06 482 1584;
www.hotel-eden.it

Grande Hotel de la Minerva €€€

The Minerva does not yet have the cachet of Rome's other five-star hotels, but none of its upmarket rivals can claim such a central position – immediately behind the Pantheon and church of Santa Maria sopra Minerva. The hotel was first converted by Holiday Inn in the 1980s, but has since left the chain and enjoyed another makeover that has improved still further the 137 rooms and suites and public areas. Service is excellent, the facilities are the equal of – and often superior to – similarly starred hotels, and little can beat the prospect as you step from the hotel's front door.

🚪 195 D3 ✉ Piazza della Minerva 69
☎ 06 695 201; fax: 06 679 4165;
www.hotel-invest.com

Hotel d'Inghilterra €€€

A 19th-century gentleman on the Grand Tour would feel more than at home in the four-star Inghilterra, which has remained the best of Rome's traditional old-world hotels since it opened in 1850. The hotel's aristocratic air comes in part from the building itself, the 15th-century former Palazzo Torlonia, but also from the opulent common areas, period furniture and oriental carpets, precious Neapolitan paintings, and fine collection of prints and pictures. Past guests have included composer Franz Liszt and writer Ernest Hemingway. The atmosphere at the Inghilterra may be too decorous and dignified for some, and not all 88 rooms are as spacious as they could be – those on floors four and five tend to be larger. The position is good, however, in a quiet side street close to the shopping district around Via Condotti.

🚪 195 E5 ✉ Via Bocca di Leone 14
☎ 06 699 811; fax: 06 6992 2243;
www.hotelinghilterraroma.it

In Parione €€

The recently upgraded three-star hotel is one of several hotels, like the Campo de' Fiori (➤ 35) whose small size is more than compensated for by a perfect position close to Campo de' Fiori and the heart of the old city. All 16 rooms are immaculately kept by the charming Italian couple who own the hotel, and all have private bathrooms or shower rooms. There is a small bar but no restaurant. All major credit cards are accepted.

🚪 194 C2 ✉ Via dei Chiavari 32
☎ 06 6880 2560; fax: 06 683 4094;
www.inparione.com

Navona €

Never mind that this hotel only has a one-star rating: its position is unbeatable – just a minute from Piazza Navona; it is in a quiet side street away from the hustle and bustle; the vast majority of its 21 rooms have been renovated to a standard that makes a nonsense of its lowly star rating; and the owners are a friendly Italo-Australian couple who make light of any communication problems.

The poor breakfast is the only drawback (take it in a nearby bar instead) and air-conditioning, if you want it, commands a hefty supplement. Parts of the building, which was built over the ancient Baths of Agrippa, date back to the 1st century AD. English poets Keats and Shelley once occupied the top floor.

Credit cards are not accepted here. If the hotel is full, the owners may suggest you stay in

e smarter, co-owned and slightly
ore expensive Zanardelli hotel just
orth of Piazza Navona.

🏠 194 C3 ✉ Via dei Sediari 8
☎ 06 686 4203; fax: 06 6880 3802;
www.hotelnavona.com

iazza di Spagna €€

e three-star Piazza di Spagna is
ot on the piazza, but in a side
reet near by, a better location
ecause it is considerably quieter.
he attractive old building is covered
 creeper and though its 17 rooms
e not enormous, their facilities are
od: all rooms have air-conditioning, TV and telephones, and a private
athroom. The location, especially if
ou intend to do a lot of shopping,
uld not be better.

🏠 195 E5 ✉ Via Mario de' Fiori 61
☎ 06 679 6412; fax: 06 679 0654;
www.hotelpiazzadispagna.it

inascimento €

his three-star, mid-range hotel
ccupies an old building in an
xcellent central location just to the
est of Campo de' Fiori: it also lies
ose to appealing streets such as Via
ei Branchi Vecchi, Via Giulia and
a del Governo Vecchio. Although its
9 well-equipped rooms may not be
e largest on offer in Rome, all have
een attractively refurbished.

🏠 194 B3 ✉ Via del Pellegrino 122
☎ 06 687 4813; fax: 06 683 3518;
www.hotelrinascimento.com

calinata di Spagna €€€

hat you pay for this three-star
otel might buy you a bigger room
sewhere, but it would take a
onsiderable sum to purchase
 setting quite as romantic – the
otel sits at the top of the Spanish
teps looking down over Keats'
ouse and the Piazza di Spagna.
ome of the 16 traditionally
rnished rooms are small, but
l are charming, as are the old
visting staircases and secret little
of garden.

🏠 195 F5 ✉ Piazza Trinità dei
Monti 17 ☎ 06 679 3006; fax: 06 6994
0598; www.hotelscalinata.com

Smeraldo €

Renovation means that this two-star
hotel has added a modern and
comfortable aspect to a good
location, just a couple of minutes'
walk from the Campo de' Fiori.
Bathrooms are all new, most of the
35 rooms have TV and air-conditioning, and the public spaces are well
presented. Though breakfast is
available, it offers relatively poor
value for money – try one of the
local bars instead.

🏠 194 C2 ✉ Vicolo dei Chiodaroli 9
☎ 06 687 5929; fax: 06 6880 5495;
www.hotelsmeraldoroma.com

Teatro di Pompeo €€–€€€

In Rome you walk through history,
but in this three-star hotel you can
sleep in it as well. On a quiet square
north of Campo de' Fiori, the hotel
occupies the site of the ancient
Theatre of Pompey, which dates
from the 1st century BC. Parts of
the original building can still be
seen in the remarkable rough-stone
vaulted dining-room and elsewhere.
History aside, this is a pleasant
hotel thanks to a welcoming owner,
modest size – just 13 rooms – and
the charm of many of the rooms:
the attic rooms with their beamed
ceilings and terracotta floors are
among the nicest. Rooms have TVs
and air-conditioning.

🏠 194 C2 ✉ Largo del Pallaro 8
☎ 06 6830 0170; fax: 06 6880 5531;
www.hotelteatrodipompeo.it

Trastevere €€

The friendly two-star Trastevere is
the best of only a handful of hotels
in the lively, old-fashioned Trastevere
district (▶ 95–98). Though the 20
rooms are quite small, they have
bright, modern bathrooms, terracotta
floors and wood panelling. Four
private apartments with kitchens
are good value if there are more
than two of you or if you are staying
more than a few nights. It can be
noisy later in the evenings.

🏠 197 E1 ✉ Via Luciano Manara 24
☎ 06 581 4713; fax: 06 588 1016;
www.hoteltrastevere.net

Food and Drink

Eating out is one of Rome's great pleasures. The city has a huge range of restaurants, from humble trattorias to chic hotel dining-rooms. Prices are generally reasonable, and there are plenty of places where you can get inexpensive snacks and sandwiches. In summer – as an extra bonus – it's often possible to eat outside.

Don't be put off by Rome's specialities, many of which require a strong stomach (► 18–19), because most restaurants offer a broad range of famili Italian dishes.

■ Differences between types of restaurants in Italy are becoming increasingl blurred. An *osteria* was once the humblest type of eating place, but now tends to describe new and unstuffy restaurants serving simple, often innovative, food in relaxed surroundings. Anywhere described as a *pizzeria* is likely to be even simpler; it will often serve a few pastas, salads and other dishes as well as pizzas. A *trattoria* is the general name for a traditional and unpretentious restaurant, while *un ristorante* is usually smarter and more expensive. A smart and expensive restaurant in Rome, more tha most cities, does not guarantee good food; often you can eat well in the humblest places.

■ For most of the eating places listed in the guide it is well worth trying to **reserve**, the exception being pizzerias, which rarely take reservations. For the more popular restaurants you may even need to reserve a few days in advance.

■ Menus begin with *antipasti* (hors d'oeuvres), followed by *il primo* (pasta, gnocchi, risotto or soup) and *il secondo* (meat or fish). Vegetables (*il contorno*) or salad (*insalata*) are usually served separately from the *seconc* For dessert you can choose between *il dolce*, *formaggio* (cheese) and *frutt* (fruit). Puddings are often disappointing; buying an ice-cream from a *gelateria* can be a better choice (see panel).
You're not obliged to wade through all the courses on the menu, and none but the top-ranking restaurants should mind if you just have a salad and a plate of pasta, especially at lunch.

Ice-cream Etiquette

Choose whether you want your ice-cream in a cone (*un cono*) or a cardboard cup (*una coppa*). Both come in different sizes, costing from about €1 for the smallest portion to €2.50 or more for the largest. You name your price and then choose flavours from the tubs laid out in front of you – usually you can choose a mixture of one, two or three flavours, even in the cheapest price band. You will usually be offered a topping of optional – and usually free – whipped cream (*panna*).

■ Romans take **lunch** (*il pranzo*) after about 12:30pm and **dinner** (*la cena*) from 8pm. The famous long Roman lunch followed by a lengthy siesta is largely a thing of the past, except on Sunday, which is still an excuse for a big traditional lunchtime meal.

■ **Service** (*servizio*) and *pane e coperto* (bread and cover charge) may bump prices up in all restaurants. Both should be itemised on the bill. If a servi charge is not included, then you should **tip** at your discretion up to about ten per cent: in less expensive places it's enough to round up to the nearest €2.50 or €5.

The **bill** (*il conto*) should be a properly printed receipt. If all you receive is prices scrawled on a scrap of paper then the restaurant is breaking the law and you are entitled to request a proper bill (*una ricevuta*).

ting Cheaply

Many restaurants, especially around Termini railway station, offer a set-price tourist menu (*un menù turistico*), but the quality and quantity of food are often poor.

Keep costs down by drinking **house wine** (*vino della casa*), usually a good white Frascati or similar, available in a quarter-litre (around a half-pint) carafe (*un quartino*) or half-litre (around 1 pint) jug (*un mezzo litro*).

Most bars offer **sandwiches** (*tramezzini*), which are invariably made from the blandest white bread with crusts removed. Far better are *panini*, or filled rolls, which you can often have heated (*riscaldato*).

Pizza by the slice (*pizza al taglio*) is often sold from tiny hole-in-the-wall bakeries, but check the quality of the topping; in the worst places it amounts to no more than a smear of tomato.

A *pasticceria* specialises in cakes and pastries. A *torrefazione* is a bar that also roasts coffee for retail sale.

Best For

To sample the best that Rome has to offer, try the following places

… **Tazza d'Oro** (➤ 94) for coffee

… **La Rosetta** (➤ 108) for fish

… **Gelateria di San Crispino** (➤ 138) for ice-cream

… **Leonina** (➤ 73) for pizza by the slice

… **Agata e Romeo** (➤ 136), **Il Convivio** (➤ 107) or **La Terrazza** (➤ 137) for a romantic meal

… **Bar della Pace** (➤ 108) for people-watching

---

hat to Drink

The first drink of the day is generally **coffee** (see panel below), usually as a cappuccino accompanied by a sweet croissant (*un cornetto*). After lunch or dinner, Italians always drink an espresso, *never* cappuccino.

Coffee Essentials

• *un espresso* (or, more colloquially, *un caffè*) – an espresso coffee (short and black)

• *una doppia* – double espresso

• *un lungo* – espresso with a little more water than usual

• *un macchiato* – espresso with a dash of milk (literally "stained" with milk)

• *un caffè corretto* – espresso with a dash of whisky or other liqueur

• *un cappuccino* – espresso with added frothed milk

• *un caffè latte* – cappuccino with more milk and no froth.

• *un americano* – espresso with lots of hot water added to make a long drink

• *un caffè Hag* – decaffeinated coffee

• *un caffè freddo* – iced coffee. It is usually served with sugar already added. Ask for "*amaro*" if you want it without sugar

• *un cappuccino freddo* – iced milky coffee

- **Tea** (*un tè*) is common, but the Romans take it with lemon (*un tè al limone*) and without milk. If you want tea with milk, ask specifically for *un tè con latte* – sometimes you may have to insist on *latte freddo* (cold milk) otherwise it'll be the warm milk used for cappuccinos.
- **Mineral water** (*acqua minerale*) is widely drunk with meals, either fizzy (*acqua gassata*) or still (*acqua non gassata*). If you want a glass of water in a bar ask for *un bicchiere d'acqua*. If you're happy with tap water – and Rome's water is generally very good – ask for a free *bicchiere d'acqua dal rubinetto* or *acqua normale*.
- Bottled **fruit juice** (*un succo di frutta*) is often drunk at breakfast, and comes in a wide variety of flavours. Freshly squeezed juice is *una spremuta* of either orange (*una spremuta d'arancia*), grapefruit (*...di pompelmo*) or lemon (*...di limone*). Lemon Soda (the brand name), a bitter lemon drink, is another good soft drink.
- **Beer** (*birra*) is generally lager, but darker British-style beer (*birra scura, nera* or *rossa*) is sometimes available. The cheapest way to buy beer is from the keg: ask for *un birra alla spina* and specify the size – *piccola* (small; 20–25cl/6.76–8.5 fluid ounces), *media* (medium; 40cl/13.5 fluid ounces) or *grande* (large; up to a litre/33 fluid ounces). Bottled beers are usually more expensive, except for Italian brands such as Peroni or Nastro Azzurro.
- **Aperitifs** include fortified wines such as Martini, Cinzano and Campari. Note that if you ask for a Campari Soda it comes ready mixed in a bottle; for the real thing ask for *un bitter Campari*. You'll often see people drinking a lurid orange-coloured aperitif – this is the non-alcoholic Crodino. Prosecco, a good white sparkling wine from northeast Italy, is another good *aperitivo*. Gin and tonic is simply *gin e tonica*.

  After dinner, most (male) Romans drink brandy (Vecchia Romagna is the best brand), *limoncello* (lemon-flavoured alcoholic drink), or *amaro*, literally "bitter". The last is the most Italian drink, the best-known brand being the very bitter Fernet Branca: a good and less demanding brand is Averna. Romans may also have *grappa* after a meal, a strong clear *eau de vie*, or sweeter drinks such as the almond-flavoured Amaretto or aniseed-flavoured Sambuca (sometimes served with added coffee bean).

Bar Etiquette

Waiter service at a table costs twice or three times as much as ordering and standing at the bar. Prices for bar service and sitting (*tavola* or *terrazza*) should be listed by law somewhere in the bar. If you do sit down, remember you can occupy your table almost as long as you wish. Ordering at the bar means paying first, which you do by stating your order at the separate cash desk (*la cassa*). After you've paid, the cashier will give you a receipt (*lo scontrino*) which you then take to the bar and present to the bar person (*barista*). If service seems slow, a coin placed on the bar as a tip with your *scontrino* often works wonders. Never try to pay at the bar, and never pay the standing rate and then to try to sit at a table.

Web Guide

For the latest information on restaurants, the following websites may be useful:

www.gamberorosso.it – a site devoted to restaurants and eating out in Rome
www.enjoyrome.com – with information, listings and good web links
www.romaturismo.it – good for general visitor information

Shopping

ome might not be in the same shopping league as London, Paris or
ew York, and even in Italy takes second place to Milan, yet it has plenty
top designer stores, as well as countless specialist shops and many
teresting markets.

The largest concentration of **designer, accessory and luxury goods** shops are
concentrated in the grid of streets surrounding **Via Condotti**, or Via dei
Condotti (➤ 139).
Less expensive clothes and shoe shops line several key streets, notably Via
del Corso – which you'll find packed with shoppers on Saturdays – Via del
Tritone and Via Nazionale. Shoes and clothes generally are good buys, as
are food, wine, accessories such as gloves, leather goods, luxury items and
fine antiques.
Other smaller streets have their own specialities: **antiques and art galleries,**
for example, on Via dei Coronari, Via Giulia, Via del Babuino, Via del
Monserrato and Via Margutta; paper and wickerwork on Via Monterone;
religious ephemera and clothing on Via dei Cestari. Via del Governo Vecchio
or Via dei Banchi Nuovi, for example, are dotted with second-hand stores,
jewellers and small artisans' workshops.
Rome does not offer much in the way of one-stop shopping: there are only
one or two **department stores** in the centre (the best is **La Rinascente**
➤ 140) and no shopping malls.
The city has several fine **markets**, notably the picturesque **Campo de' Fiori**
(➤ 80–81), the bigger and more prosaic covered market in the **Ex-caserma
(barracks) Sani** near Piazza Vittorio Emanuele (this is central Rome's main
market, open Monday to Saturday 10am to 6pm), and the famous Sunday
flea market at **Porta Portese** southwest of the centre near Porta Sublicio in
Trastevere. Porta Portese is reputedly the largest flea market in Europe,
with around 4,000 stalls selling anything and everything, from antiques to
organic food. It becomes extremely crowded by mid-morning, so try to
arrive early (it finishes at 2pm). The market is particularly popular with
pickpockets, so keep a close eye on your belongings at all times.
Most food **shopping** is still done in tiny neighbourhood shops known as
alimentari. These sell everything from olive oil and pasta to basic toiletries.
They usually have a delicatessen counter, where you can have a sandwich
(*panino*) made up from the meats and cheeses that are on display.
Rome shop assistants have a reputation for aloofness, especially in smarter
boutiques. If they pretend you don't exist, ignore them or politely ask for
help: the phrase is *mi può aiutare, per favore?*
Don't be tempted to bargain – **prices are fixed**. Prices may drop in sales:
look for the word "*saldi*".

Opening Times

In the **city centre**, opening times are fast becoming closer to those of
northern Europe, that is, Monday to Saturday 9am to 7 or 8pm. Even those
shops that still close for lunch often close for only an hour or so from 1pm
rather than observing the 1pm to 4pm break of times past.
The vast majority of shops are **closed on Monday morning**. Many food shops
close on Thursday afternoon in winter and Saturday afternoon in summer.
In August many stores close completely for weeks at a time (*chiuso per ferie*
is the tell-tale sign – closed for holidays).

Entertainment

You won't find a great deal of world-class classical music, opera, ballet and other cultural entertainment in Rome, but the city does offer fine jazz and church music, and has a sprinkling of good clubs and live music venues.

Information

- Information on most cultural activities and performing arts can be obtained from the main visitor centre and information kiosks around the city (► 3
- The main **listings** magazine is roma c'è (www.romace.it), an invaluable weekly publication with details of classical and other musical events, theatre, dance, opera, nightclubs, current museum and gallery opening times, shopping, restaurants and much more: it also has a summary of key events and galleries in English at the back. It can be obtained from most newspaper stands and bookstores. The English-language Wanted in Rome (www.wantedinrome.com) is published every other Wednesday.
- If you read some Italian, listings can be found in Time Out Roma (issued on Thursday); Trovaroma, a "what's on" insert in the Thursday editon of La Repubblica newspaper; or daily editions of newspapers such as Il Messaggero (which has a detailed listings supplement, Metro, published on Thursdays).
- Alternatively, contact box offices listed in individual chapters – although sales staff may not speak much English – or keep your eyes peeled for posters advertising events such as small church recitals or one-off concerts

Tickets

Rome does not yet have major one-stop ticket agencies, nor do all venues accept reservations and pre-payment with credit cards over the phone. Often you are obliged to visit individual box offices before a performance. The alternative is to visit a ticket agency such as **Orbis** (Piazza dell'Esquilino 37, tel: 06 474 4776, open Mon–Sat 9:30–1, 4–7:30). They will give you information only over the phone; if you want tickets you must visit in person. Tickets for some classical, jazz and other concerts are also available from Ricordi music stores, of which there are five, and from Hellò Ticket (toll-free in Italy 800 907080; www.helloticket.it).

Nightclubs

- Where nightclubs are concerned, be aware that a popular club one year can lose its following or re-emerge with a facelift and new name by the next.
- Discobars are popular across the city – smaller than clubs but with room to dance as well as drink and talk.
- Long-established **gay bars and clubs** include L'Alibi (► 112). Other clubs such as Piper (► 142) often have gay nights.
- For most clubs **admission prices** are high, but entry often includes the price of your first drink. For tax and other reasons, some clubs or bars define themselves as private clubs, which in practice means you have to fill out a (usually free) membership card. Remember, too, that many clubs close during summer or move to outdoor or seaside locations beyond the city.

Classical Music

The key classical music and opera venues and companies remain fairly fixed, but one area of classical music which is subject to change is the location of the city's various outdoor summer concert cycles. These can be one of the city's best cultural attractions, if only because of the lovely settings. Contact visitor centres for current information.

The Ancient City

Getting Your Bearing

What remains of ancient Rome is not confined to a single ar of the modern city. Buildings and monuments from the era empire and earlier are scattered far and wide, yet the heart the old city – around the Capitoline, Palatine and Esquiline hills – still boasts the largest present-day concentratic of ancient monument

VIA C BATTISTI

VIA D PLEBISCITO

Colonna Traiano **5**

LARGO MAGNANAPOLI

VIA PANISPERNA

Piazza Venezia **1**

Mercati Traianei

VIA DI SAN MARCO

VIA DEI SERPENTI

VIA DEL

Monumento a Vittorio Emanuele II
S Maria in Aracoeli

CAVOUR

VIA

Fori Imperiali **4**

PIAZZA DI SAN PIETRO IN VINCOLI

San Pietro in Vincoli **8**

Capitolino **2**

PIAZZA DEL CAMPIDOGLIO

Palazzo Nuovo **3**

VIA DEGLI ANNIBALDI

FORI IMPERIALI

Pa di Tre

Palazzo dei Conservatori **Musei Capitolini**

Monte E

VIA

Domus Aurea **9**

Foro Romano **6**

Colle Oppio

PIAZZA DEL COLOSSEO

C

LUNG DI PIERLEONI

VIA PETROSELLI

Monte Palatino

SACRA

Colosseo **7**

VI

Arco di Costantino

V DI SAN GREGORIO

CLAUDIA

As such it makes an excellent point from which to start your visit, placing into context much of what you'll see else-where in the city. The itinerary starts where Rome itself probably started, on the Capitoline Hill, close to the busy Piazza Venezia. This piazza is the hub of the modern city, roads leading off from it to the four points of the compass: Via del Corso to the north and Piazza del Popolo; Corso Vittorio Emanuele II to the west and St Peter's; Via IV Novembre to the east and Stazione Termini; and Via dei Fori Imperiali to the south and the Colosseum.

Parco del Celio

Villa Celimontana

Previous page: The Colosseum
Right: Statues of Castor and Pollux, Piazza del Campidoglio

he Capitoline Hill, however, was the
arly focus of the ancient city. From its
opes you can look over and then
xplore the open spaces of the Roman
orum (Foro Romano), the social, politi-
al and mercantile heart of the old Roman
mpire. From here it's only a few steps to
e Colosseum, the greatest of all ancient
oman monuments, and then on to a qui-
er residential area and your first church,
an Clemente, a fascinating historical
ybrid which contains a beautiful
edieval interior, the remains of an older
h-century church, and the partially
xcavated ruins of a Roman temple.

Just a few minutes' walk away stands
San Giovanni in Laterano, Rome's
cathedral church, and among the
most important churches in the
city after St Peter's. In between
times you can take time out in
the park of the Colle Oppio,

0 ———— 250 metres

0 ———— 250 yards

The huge hands in the courtyard of the Palazzo dei Conservatori are always popular with children

VIA

VIALE A MANZONI

VIA EMANUELE

CANA

MERULANA

I IN LATERANO

FILIBERTO

PIAZZA DI SAN GIOVANNI IN LATERANO

IA AMBA ARADAM

12 San Giovanni in Laterano

PIAZZA DI PORTA S GIOVANNI

VIA SANNIO

PIAZZALE APPIO

st a few moments from either the
olosseum or San Clemente. And if you
ill have time to kill, you can retrace
our steps to the Capitoline Hill and
xplore the Capitoline museums, which
e filled with artistic masterpieces from
e Roman era.

Begin your stay in Rome by exploring some of the city's greatest monuments, starting on the Capitoline Hill and moving to the Forum and Colosseum before concluding with two of Rome's most important churches.

The Ancient City in a Day

9:00am

Begin the day by walking to busy **❶ Piazza Venezia** (➤ 66), taking time to admire the colossal Monumento a Vittorio Emanuele II and **❺ Colonna Traiana** (➤ 68). Then climb the shallow ramp of steps near the piazza's southwest corner to Piazza del Campidoglio (below).

9:30am

Explore the lovely church of **Santa Maria in Aracoeli** (➤ 49) and admire the view from the terrace of the Monumento a Vittorio Emanuele II. Then take the lane from the piazza's left-hand corner, admiring the Arco di Settimio Severo, a Roman triumphal arch ahead

10:00am

Follow the steps here down to one of five scattered entrances to the **❻ Roman Forum** (➤ right, 50–55), some of the world's most historic and romantic ruins.

12:30pm

After seeing the Forum you emerge close to the **7 Colosseum** (► right, 56) and **Arco di Costantino** (► 58). You can visit them now or save them for after lunch. You could take a snack lunch in Cavour 313 wine bar (► 72), one of the cafés in the streets east of the Colosseum, a fuller meal in Nerone (► 73), or buy picnic provisions in Via Cavour and head for the Colle Oppio.

1:30pm

Spend time in the **10 Colle Oppio** (► 71), in particular the **9 Domus Aurea** (► 69) – remember that you need to reserve a tour ahead, and look at the Colosseum and Arco di Costantino if you haven't already done so.

3:30pm

Walk a short distance on Via di San Giovanni in Laterano to **11 San Clemente** (► 61–63), in time for when it opens in the afternoon. The church not only has a lovely medieval interior – complete with superb frescoes and early mosaics – but also two fascinating subterranean places of Christian and pagan worship from earlier eras (left).

4:30pm

Make your way along one of the quieter side streets – notably Via dei Santi Quattro Coronati – towards the soaring San Giovanni in Laterano, the cathedral church of Rome and one of the most important places of worship in the city.

5:30pm

Explore **12 San Giovanni in Laterano** (right, ► 64–65), not forgetting its ancient baptistery and cloister, the latter graced with countless superbly decorated columns. Then take a bus or Metro if you don't want to retrace your steps to the Colosseum and Piazza Venezia.

Capitolino

The Capitolino, or Capitoline Hill, is the smallest but most important of Rome's original Seven Hills. Home to Bronze Age tribes as early as the 14th century BC, it formed the city birthplace, eventually becoming the hub of its military, religious and political life. Its history, central position and many sights make it the perfect introduction to the ancient city.

Today, much of the Capitolino has been obscured by the Monumento a Vittorio Emanuele II, the huge white edifice that dominates **Piazza Venezia** (► 66). In earliest times, however, the hill had two distinct crests: one to the north, which was known as the *Arx*, or Citadel, and is now the site of the church of Santa Maria in Aracoeli; and one to the south, known as the *Capitolium*, which is now largely given over to palaces such as the Palazzo dei Conservatori.

Between the two lay the *Asylum*, an area reputedly created by Romulus as a place of sanctuary, the aim being to attract refugees to the fledgling city. Today this area is occupied by **Piazza del Campidoglio**, a square largely laid out by Michelangelo and bounded by Rome's town hall, the Palazzo Senatorio (to the rear), and the Musei Capitolini, or Capitoline Museums, to either side (► 66–67).

Start your visit in Piazza d'Aracoeli. Ignore the steps to Santa Maria in Aracoeli – there's an easier entrance to the church in the piazza above – and climb the shallow stepped ramp (1536), or *cordonata*, in front of you. This was designed by Michelangelo for the triumphal entry of Emperor Charles V into Rome, and

Renaissance frescoes by Pinturicchio i Santa Maria Aracoeli

The equestrian statue of Emperor Marcus Aurelius in the Piazz del Campidoglio

is crowned by two huge Roman statues of Castor and Pollux placed here in 1583. At the heart of the piazza stands a copy of a famous equestrian statue of Emperor Marcus Aurelius – the original is in the Palazzo Nuovo on your left, part of the Capitoline Museums (the rest of the museum is in the Palazzo dei Conservatori on your right).

Head for the space between the Palazzo Nuovo and Palazzo Senatorio, where you'll find steps on the left that take you into **Santa Maria in Aracoeli** (and the entrance to the Monumento a Vittorio Emanuele II ► 66), a church already considered ancient when it was first recorded in AD 574. The church is filled with chandeliers, ancient columns and a beautifully decorated ceiling. It also contains frescoes on the *Life of San Bernardino* (1486) by the Umbrian artist Pinturicchio (in the first chapel of the right, or south, aisle), and the *Tomb of Luca Savelli* (1287), attributed to the Florentine sculptor Arnolfo di Cambio (on the left side of the south transept).

TAKING A BREAK

The Capitoline Museums have a café (entrance on the lane to the right of Palazzo dei Conservatori; no museum ticket required), as does the terrace of the Monumento a Vittorio Emanuele II.

Santa Maria in Aracoeli
✠ 195 F2 ✉ Piazza d'Aracoeli ☎ 06 679 8155 ⑩ Daily 9–12:30, 2:30–5:30 🍴 Cafés in Capitoline Museums and on terraces of Monumento a Vittorio Emanuele II 🚇 Colosseo 🚌 40, 44, 46, 60, 63, 64, 70, 75, 81, 85, 87, 175 and all other services to Piazza Venezia 🎟 Free

---

CAPITOLINO: INSIDE INFO

Top tips Be sure to walk through the passages to the left and right of the Palazzo Senatorio for views over the Roman Forum (► 50–55).

• It is worth visiting the Monumento a Vittorio Emanuele II (tel: 06 699 1718), the entrance to which is rather hidden at the top of the steps that also give access to Santa Maria in Aracoeli. Walk down the short corridor to emerge on the monument's colossal terraces, with superb views of the Fori Imperiali, and an excellent outdoor café. Café and monument open daily 9:30–5:30 (4:30 in winter). Free.

Roman Forum

The Roman Forum (Foro Romano) was the heart of the
Roman Empire for almost 1,000 years. Today, its once might
ensemble of majestic buildings has been reduced almost to
nothing, yet the surviving ruins provide a romantic setting
in which you can still catch a glimpse of the glory that
was Rome.

Exploring the Forum

When exploring the Forum,
it's essential to remember
the site's 3,000-year history,
and the degree to which
monuments over this period
were built, rebuilt, moved,
destroyed, adapted, plundered
or left to fall into wistful ruin.
Be warned, therefore, that
only a handful of structures
such as the Arco di Settimio
Severo or the Basilica di
Massenzio hint at their original size or layout.

    If monuments are all you
seek from the site, you will
probably leave disappointed,
or at best bemused by the
jumble of stones and
columns. The trick here is to
enjoy the beauty and romance
of such ruins, and appreciate
their historical associations:
after all, you are literally
walking in the footsteps of Julius Caesar, Nero, Caligula,
Claudius, Hadrian and countless other resonant names from
antiquity. With this in mind, allow anything up to two hours
to amble around the site, more if you decide to walk up and
see the Palatino.

*Though little
remains of the
Forum's forme
glory (left and
below), it is
still one the
city's most
captivating ar
romantic sites*

Marsh to Majesty

The Forum was not Rome's original heart – that honour probably went to a fortress hamlet on the more easily defended
Capitoline Hill to the northwest. The future hub of the empire
actually began life as the "Velabrum", a marshy inlet of the
Tiber between the Capitoline and Palatine hills. This was the
area that featured in the myth of Romulus and Remus (► 7),
for it was here that the twins were found and suckled by the
she-wolf, and here that Romulus – according to legend –
founded Rome in 753 BC.

During the Iron Age, the area probably served as a cemetery for villages on neighbouring hills, and later as a meeting place, common land and rubbish tip for the shepherds and other inhabitants of these early settlements. It was at this point that the Forum may have acquired its name, for "*forum*" comes from a word that means "beyond" or "outside the walls" (*fuori* in modern Italian still means "outside").

As Rome prospered, so the area was drained by the 1st-century BC Cloaca Maxima, or Great Drain, and became the obvious place to build not just shops and houses, but temples, courts, basilicas and the other great buildings of state. Successive emperors, consuls and other prominent power-brokers vied with one another to leave ever-grander memorials to their military and political achievements. This state of

ins on the latine Hill ove the man Forum

Hill of Palaces

The Palatino, or Palatine Hill, which rises above the Forum to the south, is one of Rome's Seven Hills. Sometimes called Rome's Beverly Hills, the area contains ruins of grand palaces built after the 1st century BC by the city's rich and powerful (the word "palace" comes from Palatino). You come here not so much for monuments – the ruins are even more confusing than those of the Forum – but to enjoy the area's gardens, shady walks, fountains, small museum, orange groves and pretty views over the Forum. It's a charming, atmospheric place, and though the admission is a little expensive, the same ticket is valid for the Colosseum.

affairs continued until about the 2nd century AD, when a growing shortage of space meant that political power followed the emperors to their new palaces on the Palatino, or Palatine Hill. Trade and commerce, meanwhile, moved to the Mercati di Traiano (➤ 68), while new building projects were diverted to the nearby Fori Imperiali, or Imperial Fora (➤ 67–68).

After the fall of Rome, the site declined swiftly; many of the monuments tumbled, and much of the stone was plundered for building Rome's medieval churches and palaces. By the 16th century the Forum was little more than an overgrown meadow. Excavations began around 1803, but remain far from complete. Major excavations to explore previously untouched ground around the Curia and Argiletum began in 1996, and are now proceeding apace here and elsewhere, although much remains to be uncovered, not least under the Via dei Fori Imperiali.

Above: Most visitors to Rome are drawn to the Forum

The Forum

You enter the Forum alongside the **Arco di Settimio Severo**, a huge arch raised in AD 203 to mark the tenth year of the reign of Emperor Septimius Severus. It also commemorated the minor military victories of his sons, Geta and Caracalla, hence the battle scenes depicted in the large marble reliefs. To the left and a little in front of the arch, a line of stones indicates the remains of the **Rostra**, or orator's platform, the place at which Mark Antony reputedly made his "Friends, Romans, countrymen" speech after the assassination of Julius Caesar. The platform took its name from the bronze prows (*rostra*) from ships captured by the Romans in battle which decorated it. They have given their name to the speaker's "rostrum" ever since.

The eight-columned **Tempio di Saturno** (Temple of Saturn) to the south is one of the Forum's oldest temples – it dates from around 497 BC – perhaps because Saturn, a god of agriculture, was one of Rome's most venerated gods from earliest times: the ancient Romans believed the city's initial prosperity and power was based on its agricultural prowess.

Many of the ruins in the Forum are ov 2,000 years old

Walking away from the Capitoline Hill above, you pass the patchy **Basilica Giulia** on your right, begun by Julius Caesar in 54 BC to complement the Basilica Aemelia opposite. The nearby **Tempio di Castore e Polluce**, or Temple of Castor and Pollux, was supervised by the city's *equites*, or knights, and was home to the Empire's weights and measures standards. To its south is the infrequently open **Santa Maria Antiqua**, the Forum's most important Christian building: it was converted from an earlier pagan monument in the 6th century.

Cutting through the Forum is the **Via Sacra**, once the Forum's principal thoroughfare and the route taken by

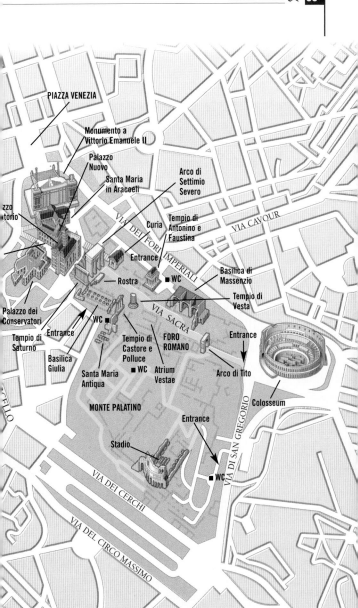

PIAZZA VENEZIA

Monumento a
Vittorio Emanuele II

Palazzo
Nuovo

Santa Maria
in Aracoeli

Arco di
Settimio
Severo

VIA CAVOUR

zzo
torio

VIA DEI FORI IMPERIALI

Curia

Tempio di
Antonino e
Faustina

Entrance

Basilica di
Massenzio

Rostra

WC

Tempio di
Vesta

Palazzo dei
Conservatori

VIA SACRA

Entrance

WC

Tempio di
Saturno

Entrance

Tempio di
Castore e
Polluce

FORO
ROMANO

Entrance

Basilica
Giulia

Arco di Tito

Santa Maria
Antiqua

WC

Atrium
Vestae

VIA DI SAN GREGORIO

Colosseum

FELLO

MONTE PALATINO

Entrance

Stadio

WC

VIA DEI CERCHI

VIA DEL CIRCO MASSIMO

he Forum and Palatine Hill

victorious generals and emperors parading the spoils of war. On your left as you walk along the surviving flagstones are the ruins of the Basilica Aemilia, built in 179 BC as a business and moneylending centre. The large brick building ahead of you and to the right is the much-restored **Curia**, or Senate House, probably completed by Augustus in 28 BC, when it became the meeting place of Rome's 300 or so senators.

The area to the Curia's right is the **Argiletum**, the site of a now-vanished temple that once held a statue of Janus, the two-faced god. Its twin doors were kept open in times of war and closed in times of peace: in 1,000 years, it is said, they were closed on only three occasions. In front of the Curia is the **Lapis Niger**, or Black Stone (protected by railings), a black marble slab, which marks the site of a sanctuary to the god Vulcan. A staircase leads to a chamber beneath the shrine,

The Tempio di Saturno (centre), with the unmistaka Arco di Settim Severo to its l

where you'll see a headstone inscribed in Latin dating from the 6th century BC (the oldest example ever found). Modern scholars believe the inscription warns against profaning the sacred site.

The **Tempio di Antonino e Faustina**, built in AD 141 by Emperor Antoninus to honour his wife, Faustina, is beyond the Curia. It makes a good introduction to the site, mainly because it is so well preserved, its survival due to its consecration as a church in the 11th century. Some of the oldest graves ever found in Rome were uncovered close by.

Beyond this point and the Temple of Castor and Pollux are the **Tempio di Vesta** and **Atrium Vestae**, respectively the Temple and House of the Vestal Virgins. It was in the temple that the Vestal Virgins tended Rome's sacred flame, a symbol of the city's continuity.

Beyond the Atrium on the left stands part of the **Basilica di Massenzio** (begun AD 306), one of the Forum's most impressive monuments: in its day it would have been still more awe-inspiring, for what remains is only a single aisle of what was once a 100m (110-yard) nave. Remarkably, only one of what

e impressive
nains of the
um's market

originally must have been dozens of columns from the basilica still survives, and now it stands in front of the church of Santa Maria Maggiore (► 118–119).

The Forum's last major monument before the Colosseum is the **Arco di Tito**, Rome's oldest triumphal arch, built in AD 81 by Emperor Domitian to honour Titus (Tito), his brother and predecessor as emperor. Titus' most famous victory was over the Jews in AD 70, and the arch's beautiful reliefs depict a series of scenes of the emperor's triumphal return to Rome with spoils from the campaign.

TAKING A BREAK

There are no places for refreshments inside the Forum: the nearest cafés are to be found off Piazza del Campidoglio (► 49), the grid of streets east of the Colosseum, or in Via Cavour. For a light snack in the last, try **Cavour 313** (► 72), an informal wine bar.

➕ 201 E4 ✉ Entrances by Arco di Settimio Severo, Largo Romolo e Remo, by Arco di Tito and off Via del Teodoro ☎ 06 699 0110 or 06 3996 7700
🕐 Forum and Palatino: Daily 9–one hour before sunset; occasional later opening 🚇 Colosseo 🚌 75, 85, 117, 175, 810, 850 to Via dei Fori Imperiali
🎟 Forum: free. Palatino: expensive. Combined pass available to Palatino and Colosseum (► 190)

ROMAN FORUM: INSIDE INFO

Top tips Before exploring the Roman Forum, **enjoy an overview of the site** from the steps and terraces on the rear eastern side of the Campidoglio, accessed from Piazza del Campidoglio. Steps from the balconies lead down to one of the Forum entrances alongside the Arco di Settimio Severo.
• Avoid visiting the Forum in the heat of the afternoon – there is little shade on the site and sightseeing can be uncomfortable.
• If you only have **limited time** to spend exploring the Forum, the most significant among the ruins (and sites definitely not to be missed) are the Curia, Arco di Settimio Severo, Tempio di Vesta and Basilica di Massenzio.

Colosseum

Little else in Rome is likely to compare with your first sight of the Colosseum (Colosseo), once the scene of gladiatorial combat and other entertainment, and now the city's most majestic and awe-inspiring ancient monument.

First Impressions

To grasp the Colosseum's scale you need to admire it from afar. The best place for an overview is the Colle Oppio, a park to the northeast of the monument, or the belvedere (Largo Agnes) immediately above the Colosseo Metro station exit (best reached from Via Cavour via Via del Colosseo or up the steps just to the right of the Metro as you face the station exit). The more usual viewpoint – the open ground to the amphitheatre's west, alongside the flank of the Roman Forum – is less satisfactory. The entrance to the monument's upper levels is close by, and from here you can walk around a part of the exterior well away from the roaring traffic that blights the Colosseum's surroundings: you can also admire the Arco di Costantino from the same point (▶ panel, page 58).

The Colosseum is the largest surviving monument from Roman antiquity

Gladiatorial combats in the Colosseum involved men, women and animals

Early Days

The Colosseum was begun around AD 70 by Emperor Vespasian. Its inspiration was the Teatro di Marcello and its site one that had previously been used for an artificial lake annexed to Nero's palatial Domus Aurea, or Golden House (► 69). The area's marshy conditions proved problematic, and required the laying of enormous drains – many of which still survive – and the creation of immense foundations. The costs of building the monument were met by the spoils of war, in this case the Romans' triumph over the Jews in AD 70, which realised 50 tonnes of gold and silver from the temple of Jerusalem alone. Jewish slaves captured in the campaign provided the labour force.

By the time of Vespasian's death in AD 79, the monument had been completed to its third tier. Additions were made by Vespasian's son, Titus, who inaugurated the Colosseum in AD 80 with celebrations that saw the slaughter of 5,000 animals and 100 days of festivities.

The completed structure was an architectural triumph. Its simple design has provided a model for stadia to this day, with tiered seating and 80 exits, or *vomitoria*, that allowed huge crowds – estimates of the Colosseum's capacity range from 50,000 to 73,000 people – to leave the stadium in minutes. Above the seating, a vast sailcloth roof, or *velarium*, could be pulled into place by sailors of the Imperial fleets to shade spectators from the elements. It was supported by 240 wooden masts, the supports and sockets for which you can still see in a ring below the structure's uppermost cornice.

Inside the Colosseum

Inside, the monument is perhaps less spectacular, if only because much of the original seating and flooring

The wooden floor that once covered the stage area was destroyed by fire, and today the Colosseum's complex sub-structure is clearly visible

Arco di Costantino

In any other context, the Arch of Constantine (AD 315) would be a major monument. Being overshadowed by the Colosseum, it is often ignored in favour of its neighbour. A triumphal arch like the Arco di Tito and Arco di Settimio Severo in the Roman Forum (▶ 55 and 52), it was raised to commemorate the triumph of Emperor Constantine over Maxentius, his imperial rival, at the Battle of Milvian Bridge (AD 312) just north of Rome. It is the city's largest and best-preserved arch, and one of the last major monuments built in ancient Rome.

Most of its materials were pilfered from other buildings. These included many of the sculptural reliefs, notably the eight reliefs framing the inscription, which portray scenes of an emperor at war or engaged in civic duties. They were probably removed from a monument raised to celebrate victories by Marcus Aurelius in AD 176. Wherever the face of Aurelius appeared, masons simply recarved the reliefs to portray Constantine.

The same happened in the arch's central passage, where the two main reliefs show scenes carved during the reigns of Domitian or Trajan. With a little judicious recarving and relabelling (*Fundator quietis* – "founder of calm"), the panels were altered to show Constantine riding into battle against the barbarians (on the monument's west side) and being crowned by the figure of Victory.

have disappeared. A major fire in AD 217 devastated the upper levels and wooden arena (from the *arena*, or sand, used to cover the stage area). Other fires and earthquakes over the next 400 years further damaged the structure. By the 6th century the arena was being used as workshops and a cemetery; by 1320 the entire south side of the monument had collapsed. This and other parts of the building were then ransacked for building stone, most of which found its way into churches, roads, wharves and palaces such as the Palazzo Venezia, Palazzo Farnese and Palazzo Barberini. The

ght: Many of
e sculptural
iefs on the
co di
stantino
ere lifted
om older
onuments and
modelled for
eir new home

desecration ceased in 1744, when Pope Benedict XIV consecrated the site in memory of the Christians who had supposedly been martyred there.

Contrary to popular myth, however, few if any Christians
were killed in the Colosseum, whose primary function was to
stage gladiatorial and other games. Today, you can look down
on the maze of tunnels and shafts that lay under the stage, the
means by which the games' animals, gladiators and other pro-
tagonists were brought to the stage from distant pens. Clever
plumbing, it's said, also meant the stage area could be flooded
to present mock sea battles.

Spectators were rigidly segregated by status and sex, and
they were expected to dress specially for the occasion. The
emperor and Vestal Virgins faced each other at the lowest
levels in special boxes. Alongside them, on wide platforms, sat
the senators, all of whom were expected to dress in white
togas and bring their own chairs (*bisellia*). Above them sat the
knights and aristocrats, then came the ordinary Roman citizens (*plebeians*) and finally – some 40m (130 feet) up and 50m
(165 feet) from the stage – the women, slaves and poor
(though few women, by all accounts, ventured to the games).
Some groups had separate sections, notably soldiers, scribes
and heralds, and some were banned altogether, namely
gravediggers, actors and retired gladiators. A special official, or
designator, kept everyone in their rightful place.

Emperors and spectators often had control over a protago-
nist's destiny. A wounded man could appeal for mercy by

ove left:
as-relief
m the Arco
Costantino

t: Stone from
Colosseum
s plundered
build many
Rome's
rches and
aces

raising a finger on his left hand; the wave of a handkerchief would then indicate a reprieve, while the sinister and still-familiar downturned thumb meant death. The wounded were often dispatched in any case, regardless of the crowd's verdict, and those who tried to escape by feigning death, would be poked with red-hot irons to discover if they were still alive.

TAKING A BREAK

Avoid the expensive cafés and bars in the monument's immediate vicinity. Alternatives are available in **Via Cavour** or the streets off **Via di San Giovanni in Laterano** to the east. For a snack lunch try **Café Café** (➤ 72) or, if you want a more substantial meal, **Nerone** or **Pasqualino** (➤ 73).

➕ 201 F4   ✉ Piazza del Colosseo, Via dei Fori Imperiali   ☎ 06 3996 7700; online booking at www.pierreci.it   🕐 Interior: Daily 9—one hour before sunset   🚇 Colosseo   🚌 30B, 75, 85, 87, 117, 175, 186   💷 Expensive. Combined ticket with Palatino

The floodlit Colosseum is one of Rome's unmissable sights

COLOSSEUM: INSIDE INFO

Top tips Return to the Colosseum after nightfall, to see the monument when it is spectacularly floodlit.
• The Colosseum's rather hidden entrance is on its southernmost side.
• Climb to the monument's **upper tiers** for a proper idea of the structure's size and the complexity of the tunnels below the stage area.
• If all the bustle wears you down, walk to the nearby Colle Oppio park (➤ 71).
• "Gladiators" outside the Colosseum often expect to be paid if you take their picture.

In more detail Before delving inside, spend time looking at some of the exterior's easily missed details, notably the half-columns framing every arch, which are Doric at ground level, Ionic on the second tier and Corinthian on the third; the arrangement was a direct copy of the Teatro di Marcello. Also note the many holes pockmarking the building, most of which originally held the 300 tonnes of iron clamps that helped bind the blocks of stone.

San Clemente

ttle in San Clemente's deceptively plain exterior suggests
ou are looking at one of Rome's most remarkable churches.
ot only is the building home to the city's loveliest medieval
terior – complete with some sublime frescoes and mosaics
but it also contains two earlier places of worship that span
000 years of religious observance.

San Clemente divides into three components, stacked one on
top of the other: a 12th-century church above a 4th- or 5th-
century church which sits on a late 2nd-century Mithraic
temple. The church alone would be worth a special visit, but
the two lower structures make the complex unmissable. Note
that you enter the main church via a side door on Via di San
Giovanni in Laterano. You should allow around 40 minutes
here, more if you are interested in the temple and excavations
on the lowest level.

The main body of the church at ground level was built
between 1108 and 1184 to replace the church that now lies
beneath it, which was destroyed by Norman raiders in 1084.
Inside, it retains Rome's finest medieval interior, most of the
city's churches having been modified in the baroque age – only
Santa Maria in Cosmedin (► 176) rivals San Clemente.

The highlights are many. Among the paintings, pride of
place goes to a Renaissance **fresco cycle** on the *Life of
St Catherine* (1428), one of only a handful of works by the
influential Florentine artist Masolino da Panicale (it's in the
rear left aisle chapel, to your right as you enter).

dieval
saics and
scoes adorn
e apse of San
emente

Among the **mosaics**, the star turn is the 12th-century *Triumph of the Cross*, which forms a majestic swathe of colour across the apse. Scholars think its design was based on that of a similar mosaic that was lost when the earlier church was destroyed in the 11th century. The work is full of detail and incident: note in particular the 12 doves on the cross, symbols of the Apostles, and the four rivers of paradise which spring from the cross, their waters quenching the thirst of the faithful, represented here by stags. The imposing 14th-century tabernacle below and to the right is by the Florentine sculptor Arnolfo di Cambio.

More noticeable than either the frescoes or the mosaics, however, is the **choir screen** (5th–9th century), whose marble-panelled walls dominate the nave. Such screens were a typical feature of early medieval churches but are now rare. Many of the panels were salvaged from the earlier church, while various of the columns originally hailed from the Foro Traiano (Trajan's Forum) in the Fori Imperiali (➤ 67). Equally beautiful and almost as venerable are the pulpit, candleholder and altar canopy, or *baldacchino*.

Steps accessed from the rear right-hand (south) side of the church take you down to what remains of the earlier church, the existence of which was only discovered in 1857. The remains here are relatively scant, although traces of very early frescoes survive, some dating back to the 5th century.

Far more is to be gained by dropping down yet another level, where you encounter the remains of two Roman-era buildings, parts of which are still only partially excavated. Almost the first thing you encounter is the cast of a **Mithraic altar**. Mithraism was a popular Roman cult that survived into

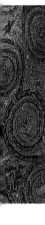

**x: A 15th-
tury fresco
Masolino da
icale**

*e Triumph of
e Cross
ve the high
ar dates from
12th
ntury. The
doves
mbolise the
ostles*

the Christian era. The bull was one of Mithraism's main symbols, hence the beast portrayed on the altar being killed by the god Mithras, along with the figures of torch-bearers and a snake, a symbol of regeneration. The cult was finally suppressed in AD 392.

This subterranean area of the church also includes part of a **Roman house** in which a *mithraem*, or place of worship, had been installed in the central room, probably towards the end of the 2nd century. Such temples were meant to replicate Mithras' cave, so doors would have been blocked or narrowed to a slit to allow sunlight to strike the cult's icons and images. Benches were installed to enable the initiates to take meals and worship communally.

The house itself has been proved to be older, archaeologists having discovered date-stamps corresponding to the reign of Domitian (AD 90–6) on the steps of the ancient staircase. In their day, these steps led from the ground-floor level of the house into its basement. Excavations suggest that the temple was walled up close to the year of Mithraism's 4th-century suppression, but that the basement continued to be used for a further six centuries.

The layout of the second structure here corresponds in part to that of a *horrea*, or warehouse, and may well have been a granary, although some early theories suggest it may have been the site of workshops belonging to the imperial mint, the *Moneta Caesaris*. Newer theories suggest the site contains two buildings, one being commercial premises, the other a house built over these premises which belonged to a wealthy Roman Christian. This Christian, so the theory goes, went by the name of Clemente, and founded a church on the site dedicated to his saintly namesake.

TAKING A BREAK

There are many small bars on Via di San Giovanni in Laterano and adjoining streets where you can stop for a coffee, a cool drink or a quick bite to eat. **Café Café** (► 72) is good for snacks.

🚇 202 A4 ✉ Via di San Giovanni in Laterano ☎ 06 7045 1018 or 06 774 0021 🕐 Church and excavations: Mon–Sat 9–12:30, 3–6, Sun 10–12:30, 3–6; closed during services 🚇 Colosseo 🚌 75, 85, 87, 117, 175 to Piazza del Colosseo or 85, 117, 850 to Via di San Giovanni in Laterano 🎟 Church: free. Excavations: inexpensive

SAN CLEMENTE: INSIDE INFO

Top tip Remember that San Clemente is closed at lunchtime until mid-afternoon, and access to the church is not permitted during services.

In more detail If the main door of the upper church is open, try to look outside at the *quadroporticus*, the distinctive square colonnaded courtyard that fronts the main facade. Such courtyards were once common features of early Roman basilica churches – rectangular churches with simple naves and no transepts – but are now rare.

San Giovanni in Laterano

San Giovanni in Laterano, not St Peter's, is the cathedral church of Rome; St Peter's lies in the Vatican, a separate sovereign state. Even without its exalted status, however, th great church would be worth visiting, both for its soaring facade and the beauty of its interior, cloister and baptistery.

San Giovanni in Laterano has venerable origins. It was in a Roman palace on the site, that Constantine, the first Christian emperor, met Pope Miltiades in 313, and here that Constantine raised the city's first officially sanctioned church (over what had been the barracks of his personal guard). From earliest times it housed the *cathedra*, or throne, of the Bishop of Rome. The church's importance continued for centuries – for example, popes were crowned here until the 19th century. During this time, the original church was destroyed by the Vandals, and subsequent churches on the site were repeatedly replaced or restored following fires and earthquakes.

In the portico at the foot of the immense **facade** (built in 1735) stands an ancient statue of Constantine, while to its right are the church's main bronze **doors**, which were brought from the Curia, or Senate House, in the Roman Forum (► 50–55). The church's restrained **interior** (1646–50) is largely the work of the baroque architect Borromini, who thoughtfully retained the nave's earlier gold-hued and beautifully ornate **ceiling**. The ceiling aside, the interior contains relatively little in the way of great art, but you shouldn't miss the papal altar and canopy

---

SAN GIOVANNI IN LATERANO: INSIDE INFO

Top tips While visiting San Giovanni you might wish to visit the **flea market** (open Mon–Fri 10–1, Sat 10–5) held along nearby Via Sannio, a right turn just through Porta San Giovanni.
• If you baulk at the long walk back to the city centre from San Giovanni, consider taking the Metro from nearby Giovanni Metro station (just beyond Porta San Giovanni).

In more depth Stand with your back to San Giovanni's facade. The building ahead of you and a little to the left contains the **Scala Santa**, or Holy Staircase, 28 wood-covered marble steps reputedly removed from Pontius Pilate's palace in Jerusalem. Constantine's mother is said to have brought them to Rome, since when, as the steps Christ ascended during His trial, they have been an object of veneration for the pilgrims who climb them on their knees.

**Right: Baroque
architect
Francesco
Borromini
remodelled
much of San
Giovanni's
sumptuous
interior**

(begun in 1367) at the main crossing, where, until latterly, only a pope could officiate. It reputedly holds the skulls of saints Peter and Paul, and part of a wooden table said to have been used by St Peter.

San Giovanni's real glory is its **cloister** (1215–32), entered off the church's left (north) side, a tranquil corner with dozens of variously shaped columns, many adorned with exquisite Cosmati work (an inlay of coloured stones and marbles).

Outside the church to its rear – you need to exit the building and bear left – is Constantine's San Giovanni in Fonte, or **Baptistery of St John**, a building whose octagonal plan provided the blueprint for baptisteries across Italy for centuries to come. Some of the building has been altered over the years, but significant older parts survive, notably the 5th-century mosaic in the north apse and the Chapel of St John (461–8), which preserves its original doors.

✚ 202 C3 ✉ Piazza di San Giovanni in Laterano ☎ 06 6988 6433. Scala Santa: 06 772 6641 🕐 Church: daily 7–6:45. Cloister: daily 9–noon, 4–6. Baptistery: daily 9–noon, 4–7. Scala Santa: daily 6:30–noon, 3–6. Note that times can vary without notice 🍴 Cafés in Via di San Giovanni in Laterano 🚇 San Giovanni 🚌 3, 16, 81, 85, 87, 117, 218, 360, 590, 650, 714, 810, 850 💰 Church, Scala Santa, Baptistery: free. Cloister: inexpensive

---

**Above:
numerous
statues adorn
San Giovanni's
soaring facade,
a prominent
feature of
Rome's skyline**

**The cloister
provides a
small oasis of
tranquillity**

At Your Leisure

1 Piazza Venezia

Piazza Venezia is the key to central Rome, a huge traffic-filled square from which some of the city's major streets strike off to the four points of the compass. But while you will probably pass through the piazza many times, it is not a place with many important things to see – save for the huge white edifice on its southern flank, the **Monumento a Vittorio Emanuele II**. This marble monolith, built between 1885 and 1911, commemorates the unification of Italy and the country's first king, Vittorio Emanuele. It is also called the Altare della Patria, of Altar of the Nation – the tomb of Italy's Unknown Soldier is here – but Romans know it as the "typewriter" or "wedding cake" after its huge marble tiers. Its terraces (➤ 49) offer superb views.

On the square's west side stands the **Palazzo Venezia** (1451), which for 200 years between 1594 and 1797 was the property of the Venetian Republic – hence its name and the name of the square. The *palazzo* is known for the balcony from which Mussolini once harangued crowds in the square below – the dictator kept an office in the building – and for the underrated **Museo di Palazzo Venezia**, used for temporary exhibitions and noted for its permanent collection of medieval paintings, textiles, ceramics, jewellery and other decorative arts. If it's open, you should also look into **San Marco**, a church best known for its beautiful gilt ceiling and magnificent 9th-century apse mosaic.

🖪 195 F2

Museo di Palazzo Venezia

🖪 195 E2 ✉ Via del Plebiscito 118
☎ 06 328101 or 06 6999 4318;
www.ticketeria.it ⏰ Tue–Sun 8:30–7:30
(hours vary for temporary exhibitions)
🍴 Cafés in Via delle Botteghe Oscure
🚇 Cavour 🚌 All services to Piazza
Venezia 🎫 Museum: moderate

3 Musei Capitolini

On the left (north) side of Piazza del Campidoglio stands the **Palazzo Nuovo**, whose inner courtyard contains the colossal Roman statue of a river god, Marforio, a favourite with

Fragments of a massive statue of the Emperor Constantine I in the courtyard of the Palazzo dei Conservatori

photographers. Inside the portico is a celebrated **equestrian statue** of Marcus Aurelius (AD 161–80); it originally stood in the piazza outside, but was brought inside after restoration for safekeeping (the statue outside is a copy). It is only such statue to survive from this period, and throughout the Middle Ages was repeatedly referred to by artists and writers. Oth

4 Fori Imperiali

The Fori Imperiali, or Imperial Fora, are five fora built when lack of space in the old Roman Forum forced emperors from Julius Caesar onwards to look elsewhere for their

oms in the
llery contain a
ealth of antique
alpture, the highlights of which
e statues of the *Dying Galatian* and
e *Capitoline Venus*, both Roman
pies of Greek originals.

Across the piazza, the **Palazzo dei
nservatori** (linked by underpass to
e Palazzo Nuovo) houses the rest of
e museums' collections – begun in
71 by Pope Sixtus IV – mainly
rther pieces of sculpture. Highlights
clude the Spinario (a 1st-century BC
onze of a boy), the famous She-Wolf
atue, probably an Etruscan bronze
ting from the 5th or 6th century BC
d works by Caravaggio, Veronese,
ntoretto, Rubens, Van Dyck and
llini. Some 400 of the museum's
alptures have been relocated to
ntrale Montemartini, a converted
wer station at Via Ostiense 106
uth of the city).

195 F2 Piazza del Campidoglio
1 06 6710 2475 or 06 3996 7800;
www.museicapitolini.org for bookings
 Tue–Sun 9–8 (last ticket 7pm)
 Museum Café Colosseo All
services to Piazza Venezia
 Expensive

grandiose architectural schemes.
Much of their area was lost when
Mussolini forced the huge Via dei
Fori Imperiali road through their
heart in the 1930s. Guided tours of
the site led by an archaeologist are
now available, though you can also
easily admire the fora while walking
down Via dei Fori Imperiali.

Walking away from Piazza Venezia
on this street, the first forum you
come to on the left is the **Foro
Traiano**, or Trajan's Forum
(AD 104–113). This is the most
impressive of the five, and contains
their single greatest monument, the
Colonna Traiano (▶ 68). In its day,
this forum was so vast and splendid
it was considered one of the world's
architectural wonders. Today, it's a
sunken space of shattered columns
and crumbling walls: only the forum's

**Little remains visible today of the once
vast Foro Traiano**

Roman-era markets, the **Mercati di Traiano**, entered some distance away at Via IV Novembre 94, preserve anything of their original grandeur.

Alongside Trajan's Forum to the right is the **Foro di Augusto**, or Augustus' Forum (begun in 42 BC), part of an immense rebuilding project initiated by Augustus that led to his famous boast, "I found Rome brick and left it marble." The most striking ruins here are the distinct remains of the Temple of Mars Ultor. Across the road lies the **Foro di Cesare**, or Caesar's Forum, the first of the Imperial Fora, built by Julius Caesar between 54 and 46 BC. Only small areas of the site have

been excavated, much of which lies beneath Via dei Fori Imperiali. There is even less to see of the remaining fora: the **Foro di Nerva** (AD 96–8), whose best surviving relic is a frieze on the colonnade at the corner of Via Cavour and Via dei Fori Imperiali, and the **Foro di Vespasiano** (AD 71–5), also known as the Foro della Pace, whose former library contains the present-day church of Santi Cosma e Damiano.

➕ 201 E5
Mercati di Traiano
➕ 201 E5 ✉ Via IV Novembre 94
☎ 06 679 0048 🕐 ➕ Apr–Sep, Tue–Sun 9–6:30; rest of year Tue–Sun 9–4:30 🚇 Cavour or Colosseo 🚌 40, 64, 70, 170 💶 Expensive

🔢 Colonna Traiano

Trajan's Column rises as a lonely, majestic sentinel from the ruins of Trajan's Forum. Built in AD 113, it was raised to mark two victorious military campaigns over the Dacians who lived in what is now Romania. Like triumphal arches, such columns were typical of Roman victory monuments, and likewise also invariably contained friezes and reliefs recording details of a campaign's battles and events. Here, the reliefs run in a remarkable spiral – over 200m (650 feet) of exquisitely carved marble, containing a continuous 155-scene sequence with over 2,600 figures portrayed two-thirds of life size. The importance of the column is in the intense detail of these scenes, detail which has allowed scholars to learn much about the mechanics of the Roman military machine.

One reason for the column's survival is that it formed the bell-tower of a Christian church, San Nicola de Columna. When this was demolished in the 9th century, the column became the first archaeological monument to be designated for protection by Rome's papal rulers. The structure comprises 29 vast drums of marble – eight for the base, nineteen for the column and two for the summit pedestal. Inside is a spiral staircase carved from the solid stone, a miracle of Roman engineering but a miracle withheld from public view, for the column can only be admired from the outside. The figure crowning the summit is St Peter, added in 1588, replacing a bronze statue of Trajan, whose ashes once resided in a golden urn at the column's base.

➕ 201 D5 ✉ Via dei Fori Imperiali
🚇 Cavour 🚌 Services to Piazza Venezia

St Peter's Chains

San Pietro in Vincoli was built in 432, reputedly on the site where St Peter was condemned to death during the persecutions of Nero. The church takes its name from the highly venerated chains (*vincoli*) that you see in a casket under the main altar. There are actually two sets of chains: one is believed to have been used to bind Peter in Jerusalem, the other thought to have been used to shackle him in Rome's Mamertine prison. When the two were eventually united they miraculously fused together.

San Pietro in Vincoli

takes only a couple of minutes to walk to this church from the Colosseum, and only a little longer to see its main attraction – an imposing **statue of Moses** (1503–13), one of Michelangelo's sculptural masterpieces. The statue was conceived as part of a 42-figure ensemble designed to adorn the tomb of Pope Julius II, one of Michelangelo's principal patrons. In the event the project was never realised, although it would torment Michelangelo for much of his life – he referred to it as this "tragedy of a tomb". Instead he was distracted by other works such as the Sistine Chapel – another Julius commission – and then after Julius' death deprived of funds by popes who saw little glory in funding their predecessor's obsession.

The statue of Moses hints at what might have been, a monumental figure captured at the moment he receives the tablet of the Ten Commandments (shown here under his right arm). Michelangelo left a famous signature in the statue's beard – his profile – and gave Moses a wonderfully equivocal expression as he watches the Israelites dance round the golden calf, his look of divine illumination at receiving the tablets mixed with fury at his people's faithlessness and idolatry. Note, too, the figure's horns, which

represent beams of light, features ascribed to Moses in the iconography of many medieval paintings and sculptures. The main flanking statues are also by Michelangelo, and represent Rachel and Leah, symbols of the active and contemplative life. The other figures, which are noticeably less successful, are the work of Michelangelo's pupils.

✚ 201 F5 ⊠ Piazza di San Pietro in Vincoli 4a ☎ 06 488 2865 🕓 Daily 8–12:30, 3:30–7 (6, in winter) 🍴 Nerone (➤ 73) 🚇 Colosseo or Cavour 🚌 75 to Via Cavour or 75, 85, 87, 117, 175 or 186 to Piazza del Colosseo 🎫 Free

Michelangelo's masterpiece in San Pietro in Vincoli depicts Moses receiving the Ten Commandments

❾ Domus Aurea

The Domus Aurea, or Golden House, was built as a colossal pleasure dome by Nero after the fire in AD 64 during

Beneath the Colle Oppio, a peaceful park in the centre of Rome, lies the Domus Aurea

which the emperor famously "fiddled while Rome burned". It centred on the present-day site of the Colle Oppio, but extended across a quarter of the ancient city. Parts of the much-reduced complex (now underground) are open, having been closed to the public for many years. To visit, you must join a guided tour and reserving ahead is essential. At the time of writing the complex is undergoing restoration and may be closed from time-to-time.

The house's scale and splendour must have been almost beyond imagining. Most surfaces were covered in

Off the Beaten Track
The little-known park of **Villa Celimontana** south of the Colosseum (entered from Via della Navicella) is a good place to escape from the rigours of sightseeing. The area around the park is also relatively quiet and unexplored, with interesting churches like Santa Maria in Domnica and Santo Stefano Rotondo (► 16–17), and little lanes such as Viale del Parco and Clivo di Scauro which lead to Santi Giovanni e Paolo.

gold leaf, hence its name. Ceilings were carved with ivory and held concealed vents that sprayed a mist of scent or petals into the rooms below. The approach was some 2km (1 mile) long, and flanked by triple colonnades, while the gardens featured a lake overshadowed by a 35m (115-foot) statue of Nero – the largest statue ever made in antiquity, larger even than the Colossus of Rhodes.

Enthusiasm for the palace died with Nero in AD 68. Pressure of space then meant that much of the building was sacrificed in favour of projects such as the Colosseum and a huge baths complex – Rome's first – built by Trajan in 104. So much was lost, in fact, that it was only in 1490 that excavations first brought a portion of its remains to light. Among other things, the discovery revealed magnificent frescoes which greatly influenced Renaissance artists such as Raphael, whose Stanze in the Vatican borrowed heavily from the wall paintings (► 150–151). Another magnificent work of art found in the area was the *Laocoön*, one of the greatest of all ancient statues (► 148).

Today, visitors can see ancient wall paintings, brick-vaulted chambers, rooms and passageways, most of which would once have been faced with marble.

the Esquiline Hill, one of the original Seven Hills. It takes its name from one of the hill's two summits, the *Cispius* and *Oppius*. Although just across the street from the Colosseum, it is little used by visitors, but locals,

Much of the surroundings, including Trajan's baths, have never been excavated, offering the tantalising prospect that many more masterpieces still lie concealed.

🚹 201 F4 ⊠ entrance in Colle Oppio park ☎ Advance booking obligatory: 06 3996 7700; www.pierreci.it
🕔 Tue–Fri 10–4 (but check for restoration closures) 🚇 Colosseo
🚌 30B to Via Labicana or services to Piazza del Colosseo (➤ 60)
🎫 Moderate (plus booking fee)

🔟 Colle Oppio

The Colle Oppio is central Rome's most convenient park, a pretty area of grass, walkways, trees and archaeological remains spread over the slopes of

make full use of its café and quiet corners, particularly on Sundays. The park's loveliest area of grass, only faintly shaded by slender palms, is the section right by the entrance across from the Colosseum.

The park makes a pleasant way of reaching Santa Maria Maggiore (➤ 118–119) or Palazzo Massimo alle Terme (➤ 120–123), avoiding the busy Via Cavour and other roads. One important word of warning, though: avoid the park at night.

🚹 202 A4 ⊠ Via Labicana 136
🚇 Colosseo

For Kids

The Forum may be a little too ruined for young imaginations to deal with but the scale of the **Colosseum** and its gladiatorial associations (➤ 56–60) should fire youngsters' minds. Children should also enjoy the dank and mysterious Mithraic bowels of **San Clemente** (➤ 61–63), and curious one-offs such as the huge hands and feet in the courtyard of the **Musei Capitolini** (➤ 66–67) and Bernini's eccentric elephant outside the church of Santa Maria sopra Minerva (➤ 94). The **Colle Oppio** park is a favourite among families – buy kids a drink, ice-cream or picnic in streets to the south. On Sundays, street performers can often be found on the nearby Via dei Fori Imperiali.

Where to...
Eat and Drink

Prices
Expect to pay per person for a meal, excluding drinks and service

€ under €20   €€ €20–40   €€€ over €40

The area of Rome that embraces the Capitoline Hill, Colosseum and Roman Forum is almost entirely given over to monuments, and the number of restaurants is correspondingly small. Though most are aimed at tourists, there are a handful of good places in the side streets close to the main sights.

Antica Birreria "Peroni" €
Don't be tempted into the overpriced cafés or snack bars on Piazza Venezia. Instead, walk just round the corner to this *birreria*, or beer hall. The term is slightly misleading for what is more a large, pleasant bar and simple restaurant. You could just have a beer: it's worth a visit simply to admire the original art nouveau interior. Romans pack the place at lunchtime to take advantage of the handful of inexpensive but well-prepared pasta and other dishes (though it is little known to visitors to the city). Service is canteen style; the seating is at simple wooden tables. The atmosphere is lively but not intimidating.

🚹 195 F3 ☒ Via di San Marcello 19
☎ 06 679 5310 🕒 Mon–Sat
noon–midnight. Closed 2 weeks in Aug

Antico Caffè del Brasile €
This traditional bar serves superlative coffee, for the owners roast the blends themselves. The Antico Caffè del Brasile's chief claim to fame is that Pope John Paul II came here to buy his coffee when he was still Cardinal Wojtyla. In days past, huge sacks of coffee sat below vast roasting machines to the rear. EU directives meant these had to go, but if some of the Brasile's authentic charm has gone, the quality – and range – of coffees and hot chocolate to buy or drink on the premises is still outstanding. The bar is on a side street off the north side of Via Cavour.

🚹 201 F5 ☒ Via dei Serpenti 23
☎ 06 488 2319 🕒 Mon–Sat
6am–8pm, Sun 7–7. Closed 2 weeks
in Aug and Sun in Jul

Binario 4 €
Binario 4 is a recent arrival in an area with relatively few acceptable restaurants. Within easy walking distance of the Colosseum and San Clemente, this informal osteria-style restaurant serves well-executed traditional dishes that change daily, with specials posted on a blackboard.

🚹 202 A4 ☒ Via di San Giovanni in
Laterano 32 ☎ 06 700 5561
🕒 Wed–Mon 12:30–2:30, 7:30–11,
Tue 12:30–2:30

Café Café €
A tiny, one-room café-restaurant just seconds from the Colosseum with a cosy, ochre-coloured interior, Café Café serves good cold snacks, with one or two hot dishes daily. It is perfect for lunch, tea, coffee or a glass of wine.

🚹 201 F4 ☒ Via dei Santi Quattro
(Coronati) 44 ☎ 06 700 8743
🕒 Daily 11am–1am. Closed Aug

Cavour 313 €
This popular and long-established wine bar is surprisingly little patronised by non-Romans despite being less than a minute's walk from the main entrance to the

Roman Forum. First impressions inside are of rather plain and uninspiring wood-dominated decor, but don't be put off: the atmosphere is informal and friendly, the many good hot and cold snacks are well priced, and there's a selection of more than 500 wines (some by the glass) to choose from.

+ 201 F5 ⊠ Via Cavour 313 ☎ 06 678 5496 ⊚ Jun–Sep Mon–Sat 12:30–2:30, 7:30–12:30; rest of year Mon–Sat 12:30–2:30, 7:30–12:30, Sun 7:30–12:30

Charly's Saucière €€

The name doesn't sound Italian, and this is in fact one of Rome's very few French restaurants. An unpromising notion maybe, but this pleasant and discreet little place just south of the church of San Giovanni in Laterano has been doing good business for many years. Swiss dishes, including fondues, also feature among the menu's list of classic and immaculately prepared French staples such as fine meats, soufflés and patés.

Puddings are often outstanding. French wines, of course, predominate on the wine list. This is a good place for a more formal dinner than nearby Pasqualino (▶ 73).

+ 202 C3 ⊠ Via di San Giovanni in Laterano 268–270 ☎ 06 7049 5666 ⊚ Tue–Fri 12:30–2:30, 7:30–10:30; Mon, Sat 7:30–10:30. Closed 2 weeks in Aug

Leonina €

You can tell you're in the presence of something special by the regular long lines outside Leonina. People here are waiting for some of Rome's best *pizza al taglio*, or pizza by the slice. Prices for what is usually the most inexpensive of snacks are higher here than elsewhere, but then so is the quality of the pizza.

+ 201 F5 ⊠ Via Leonina 84 ☎ 06 482 7744 ⊚ Daily 8am–11pm

Nerone €–€€

Nerone, less than a minute's walk from the Colosseum, is the perfect spot for an inexpensive and relaxed

trattoria meal. *Antipasti* (starters) here are especially good – you can choose from Roman and Abruzzese specialities (the owners come from the Abruzzo, the mountainous region east of Rome). The dining area amounts to a couple of plain rooms, and in summer you can sit outside at a few tables on the pavement with a corner of the Colle Oppio park just across the road.

+ 201 F4 ⊠ Via delle Terme di Tito 96 (corner of Viale del Monte Oppio) ☎ 06 481 7952 ⊚ Mon–Sat noon–3, 7–11. Closed Aug

Pasqualino €–€€

Pasqualino has been around for many years, and doesn't seem to have changed in its menu, waiting staff or simple trattoria approach to cooking and eating in decades. There is often a big foreign presence here, including lively groups of trainee priests from the nearby Irish College, but also enough locals to make this a thoroughly

Roman experience. A good place to stop for lunch after seeing the Colosseum, just two minutes' walk away, or an informal dinner.

+ 202 A4 ⊠ Via dei Santi Quattro 66 ☎ 06 700 4576 ⊚ Lunch and dinner Tue–Sun. Closed 2 weeks in Aug

Trattoria Sora Lella €€

Sora Lella lies on Isola Tiberina (Tiber Island) between the Capitoline area and Trastevere district. It is worth the detour from either location, as the accomplished, authentic Roman cooking is a cut above what you'd expect of some-where that affects the informal atmosphere (but not the prices) of a simple trattoria. Sora Lella was a much-loved actress, and the restaurant was named in her honour by her son, Aldo Trabalza, after her death in 1993. Her portrait occupies pride of place alongside the bar.

+ 200 C4 ⊠ Via di Ponte Quattro Capi 16, Isola Tiberina ☎ 06 686 1601 ⊚ Mon–Sat 12:30–2:30, 7:30–10:30. Closed Aug

Where to...
Shop

This is not an area of the city for shoppers to visit with any great expectations, though you may stumble across the odd artisan's workshop, gallery, antiques shop or specialist store in the side streets off Via Cavour (the best hunting grounds are Via dei Serpenti, Via dei Boschetto and Via Madonna dei Monti). One such is **La Bottega del Cioccolato**, a vivid red chocolate shop at Via Leonina 82 (tel: 06 482 1473, Mon–Sat 9:30–7:30).

Otherwise most of the shops in the streets around Rome's ancient monuments are local food and general stores for those who live around Via Cavour (by the Forum) and in the residential enclave between the Colosseum and San Giovanni in Laterano.

Where to...
Be Entertained

Ancient monuments and cultural life generally don't mix in Rome. Outdoor concerts were once held in the Terme di Caracalla (Baths of Caracalla) south of the Colosseum, but for a variety of reasons, most significantly the preservation of the ruins, these have been suspended indefinitely. Similar restrictions mean that no productions are held at the Colosseum, Roman Forum or other sites.

MUSIC AND THEATRE

The **Teatro di Marcello** provides a summer venue for classical concerts organised by the **Associazione Il Tempietto** (Via Rodolfo Morandi 3, tel: 06 8713 1590; www.tempietto.it). Between November and July the association's concerts move indoors to the church of **San Nicola in Carcere** (tel: 06 686 9972) south of the Teatro at Via del Teatro di Marcello 46. Tickets are available from both venues about 2 hours before each performance. **San Giovanni in Laterano** is one of only a handful of churches to maintain a choir and present a sung Mass. The church is also a good place to hear organ music; the superb Luca Blasi organ is usually played during and after the 10am Sunday Mass. Contact visitor centres or the church for further details. The tiny church of **San Teodoro** in Via San Teodoro on the western flank of the Palatine Hill is also used as a concert venue by the choral association "Agimus", short for the **Associazione Giovanile Musicale** (tel: 06 3211 1001; www.agimus.it).

Theatre and dance productions are held at the **Teatro Colosseo**, east of the Colosseum at Via Capo d'Africa 5a (tel: 06 700 4932).

NIGHTLIFE

This is not an area rich in nightlife, but one of Rome's newest clubs, **Micca** (Via Pietro Micca 7a, tel: 06 8744 0079; www.miccaclub.com; Thu–Sun 10pm–3am) has opened on its fringes. A good place for a light meal or a late-night drink near Termini is the **Zest** bar in the sleek contemporary Radison SAS es. Hotel (Via Filippo Turati 171, tel 06 444 841; www.rome.radissonsas.com). If you've been out late and need a drink or bite to eat, **La Base** at Via Cavour 274 (tel: 06 474 0659) stays open until 4:30am every morning.

The Heart of Rome

Getting Your Bearings

The heart of Rome – the area bounded by the curve of the Tiber in the west and Via del Corso in the east – is often described as "Renaissance Rome" or "Baroque Rome" or even "Medieval Rome". No description is quite right, for the area is a wonderful mixture of ancient monuments, churches, palaces, streets and squares that span some 2,000 years of history.

The two itineraries in this chapter are slightly less coherent than those to other parts of the city, mainly because the more you see of the city, the harder it becomes to define its quarters in terms of historical epochs. The area covered in the first itinerary does have an atmosphere and appearance all of its own, thanks to its combination of tiny old cobbled streets, imposing Renaissance palaces, the occasional broad thoroughfare – Corso Vittorio Emanuele II is the axis around which the area hinges – and a sprinkling of larger or grander squares such as Campo de' Fiori and Piazza Navona. This is also an area where people live and work, and at times its artisans' workshops, neighbourhood shops and busy markets create the feel of a village rather than a capital city.

It is also – inevitably – scattered with remnants of Imperial Rome, among them the Pantheon, which rivals even the Forum and Colosseum, as well as a marvellous museum of antiquities, the Palazzo Altemps.

Two of Rome's most distinctive districts are also encompassed in this chapter. The medieval Jewish Ghetto, a web of streets just beyond Lungotevere di Cenci on the northern banks of the Tiber, is a mostly residential enclave of peaceful streets and small squares, with a sprinkling of more traditional restaurants and shops. Across the river lies Trastevere, a self-contained corner of the city, filled with picturesque old streets and squares. It retains much of its old working-class residential character – despite the fact that its pretty appearance has made it one of Rome's main restaurant districts. This is a good place to explore at random by day or in the evening, though it has relatively few churches, museums and monuments.

★ Don't Miss

Previous page: Raphael's Loggia of Cupid and Psyche in the Villa Farnesina

At Your Leisure

The first day of this two-day itinerary includes many highlights of medieval and Renaissance Rome – as well as one of the city's grandest ancient monuments – and is followed by a quieter day in Trastevere and the old Ghetto district. If you are short of time, you can condense the itinerary into a single day by visiting Piazza Navona, Palazzo Altemps and the Pantheon in the morning, and the Palazzo Doria Pamphilj and Trastevere in the afternoon.

The Heart of Rome in Two Days

Day One

Morning
Breakfast in **1** **Campo de' Fiori** (➤ 80–81), before exploring its wonderfully evocative morning food and flower market (left). Then head off to **2** **Piazza Farnese** (➤ 99), the Via Giulia – one of Rome's most elegant streets – and (perhaps) the small **3** **Palazzo Spada** art gallery (➤ 99–100).

Walk back to **5** **Piazza Navona** (➤ 82–85), a baroque showpiece second only to St Peter's, meander the side streets off the square – notably Via della Pace – and stop for a coffee in one of its cafés.

Just north and east of Piazza Navona lie the churches of **7** **Sant'Agostino** (➤ 100–101) home to a Raphael fresco and **8** **San Luigi dei Francesi** (➤ 102), graced with three major paintings by Caravaggio.

Lunch
Try Cul de Sac or Bar della Pace if you only want a snack lunch (➤ 108), La Carbonara (➤ 107) for an inexpensive meal alfresco or La Rosetta for a splurge (➤ 108).

Afternoon
Visit **6** **Palazzo Altemps** (➤ 86–89), one of Rome's most dazzling museums, where some of the greatest classical Roman sculpture is on display. Then make your way to the **10** **Pantheon** (right, ➤ 90–94), the most perfectly preserved of all Rome's ancient monuments.

end the rest of the afternoon exploring Via del Corso, one of the city's
in shopping streets, and the streets to its west where you will find many
eresting little specialist shops. Alternatively, visit the **11** **Ara Pacis** (► 103),
Roman monument covered in marble reliefs, and the art-filled church of
Santa Maria del Popolo (► 103–104).

Day Two

Morning

Allow an hour or so to see the rich collection of paintings at the **13** **Palazzo
ria Pamphilj** (► 104–105), and – if they are open – some extra time to join a
guided tour of the palace's private apartments.

lk to Trastevere (above) by way of Santa Maria in Cosmedin and the Ghetto
► 176–179). Alternatively, take a bus to Trastevere from Via del Plebiscito
t off Piazza Venezia.

Lunch

You can take lunch in any number of places
on your walk to, or around, Trastevere: try
Augusto in Trastevere (► 107).

Afternoon

Spend time simply exploring **15** **Trastevere's**
retty streets and squares (right, ► 95–98),
before making your way to **Santa Maria in
Trastevere**, which is usually open all day.

Trastevere has lots of places to eat, so you
may wish to extend the day and stay in the
ea for dinner without returning to your hotel.
Do this either by walking up to the **Gianicolo
ll** (► 96) above Trastevere for good views of
he city, or by visiting the church of **14** **Santa
Cecilia in Trastevere** (► 105–106).

Campo de' Fiori

Campo de' Fiori (Field of Flowers) is a place you will probably return to more than once during your stay. One of Rome's prettiest piazzas, it is the site of a wonderful outdoor market, with picturesque palaces and houses providing the backdrop for a colourful medley of stalls selling fruit, flowers and fish.

Take time to wander around these stalls and enjoy the street life: the old knife-sharpeners, the redoubtable Roman matriarchs trimming vegetables, the fishmonger bawling his wares, and the local housewives driving a hard bargain with knowing stallholders. When you have had your fill of sights, sounds and smells, pick one of the small cafés around the square and watch proceedings over a cappuccino.

In its earliest days the square really was a field of flowers: until the Middle Ages it formed a meadow that fringed the 1st-century BC Theatre of Pompey. Then it was built over and quickly became a bustling focus of city life. All manner of famous names were associated with the surrounding district: Lucretia Borgia was born locally, her brother Cesare was assassinated near by, and the artist Caravaggio murdered a rival after losing a tennis match in the square. Lucretia's father, Alessandro, better known as Pope Alexander VI, would also have been familiar with the area, for one of his mistresses, Vanozza Cattenei, ran some of the inns and brothels for which the district became celebrated.

Today, there's relatively little to see here apart from the market and the statue at its heart (▶ Inside Info). However, be

Top: The Car is a popular place to mee at night

Above: Stallholders Campo de' Fiori, Rome's prettiest mar

sure to explore some of the characterful surrounding streets, notably Via dei Cappellari (Street of the Hatters), a shadowy lane filled with furniture workshops and premises of other artisans. Also walk the short distance to Piazza Farnese to admire the square and its palace (➤ 99), and then continue to Via Giulia, one of Rome's most exclusive residential streets, to look at the church of Santa Maria dell'Orazione e Morte (➤ 100).

TAKING A BREAK

The Campo is full of small cafés and restaurants: one of the nicest is the **Caffè Farnese** (Via dei Baullari 106–7) just off the square on the corner with the grander Piazza Farnese. One of the best places for lunch or dinner is the old-fashioned **Grappolo d'Oro** (➤ 107), a few steps off the square.

✚ 194 C2 ✉ Piazza Campo de' Fiori 🚌 40, 46, 62, 64 to Corso Vittorio Emanuele II or H, 8, 63, 271, 780 to Via Arenula

CAMPO DE' FIORI: INSIDE INFO

Top tips The Campo's cafés make a perfect place for breakfast; the market is also at its least crowded early on (it runs daily except Sunday from about 6am to 2pm).
• As in any busy part of the city, be sure to keep a tight grip on your valuables.
• The Campo is also popular at night: the Vineria wine bar (No 15) and the American-run Drunken Ship (No 20–1) in the piazza's western corner are among the liveliest bars.

In more detail At the heart of Campo de' Fiori stands a cowled and rather **ominous-looking statue**, easily missed amid the debris of the market. This depicts Giordano Bruno, a 16th-century humanist and scholar who was burned at the stake on this spot in 1600 for the crime of heresy. His secular outlook suits the square, which to this day remains unusual among Roman piazzas in having no church.

Piazza Navona

None of Rome's many squares is as grand or theatrical as Piazza Navona. The magnificent piazza, one of the city's baroque showpieces, is dominated by three fountains, a ring of ochre-coloured buildings – many hung with flowers in the summer – and an almost constant throng of visitors, artists and stallholders.

Right: Street traders and artists contribute to the piazza's lively atmosphere

You will probably be tempted back here many times during your visit, although whether your budget will stretch to too many drinks at the piazza's pretty but expensive cafés is another matter. You don't need to spend money, however, simply to enjoy the area, which is an irresistible meeting and people-watching place at most times of the day and night.

Catching up with the news by the Fontana del Nettuno, one of the piazza's trio fountains

The piazza's distinctive elliptical shape betrays its origins, for the square corresponds almost exactly to the outline of the racetrack and stadium built on the site by Emperor Domitian in AD 86. This was known as the Circus Agonalis, a name which by the Middle Ages had been modified to *in agone* and the dialect *n 'agone* before arriving at the present "Navona".

All manner of activities took place here over and above games and races, not least the martyrdom of Sant'Agnese (Saint Agatha), a 13-year-old girl killed in AD 304 for her refusal to renounce her Christian beliefs and marry a pagan. She was thrown into a brothel close to the stadium, then paraded naked in the Circus, only for her nakedness to be covered by the miraculous growth of her hair. The simple oratory eventually built on the site of her death was superseded by the present church of **Sant'Agnese in Agone** (Tue–Sat 9–noon, 4–7, Sun 10–1, 4–8) on the piazza's western edge in the mid-17th century.

One of the architects involved in the church was Borromini, the great but troubled rival of Rome's other baroque superstar, Gian Lorenzo Bernini, who designed the piazza's central fountain, the **Fontana dei Quattro Fiumi** (1648), or Fountain of the Four Rivers. The fountain's four major statues represent the four rivers of Paradise, the Nile, Ganges, Plate and Danube, and the four known corners of the world – Africa, Asia, Europe and America. Note the dove on the top of the obelisk, a symbol of Pope Innocent X Pamphilj, who commissioned the work.

Innocent was also responsible for other major changes to the square, notably the creation of the Palazzo Pamphilj (left of Sant'Agnese), now the Brazilian Embassy, changes which largely put an end to the horse racing, jousting and bullfights that had taken place in the square for much of the Middle Ages. At times the piazza was also flooded, allowing the city's aristocrats to be pulled around the resultant artificial lake in gilded carriages, an echo of the so-called *naumachia*, the mock sea-battles staged by the ancient Romans under similar circumstances.

rnini's
ntana dei
attro Fiumi
etail, right)
s at the heart
the piazza

✚ 194 C3 ✉ Piazza Navona 🚇 Spagna 🚌 30, 70, 81, 87, 116, 492, 628 to
Corso del Rinascimento or 40, 46, 62, 64 to Corso Vittorio Emanuele II

Piazza Navon
is a popular
place for an
after-dinner
stroll

The Fontana o
Nettuno, at th
northern end c
the piazza

TAKING A BREAK

Most of the piazza's cafés are much of a muchness, though
those on its eastern flanks enjoy a little more sun. Two of the
best-known bars are **Caffè di Colombia** (No 89) and **I Tre
Scalini** (► 108), the latter celebrated for its sensational chocolate chip ice-cream (*tartufo*). Don't forget the ever-popular **Bar
della Pace** (► 108) near by.

PIAZZA NAVONA: INSIDE INFO

Top tips Be warned that drinks at cafés around Piazza Navona are some of the
most expensive in the city, but remember that once you've paid for your drink you
can sit at your table as long as you wish.
• Piazza Navona is busy with sightseers by day, but still busier by night, so **leave
time for an after-dinner stroll** past the floodlit fountains and the many artists and
caricaturists who set up shop here.

In more detail An often-told tale relates how Bernini deliberately designed one
of the statues on his central fountain so that it appeared to be shielding its eyes
or recoiling in horror at Sant'Agnese, the church of his great rival, Borromini. It's
a nice story, but in fact the fountain was created before the church.

Hidden gems Most visitors overlook Piazza Navona's two lesser fountains. At
the piazza's northern end stands the **Fontana del Nettuno**, or Fountain of Neptune,
which shows the marine god grappling with a sea serpent. At the southern end is
Giacomo della Porta's **Fontana del Moro** (1575), or Fountain of the Moor, whose
central figure – despite the fountain's name – is actually another marine god: the
erroneous name probably comes from the name of the sculptor, Antonio Mori,
who added the dolphin from a design by Bernini.

Palazzo Altemps

The Palazzo Altemps and its sister gallery, the Palazzo Massimo alle Terme (➤ 120), form the magnificent setting for the cream of Rome's state-owned antiquities. The Roman sculptures here are some of the city's finest, and are superbly displayed in a beautifully restored Renaissance palace.

ne Palazzo Altemps was begun around 1477, but took its
me from Cardinal Marco Sittico Altemps, its owner after
568. Altemps was a collector of antiquities, and would have
en pleased at what has become of his palace, for it now
ouses some of the most sublime sculptures of the classical
e. These sculptures form part of the collection of the Museo
azionale Romano, whose previously poorly displayed
xhibits were split between several new homes at the end of
e 1990s.

The palace and its exhibits spread over just two floors, and
nlike many similar museums don't dull the senses with end-
ss rows of anonymous busts and second-rate statues.
verything here is outstanding, with only a handful of exhibits
each room – some rooms have just one or two sculptures –
th the result that each masterpiece has the space it needs to
ine. As an added bonus, the palace itself has some beautifully
corated and frescoed rooms and chambers, not least the
all church of Sant'Aniceto and the stunning painted loggia
the first floor.

After a small medley of rooms around the ticket hall you
alk into the palace's airy central courtyard, flanked at its top
d bottom (north and south ends) by two statue-filled
cades. Start your explo-
tion by turning left, but
te that although the rooms
e numbered and named on
e gallery plan, their open-
an arrangement encourages
u to wander among the
hibits at random.

Room 7, the Room of the
erms, houses the first of the
llery's major works, two
t-century figures of **Apollo
e Lyrist**, both from the
dovisi collection, a major
oup of sculptures amassed
Ludovico Ludovisi, a
lognese nephew of Pope
egory XV. The collection –
rchased by the Italian gov-
nment in 1901 – forms the
re of the Altemps' displays.
other work from the collec-
n, the **Ludovisi Athena**,
minates Room 9, a statue
stinguished by the finely
rved tunic and the snake
isting to stare at the god-
ss. Room 14 contains a
onderful sculptural group
rtraying Dionysus and satyr
th a panther, full of beauti-
lly carved details such as
onysus' ringleted hair and
sped bunch of grapes.

**Left: Portrait
busts of the
caesars line
the beautiful
painted loggia
on the first
floor**

**The palazzo
is built around
a central
courtyard**

The gallery's real stars are on the first floor. To reach them, cross back over the courtyard and climb the monumental staircase close to where you first entered. This will bring you to the south loggia, where you should hunt out a 2nd-century **sarcophagus** embellished with scenes of Mars and Venus, significant because it was drawn and much admired by Renaissance artists such as Raphael and Mantegna. Room 19 at the far end of the loggia is known as the Painted Views Room – for obvious reasons.

In the next room (Room 20, the Cupboard Room), you come face to face with two sensational statues: the **Ludovisi Orestes and Electra**, a 1st-century group by Menelaus (the artist's signature can be seen on the supporting plinth), and the **Ludovisi Ares**, a seated figure (possibly Achilles) with sword and shield; the sculpture is probably a Roman copy of a Greek original and was restored by Bernini in 1622.

The gallery's finest works occupy the next room (Room 21, The Tale of Moses Room), which contains little more than two monolithic heads and a deceptively humble-looking relief. The heads are the Ludovisi Acrolith (left of the relief) and the **Ludovisi Hera**. The latter was one of the most celebrated and admired busts of antiquity, and has been identified as an idealised portrait of Antonia Augusta, the mother of Emperor

The dramatic *The Gallic Soldier and His Wife Committing Suicide* was commissioned by Julius Caesar

Claudius, who was deified by Claudius after her death and held up as an exemplar of domestic virtue and maternal duty.

Less striking, but more precious to scholars because of its unusual nature and probable age, is the central relief, the **Ludovisi Throne** discovered in 1887 in the grounds of the Villa Ludovis. Although some controversy surrounds the piece, most critics believe it is a 5th-century BC work brought to Rome from one of the Greek colonies in Calabria, southern Italy, after the Romans conquered much of the region in the 3rd century BC. The scene portrayed on the front of the "throne" probably shows the birth and welcome to land of Aphrodite (literally "born of the foam"). Panels on the throne's sides show two young girls, both seated on curious folded cushions, one nude and playing a double-piped flute, the other clothed and sprinkling grains of incense from a box on to a flaming brazier.

Three further exceptional sculptures dominate the large room (Room 26) at the end of the palace's west flank, a large salon with ornate fireplace once used for entertaining palace guests. At its heart stands the *Gallic Soldier and His Wife Committing Suicide*, one of the most dramatic and visceral sculptures in Western art. It was found with the *Dying Galatian* statue, now in the Musei Capitolini (➤ 66–67), and probably

The Ludovisi Throne is one of the gallery's best pieces. Its front panel (below) depicts the birth of Aphrodite

belonged to a group of linked statues based on three bronzes commissioned by Attalus I, king of Pergamum, to commemorate his victory over the Galatians. The marble copies here and on the Capitolino were commissioned by Julius Caesar to celebrate his victory over the Gauls. Like the Ludovisi Throne, the statue was found during construction of the Villa Ludovisi on land that once belonged to Julius Caesar. Finally, don't miss the room's superb helmeted head of Mars and the **Grande Ludovisi Sarcophagus**, a virtuoso sculpture portraying a battle scene divided into three: the victors at the top; the combatants at the centre; and the vanquished at the bottom.

TAKING A BREAK

Stop for a coffee at the ever-popular **Bar della Pace** (➤ 108), just off Piazza Navona.

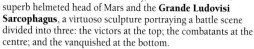

➕ 194 C4   ✉ Piazza di Sant'Apollinare 44   ☎ 06 3996 7700   🕑 Tue–Sun 9–7:45   🚍 30, 70, 81, 87, 116, 492 and 628 to Corso del Rinascimento   🎟 Moderate. Combined pass available ➤ 190

PALAZZO ALTEMPS: INSIDE INFO

Top tips If you come to Rome outside the summer months, try to **visit the Palazzo Altemps after dark**: the superb lighting in the gallery adds immense drama to many of the exhibits.

• Invest in the **gallery guide and plan** published by Electa-Soprintendenza Archeologica di Roma (available in English): it is beautifully illustrated and provides interesting background information to the main exhibits.

Pantheon

The Pantheon is the closest you'll come to a perfect Roman building. One of Europe's best-preserved ancient buildings, its majestic outlines have remained almost unchanged despite the passage of almost 2,000 years. No other monument presents such a vivid picture of how Rome would have looked in its ancient heyday.

The first sight of the Pantheon is one of Rome's most memorable moments. The initial impact is further reinforced when you move closer, for only then does the building's colossal scale become clear – few stone columns, in Rome or elsewhere, are quite as monolithic as the Pantheon's massive pillars. The building itself does not take long to admire, however – inside or out – for there's little specific to see, which means your best bet is to take in the former temple from the sanctuary of an outdoor café table in Piazza della Rotonda.

Temple to Church

The Pantheon you see today was built by Emperor Hadrian between AD 118 and 125. It largely superseded two previous temples on the site, the first having been built some 150 years earlier between 27 and 25 BC by Marcus Agrippa, the son-in-law of Emperor Augustus. This structure was damaged by a momentous fire that swept through Rome in AD 80. A second temple, built by Emperor Domitian, suffered a similar fiery fate when it was struck by lightning in AD 110.

Given this history, the large dedication picked out in bronze letters across the building's facade is puzzling, for it clearly alludes to Marcus Agrippa: *m. agrippa l. f. cos tertium fecit* (Marcus Agrippa, son of Lucius, made this in his third consulship). This apparent anomaly is evidence of Hadrian's modesty, for he habitually retained the name of a building's original dedicatee on the Roman monuments he rebuilt or restored.

Subsequent rulers were less modest, as you can see from the faint two-line inscription below in much smaller letters: *pantheum vetustate corruptum cum omni cultu restituerunt* ("with every refinement they restored the Pantheon, worn by age"). This refers to renovations supposedly made by emperors Severus and Caracalla in AD 202. Not only were the pair

Unknown Purpose

For so great a building it is remarkable that no one really knows the Pantheon's purpose. Its name suggests it was a temple devoted to "all the gods", but there is no record of any such cult elsewhere in Rome. Some theories suggest it was devoted to the 12 Olympian gods of ancient Greece, others that it was not a temple at all in the accepted sense, but rather a place where rulers would glorify themselves by appearing in the company of statues of the gods.

immodest in their claims, they were also dishonest, for it appears the restorations never took place.

Hadrian's involvement was confirmed in 1892, when archaeologists – who until then had associated the building with Agrippa – found that many of the Pantheon's bricks contained the Emperor's personal seal. Hadrian's involvement probably included the building's design, the simple squares and circles of which created a structure of near-architectural perfection.

Plenty of Roman buildings shared the Pantheon's mixed fortunes, but few survived the passage of time in such pristine form. The reason for its excellent condition is that it became a Christian church in AD 608, when Rome's then ruler, the Byzantine emperor Phocas, presented the building to Pope Boniface IV. This was the first time a temple constructed for

e 9m (30-
ot) *oculus* in
e middle of
e dome
amatically
uminates the
terior of the
antheon

pagan rites had been converted into a church – worship in such temples had previously been banned – and the change brought with it the ruling that to remove even a single stone from the site constituted a mortal sin.

Not all the building survived unscathed, however, as you'll see from the porch's exterior walls, which were once largely clad in white marble. The main body of the building to the rear was simply faced in stucco, a cheap way of imitating marble. Better preserved than the cladding are the huge columns, most of which are fashioned from Egyptian granite, together with their capitals and bases, which were carved from finest Greek Pentelic marble. Even here, though, certain contingencies had to be made: one column, for example, was brought from Emperor Domitian's villa in Castelgandolfo in the hills above Rome in 1626; two more – needed to replace damaged pillars – came from the Baths of Nero in 1666.

Damage was not always accidental, however. Sometimes it was inflicted, most notably when Emperor Constans II plundered the bronze gilding that covered many surfaces in 663–7: most of it found its way to Constantinople and was melted down and re-formed into coins. Something similar happened in 1626, when Pope Urban VIII was persuaded by Bernini, the celebrated architect and sculptor, to remove the ancient bronze gilding from the portico's wooden beams. Some 200 tonnes of metal were removed, most of which went to make Bernini's huge *baldacchino*, or altar canopy in St Peter's (► 156–161). Enough metal was left over, it's said, to provide Urban with some 80 new cannons for the Castel Sant'Angelo.

The Pantheon dome is one of the marvels of Roman engineering. It becomes progressively thinner and uses lighter materials towards its top

Dome and Interior

Walking into the interior produces a double take, for looking up at the great coffered dome reveals a 9m (30-foot) hole, or *oculus*, in the middle of the ceiling. This was a deliberate part of Hadrian's design, intended to allow those inside the building a direct contemplation of the heavens. It is also a dramatic source of light, casting a powerful beam of sunlight into the marble-clad interior on sunny days and providing a beautiful glimpse of the starlit sky on clear evenings. On startling occasions, it also allows in birds and rain.

Missing Statues

Among the treasures lost from the Pantheon over the centuries is a statue of Venus that once stood outside Agrippa's original version of the temple. The statue was celebrated for the earrings with which it was adorned, made by cutting in half a pearl that Cleopatra left uneaten after a famous bet she made with Mark Antony that she could spend 10 million *sesterces* on a single meal.

The dome is the Pantheon's greatest glory, measuring 44.4m (242.5 feet) in diameter – greater than the dome of St Peter's – exactly the same as the height of the building from floor to *oculus* (a perfect sphere would fit in the interior). This was the world's largest concrete dome until 1958, when it was superseded by the CNIT building in Paris.

The dome's distinctive coffering, or *lacunas*, was made by pouring material into moulds, just one of the cupola's many engineering subtleties. What you can't see is the way in which the dome's skin becomes thinner as it approaches its apex – from 7m (23 feet) to just 1m (3 feet) thick – so reducing its overall weight. Neither can you see the way in which progressively lighter materials were used: concrete and travertine at the base, volcanic tufa midway up, and featherlight pumice close to the *oculus*.

Lower down, little of the marble veneer you see on the walls is original, although it is thought to correspond closely to Hadrian's original decorative scheme. Much of the pavement, however, although extensively repaired, is believed to be original. Around the walls are seven alternating rectangular and semicircular niches, originally designed to hold statues, but now given over in part to the tombs of the kings and queens of Italy's monarchy (1870–1946). The third niche on the left contains the tomb of the painter Raphael (1483–1520), who was exhumed in 1833 and reburied here in an ancient Roman sarcophagus.

TAKING A BREAK

The **Tazza d'Oro** café (Via degli Orfani 84, tel: 06 678 9792; closed Sun) just off Piazza della Rotonda is considered by many to serve the best coffee in Rome, but unlike the cafés in the square, you can't sit down and there is no view of the Pantheon.

The Pantheon's main facade

🔢 195 D3 ✉ Piazza della Rotonda ☎ 06 6830 0230 🕐 Mon–Sat 8:30–7:30, Sun 9–6, public holidays 9–1; Mass Sat 5 pm, Sun 10:30am and 4:30pm 🚇 Spagna 🚌 116 to Piazza della Rotonda, or 30, 40, 46, 63, 62, 64, 70, 81, 87 and all other services to Largo di Torre Argentina 🎟 Free

---

PANTHEON: INSIDE INFO

Top tips The Pantheon is sometimes **closed on Sunday afternoon**.
• Don't look for the ticket office: the Pantheon is a church and **entrance is free**.
• **Come in the rain** to enjoy the remarkable spectacle of water pouring through the hole in the Pantheon's roof.
• The Pantheon can be seen quickly and easily in conjunction with two other smaller sights: the Caravaggio paintings in **San Luigi dei Francesi** (▶ 102) and the Gothic church of **Santa Maria sopra Minerva**, founded in the 8th century over a Roman temple to Minerva. Outside the church, look out for Bernini's elephant statue supporting an ancient Egyptian obelisk. Inside, be sure to see the frescoes of the *Annunciation* and *Assumption* by Filippino Lippi (in the Cappella Carafa in the right, or south, transept), the statue of *The Redeemer* by Michelangelo to the left of the high altar, and the tomb of Fra Angelico, patron saint of painters, who is buried in a passage at the end of the north (left) nave.

In more detail The date on which the Pantheon was consecrated as a church – 1 November, 608 – is interesting, for it marked the beginning of All Saints' Day, or the Day of the Dead. In another allusion to all the saints, as opposed to all the gods, the church was christened and dedicated to Santa Maria ad Martyres, the Virgin and the Christian Martyrs. Countless martyrs' bones and relics were brought here from catacombs around the city to mark the event.

Trastevere

rastevere means "over the Tevere", and refers to a quaint
nclave of the city on the southern bank of the Tiber (Tevere),
n area that until recently was both the most traditional part
f central Rome and the heart of its eating and nightlife
istrict. Although no longer at the cutting edge, its cobbled
treets and tiny squares are still picturesque places to explore
nd eat either by day or night.

**astevere is
l of small
rs and
staurants**

Trastevere has few hotels, so the chances are you will be
coming here on foot or by bus. It's not far to walk from most of
central Rome, and the routes you would take from places like
the Capitolino or Campo de' Fiori run through interesting parts
of the city such as the Ghetto, the Isola Tiberina and the cluster
of churches and temples around Piazza Bocca della Verità
(➤ 176). If you want to conserve your energy and catch a bus,
there's plenty of choice, as Ponte Garibaldi, the main bridge
linking the rest of Rome to Piazza Sonnino, one of Trastevere's
main squares, is a major city thoroughfare.

   As for what you should see, there are two main sights – the
fine church of **Santa Maria in Trastevere** (➤ 96), the focus of
the area's central square, and the **Villa Farnesina** (➤ 98),
which contains rooms and ceilings adorned with frescoes by
Raphael and others. Lesser attractions include the **Orto
Botanico** (➤ 98, 101), but in the final resort, this is a place to
explore and admire at random, particularly the web of streets
sandwiched between Via Garibaldi and Viale di Trastevere.

Santa Maria in Trastevere

There's nearly always something happening in Piazza Santa Maria in Trastevere: kids playing football, old men chatting, lovers canoodling, though late at night the atmosphere becomes seedier. Even when there are no people to watch, you can simply enjoy the facade of the church that dominates the square. Santa Maria in Trastevere was reputedly founded in 222, which – if true – would make it one of the city's oldest churches. It is first properly documented in 337, when a church was begun here by Pope Julius I, on the site where it was believed that a miraculous fountain of oil had flowed on the day of Christ's birth.

The mosaic in the upper apse of Santa Maria in Trastevere depicts Christ and the Virgin enthroned

Gianicolo

If you have the legs for a longer walk, then aim for the trees and greenery etched on the skyline above Trastevere. This is the Gianicolo, or Janiculum Hill, one of Rome's original "Seven Hills", and views over Rome from here make the climb worthwhile. Walk up Via Garibaldi and look at the **Fontana Paola** (1610–12), a monumental fountain created for Pope Paul V, and then see the late 15th-century church of **San Pietro in Montorio** at the top of Via Garibaldi, supposedly built over the spot on which St Peter was crucified (scholars believe he was actually martyred closer to the present-day site of the Vatican). In an adjoining courtyard stands the **Tempietto**, a tiny masterpiece of Renaissance architecture designed by Bramante, the architect partly responsible for St Peter's.

If you still have energy to burn, walk to the **Villa Doria Pamphilj**, Rome's largest park, a huge area of paths, pines, lakes and open spaces.

nta Maria in
stevere's
autiful
ade mosaics
ow the Virgin
nked by ten
ale figures

The present church dates from the 12th century, and was begun by Pope Innocent II, a member of a prominent local family. Its most arresting features are its facade **mosaics** – many Roman churches would have once been similarly decorated – which portray, among other things, the Virgin flanked by ten figures. Like the identity of the figures themselves, the identity of the mosaics' creator is not known, although Pietro Cavallini is a possible candidate, if only because he was responsible for many of the even more spectacular mosaics inside the church. For instance, Cavallini's hand can be seen in the lively mosaics of the lower apse (1290), which portray scenes from the Life of the Virgin. The scenes in the upper apse are earlier (1140), and are executed in a more old-fashioned Byzantine style.

Don't miss the church's lovely inlaid medieval pavement and the nave's ancient columns, the latter brought here from the Terme di Caracalla, a sprawling Roman baths complex 15 minutes' walk beyond the Colosseum.

prepared for
unexpected
this part of
wn

stevere is
l a largely
idential
trict

Villa Farnesina

From the church, walk northeast on Via della Scala and continue on Via della Lungara, not an exciting walk, but worth making for this beautiful Renaissance villa, built in 1511 for Agostino Chigi, a wealthy Sienese banker. Its highlight the **Loggia of Cupid and Psyche** on the ground floor, adorned with frescoes (1517) designed by Raphael but largely painted by Giulio Romano and others. Upstairs is the **Sala delle Prospettive**, a room entirely covered in bewitching frescoes containing views of Rome and clever *trompe-l'oeil* tricks of perspectiv. The adjoining room, formerly a bedchamber, contains vivid 16th-century frescoes by Sodoma.

A stone's throw from the Villa you'll find the **Orto Botanico** (► 101), at the end of Via Corsini, a turn off Via della Lungara just south of the villa. Opened 1883, its 12ha (30 acres) occupy the former gardens of the Palazzo Corsini, and spread up the slopes of the Gianicolo to the rear. It is famed for its palms and orchids, but is also a lovely place to take a shady time out from sightseeing.

TAKING A BREAK

The **Sala di Tè Trasté** (Via della Lungaretta 76, tel: 06 589 4430; open daily 5pm–2am), a civilised pocket of Trastevere calm, serves coffee, cakes and snac in a comfortable, modern setting.

Santa Maria in Trastevere
✚ 200 B4 ⊠ Piazza Santa Maria in Trastevere ☎ 06 581 4802 ⏰ Daily 7:45am–8/9pm, but may close 12:30–3:30 in winter 🚌 H, 8, 630 and 780 to Viale di Trastevere 💷 Free

Villa Farnesina
✚ 194 A2 ⊠ Via della Lungara 230 ☎ 06 6802 7268; www.lincei.it ⏰ Mon–Sat 9–1 🚌 23, 1 and 280 to Lungotevere della Farnesina or H, 8, 630 and 780 to Viale di Trastevere 💷 Moderate

At Your Leisure

Piazza Farnese

zza Farnese lies just a few steps
m Campo de' Fiori, yet it's hard to
nk of two more contrasting Roman
ares. Campo de' Fiori will always
interesting, because of its market,
t it is shabby and cramped. Piazza
nese is broad and august, graced
h elegant fountains, and unlike the
mpo, which has no buildings of
te, is dominated by the magnificent
azzo Farnese. The palace, which
housed the French Embassy since
71, is closed to the public. You can
l admire the exterior, though,
nmissioned in 1515 by Cardinal
ssandro Farnese (later Pope Paul
), and catch a glimpse through the
ge windows of Annibale Caracci's
ling frescoes (1597–1603) when
interior is illuminated at night.
ch of the stone for the palace was
ered from the Colosseum, and
ised here by the Tuscan architect
tonio da Sangallo the Younger.
en Sangallo died in 1546 he was
laced on the project by
chelangelo, who designed much of
palace's cornice, many of the
per windows and the loggia. For
e of Rome's grandest buildings, the
nch government pays the lowest
t in the city: set, before the advent
he euro, at one lira every 99 years.
e Italians pay a similarly nominal
n for their embassy in Paris.

The **fountains** in the square were
ginally massive baths of Egyptian
inite from the Terme di Caracalla.
ey were brought to the piazza in
16th century by the Farnese
ily, who used them initially as a
s or platform from which to
mire the square's various entertain-
nts (look out for the carved lilies,
Farnese family symbol). They
re turned into fountains in 1626.

➕ 194 B2 ✉ Piazza Farnese
🚌 40, 46, 62, 64, 916 to Corso Vittorio
Emanuele II or H, 8, 63, 630, 780 to
Via Arenula

🔳 Palazzo Spada

There are three modest reasons to
visit the Palazzo Spada, just a couple
of minutes' walk from Campo de'
Fiori. The first is the palace itself,
built for Cardinal Girolamo Capo
di Ferro in 1548. Much of the building's charm derives from the facade,
added between 1556 and 1560,
which is covered in beautifully
patterned stucco work. The second
is an architectural *trompe-l'oeil* created
in 1652 by the craftsman Francesco
Borromini. It involves what appears
to be a long columned corridor
between two courtyards, which is
in fact a passage a little under 9m
(30 feet) long. The illusion is
achieved by the
deliberate narrow-
ing of the
corridor and
foreshort-
ening of
the

columns. The third reason to visit is
its small collection of paintings,
among them works by Titian,
Albrecht Dürer, Jan Breughel the
Elder and Guido Reni's portrait of his
patron, Cardinal Bernardino Spada,
who bought the palace in 1632.

✚ 194 C2 ✉ Vicolo del Polverone 15B
☎ 06 687 4893; www.ticketeria.it
🕒 Tue–Sun 8:30–7:30 🍴 Cafés in
Campo de' Fiori and Piazza Farnese
🚌 H, 8, 40, 46, 64, and other services
to Via Arenula or Corso Vittorio
Emanuele II 🎟 Moderate

❹ Santa Maria dell'Orazione e Morte

After looking at Piazza Farnese, walk along Via dei Farnesi. This soon brings you to **Via Giulia**, laid out by Pope Julius II between about 1503 and 1513, and still one of the city's most elegant and coveted residential thoroughfares. It's well worth admiring, though perhaps not along its full length, for it runs for virtually a kilometre (half a mile) towards St Peter's.

Even if your itinerary doesn't take you down the street, devote a couple of minutes to the church on the junction of Via Giulia and Via dei Farnesi. Look for the unmistakable facade, decorated with stone skulls and, on the right side of the facade, looking down Via Giulia, the figure of a beaked bird – Osiris, the Egyptian god of death. A cheering inscription reads, in translation:

"Me today, thee tomorrow". Santa Maria dell'Orazione e Morte (Our Lady of Oration and Death) was on the headquarters of a religious body known as the Compagnia della Buo Morte, or the "Company of the Goc Death". Its charitable duties includ collecting the unclaimed bodies of the poor and providing them with a

Borromini's architectural *trompe-l'oeil* in the Palazzo Spada creates the illusion of a long corridor in a passage just 9m (10 yards) in length

Christian burial. The corpses were once stored in three large tunnels running down to the Tiber, all but one of which were sealed up during construction of the river's modern embankment.

✚ 194 B2 ✉ Via Giulia 🕒 Open for Mass Sun morning 🚌 23, 63, 280

❼ Sant'Agostino

The church of Sant'Agostino (1479–83) lies tucked away in the streets just north of Piazza

The *Madonna del Parto* by Jacopo Sansovino in the church of Sant'Agostino

avona. The exterior is plain and unprepossessing, although the facade is one of the earliest Renaissance vintages in the city.

The interior, which was extravagantly refurbished in 1750, is that bit more promising, and holds some unlikely treasures for so modest a church. The first is a Michelangelo-influenced fresco of the **Prophet Isaiah** (1512) by Raphael, commissioned by a humanist scholar, Giovanni Goritz, as an adornment to his tomb (the painting is on the third pillar of the left, or north side of the church).

The first chapel on the same side of the church features Caravaggio's outstanding painting, **Madonna di Loreto** (1605). Turn around, and against the west wall – the wall with the entrance door – stands a statue by Jacopo Sansovino known as the **Madonna del Parto**, or Madonna of Childbirth (1521), much venerated by pregnant women or couples wanting a child.

🔂 194 C4 ✉ Via di Sant' Agostino
☎ 06 6880 1962 🕐 Daily 8–noon,

For Kids

Children should enjoy the **Campo de' Fiori** market (➤ 80–81) and the artists and occasional street performers in **Piazza Navona** (➤ 82–85). They'll also relish the ice-cream at I Tre Scalini (➤ 108) or a trip to Bertè (Piazza Navona 108, tel: 06 687 6011, Tue–Sun 9–1, 3:30–7:30, Mon 3:30–7:30), one of Rome's oldest toy shops. Città del Sole (Via della Scrofa 65, tel: 06 6880 3805, Tue–Sat 10–7:30, Sun 11–7:30, Mon 3:30–7:30), near Piazza Navona is also good for toys.

A walk around the **Isola Tiberina** may be a winner, and the **Orto Botanico** (Largo Cristina di Svezia 24, tel: 06 4991 7107, Tue–Sat 9:30–6:30 or dusk, closed Aug, inexpensive) provides plenty of outdoor playing space (popular with local mothers with children) but no playing equipment. The Villa Sciarra, however – to the southwest of Trastevere – has a playground and mini roller-coaster.

4:30–7:30 🍴 Cafés in Piazza Navona
🚌 30, 70, 81, 87, 116, 492 and 628 to
Corso del Rinascimento 🎫 Free

🔳 San Luigi dei Francesi

The French national church
(1518–89) in Rome is easily seen on
the short walk between Piazza
Navona and the Pantheon, and it is
well worth stopping for the five
minutes it takes to see its principal
attractions: three superlative paintings by Caravaggio. The three
pictures are located in the last (fifth)
chapel on the left as you face the
altar. All three are late works

Francesco Borromini's spiral cupola at
Sant'Ivo alla Sapienza was inspired by the
sting of a bee

(1597–1602), and all demonstrate t
dramatic handling of light and shad
or *chiaroscuro* (literally "clear and
dark") for which Caravaggio was
famed. They all deal with the same
theme – the life of St Matthew – an
portray *The Calling of St Matthew* (
saint hears God's summons while
collecting taxes); *St Matthew and th
Angel* (the altarpiece); and *The
Martyrdom of St Matthew.*

➕ 194 C3 ✉ Piazza di San Luigi dei
Francesi at the corner of Via Giustiniani
and Via della Scrofa ☎ 06 6882 8271
🕐 Hours vary, but generally daily
8/8:30–12:30, 3:30–7. Closed Thu and
Sun pm 🍴 Cafés in Piazza Navona or
Piazza della Rotonda 🚌 30, 70, 81, 87,
116, 492 and 628 to Corso del
Rinascimento 🎫 Free

🔳 Sant'Ivo alla Sapienza

The fact that Sant'Ivo is rarely open
matters little, for the church's main
attraction is its extraordinary
spiralling dome and lantern, the wo
of Borromini, a leading baroque
architect and rival of Gian Lorenzo
Bernini. Borromini received his
commission from Pope Urban VIII,
member of the powerful Barberini
family, and it is said
the architect
based his spiky
and eccentric
dome on
the

s-relief from the Ara Pacis
raying the earth goddess
us

ily's symbol, the bee,
ng the bee's sting as his
piration. You'll catch a
pse of the dome if you
k from the Pantheon to
zza Navona via Piazza
t'Eustachio. For a closer
k you need to enter the
azzo alla Sapienza, part of
papal university first
nded in 1303 (roughly
slated, *sapienza* means
sdom" in Italian).

🕂 195 D3 ☒ Corso del
inascimento 40 ☎ 06 686
987 🕓 Mon–Fri 8:30–5,
at–Sun 9–noon, may close at
unchtime 🍴 Cafés in Piazza
lavona or Piazza della Rotonda
🚌 30, 70, 81, 87, 116, 492 and
28 to Corso del Rinascimento
🎟 Free

Ara Pacis

ere's no convenient way to
this Roman monument,
ich lies in an isolated posi-
n near the Tiber and to the
theast of the Castel
t'Angelo. It's well worth
king a detour, however,
the "Altar of Peace" (13–9
, now within architect
hard Meier's controversial modern
vilion (2006), contains some of the
y's best-preserved Roman bas-
efs. The altar was commissioned
the Senate to commemorate

ff the Beaten Track

o escape the hordes, visit Trastevere's
otanical gardens, **Orto Botanico**
➤ 98), off Via Corsini or the **Villa**
oria Pamphilj, a huge park on the
estern flanks of the Gianicolo. It is a
ng walk to the latter, however, so
ke either a cab or bus 870 from the
estern end of Corso Vittorio
manuele II or 115 or 125 from the
outhern end of Viale di Trastevere.

Emperor Augustus' military victories
in France and Spain. The most striking of several sculpted friezes shows
the procession that accompanied the
altar's consecration, and includes the
figures of Augustus, a number of
high-ranking Roman officials and
members of Augustus' family.

🕂 195 D5 ☒ Via di Ripetta ☎ 06
8205 9127; www.arapacis.it
🕓 Tue–Sun 9–7 🚌 224, 628, 926 to
Passeggiata di Ripetta 🎟 Moderate

🄸 Santa Maria del Popolo

This church receives fewer visitors
than it deserves, mainly because it
lies on the northern fringe of the old
city. Founded in the 11th century –
allegedly over the tomb of Emperor

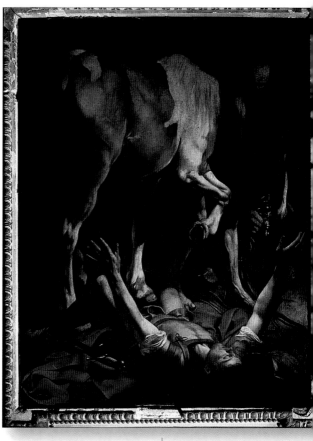

Caravaggio's *The Conversion of St Paul*, one of the artistic treasures in the church of Santa Maria del Popolo

Nero – it was much restored in later centuries by leading architects such as Bramante and Bernini. Inside, there are four outstanding artistic treasures. The first is a series of frescoes (1485–9) behind the altar of the first chapel on the right (south) side by the Umbrian Renaissance painter Pinturicchio; the second is a pair of tombs (1505–7) in the choir by Andrea Sansovino; the third is a pair of paintings by Caravaggio, *The Conversion of St Paul* and *Crucifixion of St Peter* (1601–2) in the first chapel of the left transept; and the fourth is the Cappella Chigi (1513) chapel (second on the left, or north side) commissioned by the wealthy Sienese banker Agostino Chigi. The last is noteworthy because virtually all its component parts were design by Raphael.

➕ 197 F5 ✉ Piazza del Popolo 12
☎ 06 361 0836 🕐 Mon–Sat 8–1:30, 4:30–7:30, Sun 8–7:30 🍴 Rosati
(▶ 138) Ⓜ Flaminio 🚌 117, 119 to Piazza del Popolo 💲 Free

🅱 Palazzo Doria Pamphilj
You'd never imagine looking at the Palazzo Doria Pamphilj's blackened exterior that inside it contained a multitude of beautifully decorated rooms, several of which provide a

mptuous setting for one of Italy's
ost important private art collections.
There's no shortage of great paint-
gs in Rome, but what makes the
llection here so appealing is the
auty of its palatial setting. You could
end an hour or so with the paint-
gs, and then join one of the guided
urs around parts of the palace
rmally closed to visitors. These
urs require an additional admission
on top of an already expensive
ket to see the pictures and are
nducted in Italian. Neither fact
ould put you off, as Rome offers few
portunities to see behind the scenes
so grand a private palace.

The palazzo is one of Rome's
gest, with well over 1,000 rooms,
e courtyards and four colossal
ircases. Its size – in an age when
e upkeep of such buildings is astro-
mical – is all the more remarkable
en that it's still owned, and in part
cupied, by the Doria Pamphilj
mily. This venerable papal dynasty
s created when two families were
ited by marriage: the Doria, an
portant Genoese merchant dynasty,
d the Pamphili (or Pamphilj), a
lar of the Roman aristocracy.

The family's **paintings** are
anged somewhat haphazardly on
rt of the first floor, with Flemish
d Italian works hung alongside
e another – the arrangement
eferred by Prince Andrea Doria IV
1760: a handlist is available to
ke sense of the paintings, which
e numbered rather than labelled.
e collection's most famous work is
lázquez's *Portrait of Innocent X*
650), a pope of notoriously weak
aracter. Innocent is said to have
marked of the likeness that it was
o true, too true". Most of the
eat names of Italian art are also
presented, including Caravaggio
est on the Flight into Egypt and
ry Magdalene), Raphael (*Double
rtrait*) and Titian (*Salome with the
ad of John the Baptist*).

The **guided tours** of the palace
artments take you, among other
ces, to the Saletta Rossa, or Red
om, whose walls are covered in

painted *Allegories of the Elements and
Seasons* by Jan Brueghel the Elder;
the club-like Smoking Room –
created for the English wife of a
Doria scion in the 19th century; the
Winter Garden conservatory; and the
Green Room, home to paintings that
include Renaissance masterpieces by
Lorenzo Lotti (*Portrait of a Man*) and
Filippo Lippi (*Annunciation*).

➕ 195 E3 ✉ Piazza del Collegio
Romano 2 ☎ 06 679 7323;
www.doriapamphilj.it; book tickets on
06 32810 or at www.ticketeria.it
🕐 Gallery: Fri–Wed 10–5. Apartments:
currently closed for restoration
🚇 Barberini 🚌 60, 62, 81, 492 and all
other services to Piazza Venezia
🎫 Gallery: expensive

🔢 Santa Cecilia in Trastevere

This church sits slightly west of
Viale di Trastevere and the rest of
Trastevere, but can easily be included
as part of a Trastevere stroll or a walk
from the other side of the Tiber by
way of the Isola Tiberina. Much of
its appeal is wrapped up in the story
of its dedicatee, St Cecilia, who is
said to have lived with her husband
Valerio, an important Roman patrician figure, in a house on the site in
the 4th century.
Valerio joined
his chaste
wife as a
Christian,
only to
be

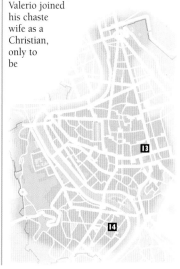

rewarded with martyrdom. Cecilia's own martyrdom was protracted: attempts to scald and suffocate her failed, and she finally succumbed to three blows to her neck, but only after singing throughout her ordeal – one of the reasons why she is the patron saint of music.

The present church is a mixture of styles, ranging from the 12th-century portico to the 18th-century facade and chill baroque interior. Several fine works of art survived the years, notably a **statue of St Cecilia** by Carlo Maderno. The sculptor was apparently present when the saint's tomb was opened in 1599, her body having previously been moved from the catacombs outside the city on the orders of Pope Paschal I in the 9th century. Maderno made a drawing of her reputedly uncorrupt body, and in his statue clearly depicted the three cuts left by the Roman executioner's unsuccessful attempts to cut off Cecilia's head. Today, the saint's tomb is in the church's crypt which can be visited, along with excavations which reveal the remains of a Roman house.

Above the church's altar is a lovely Gothic *baldacchino*, or **altar canopy** (1293), the work of Arnolfo di Cambio. The apse is adorned with a

glowing 9th-century **mosaic** which shows Pope Paschal I presenting Cecilia and her husband Valerio to Christ. The cloister features celebrated frescoes of the **Last Judgeme** (1293) by the Roman painter and mosaicist Pietro Cavallini, an impor tant contemporary of Giotto.

✠ 200 C4 ✉ Piazza di Santa Cecilia in Trastevere ☎ 06 589 9289
🕑 Church: daily 9:30–12:30, 4–6:30 (hours can vary). Cavallini frescoes: Mon–Sat 10:15–12:15, Sun 11am–12:30pm
🚌 56, 60, 75, 710, 780 🚋 8 to Viale di Trastevere

The late 16th-century statue of St Cecilia by Carlo Maderno in the church of Santa Cecilia in Trastevere

Where to...
Eat and Drink

Prices

Expect to pay per person for a meal, excluding drinks and service
€ under €20   €€ €20–40   €€€ over €40

Augusto €

Where once Rome was filled with old-fashioned trattorias straight out of a 1950s Fellini film, these days such charming restaurants are a dying breed. Augusto is one of the few survivors, serving basic but authentic Roman dishes at quite reasonable prices in one of Trastevere's prettier and quieter piazzas. Tables on the square during summer allow you to eat outdoors. Be prepared for occasional brusque service. No credit cards.

🚹 194 B1 ⊠ Piazza de' Renzi 15
🕿 06 580 3798 🕘 Daily noon–3, 8–11. Closed mid-Aug to mid-Sep

La Bottega del Vino €

Part of this shop, situated between Piazza Navona and the Pantheon, is given over to wine, but there are also tables where you can enjoy a simple lunch of cheese and cold cuts, salad and one or two daily specials. Order at the counter by the till, where you will be able to see most of the food available. Arrive early to be sure of securing a table.

🚹 195 D3 ⊠ Via del Teatro Valle 48–9 🕿 06 686 5970 or 06 6830 0475 🕘 Lunch only Tue–Sat 12.45–3 (wine shop Tue–Sat 8–8). Closed 3 weeks in Aug

La Carbonara €–€€

This popular Campo de' Fiori fixture is the best restaurant on the square, and serves perfectly acceptable food at decent prices. The large number of outdoor tables means you shouldn't have to wait too long to be seated.

🚹 194 C2 ⊠ Campo de' Fiori 23
🕿 06 686 4783 🕘 Wed–Mon 12:15–3, 7–11.30. Closed 3 weeks in Aug

Il Convivio €€€

The bill may be a shock, but it's unlikely to be as high as in the city's other top-class restaurants, and here at least you're assured of a memorable meal with good service in tasteful and intimate surroundings. The menu changes according to season and the inclinations of the chef, combining a dash of traditional Roman cuisine with creative Italian-based cooking.

🚹 194 C4 ⊠ Vicolo dei Soldati 31
🕿 06 686 9432 🕘 Dinner only Mon–Sat 8–10.30. Closed 1 week in Aug

Grappolo d'Oro €–€€

When The New Yorker magazine's former Rome correspondent wrote his farewell to the city, he based the article on observations of and from this peerless traditional trattoria close to Campo de' Fiori. Little has changed here in decades, from the seemingly ageless waiters to the traditional cooking – try the delicious ravioli alla Gorgonzola or one of the various risottos. The only difference, inevitably, is that more visitors know about the place, so arrive early: reserving a table is hit and miss.

🚹 194 C3 ⊠ Piazza della Cancelleria 80 🕿 06 689 7080 🕘 Daily noon–3, 7.30–11; closed lunch Tue–Fri in winter

Il Leoncino €

Other pizzerias in the city may be better known, but Il Leoncino, just a couple of blocks west of Via del Corso, offers the authentic Roman pizzeria experience – and is likely to be busy with locals. Pizzas are made behind an old marble-topped bar and cooked in wood-fired ovens.

195 D5 **Via del Leoncino 28, off Piazza San Lorenzo in Lucina** **06 687 6306** **Lunch: Mon–Tue, Thu–Fri 1–2:30. Dinner: Thu–Tue 6:30–midnight**

Matricianella €€

You'll need to reserve a table at this simple but snug three-room trattoria, where the plainness of the decor is more than compensated for by superb Roman food (including "fritti", or deep-fried specialities) and other more innovative dishes. Service is friendly, and you can order wine by the glass.

195 D5 **Via del Leone 3–4, off Via del Leoncino** **06 683 2100** **Mon–Sat 12:30–3, 7:30–11. Closed Aug**

Myosotis €€

The vivid modern dining-rooms and light, innovative cooking at Myosotis are something of a departure from Rome's often rather

traditional and decoratively uninspired restaurants. Service is amiable, the atmosphere relaxed, and the prices reasonable. Menus change with the season, but almost always include Roman classics such as *spaghetti alla carbonara* and a selection of fish.

195 D4 **Vicolo della Vaccarella 3–5** **06 686 5554** **Mon–Sat 7:30–11. Closed 3 weeks in Aug**

Paris €€–€€€

Paris serves some of the city's best fish and traditional Roman-Jewish cuisine (including deep-fried artichokes, pasta and chickpeas and salt cod). Other more conventional Roman and Italian dishes are also available. In fine weather there are a few tables outside, while the interior is a picture of simple elegance. A safe bet for a reliable meal in pleasant surroundings.

197 E1 **Piazza San Calisto 7a** **06 581 5378** **Tue–Sat 12:30–3, 7:45–11. Sun 7:45–11**

La Rosetta €€€

Rome has several good fish and seafood restaurants, the best and most central being La Rosetta, just a few steps from the Pantheon and Italian Parliament (the restaurant is a politicians' favourite). Prices are high – they usually are for fish – but meals here are invariably memorable and the elegant setting is perfect if you want to dress up. Reservations are essential.

195 D3 **Via della Rosetta 8–9** **06 686 1002** **Mon–Sat 1–3, 8–11:30**

BARS AND CAFÉS

Bar della Pace €

Old Rome hands may be cynical about this place just off Piazza Navona, but they still come back. By day, the bar is a pretty place for a coffee; by night it is one of the city's best and buzziest spots. The pizzeria-trattoria alongside is also good.

194 B3 **Via della Pace 3–7** **06 686 1216** **Daily 9am–2am**

Cul de Sac €

This wine bar, founded in 1968, close to Piazza Navona serves a large selection of wines, as well as a good selection of (mostly cold) snacks and appetisers.

194 C3 **Piazza Pasquino 73** **06 6880 1094** **Daily noon–4, 6–12:30**

Il Goccetto €

An intimate and cosy wine bar close to Cul de Sac (see above) that takes its wine seriously. The setting, part of a grand medieval house, is lovely, with original frescoed ceilings.

194 A3 **Via dei Banchi Vecchi 14** **06 686 4268** **Mon–Sat 11:30–2, 7–11. Closed 3 weeks in Aug and Sat lunch Jul and Aug**

I Tre Scalini €

I Tre Scalini would be just one more Piazza Navona bar were it not for its rightly celebrated *tartufo* ice-cream.

194 C3 **Piazza Navona 28–32** **06 6880 1996** **Daily 9am–1am**

Where to...
Shop

The heart of Rome is a large and varied area and the shopping opportunities here are correspondingly mixed and extensive. Small side streets often prove a happy hunting ground for specialities, notably Via dei Coronari (antiques), Via dei Giubbonari (inexpensive clothes and shoes), Via Giulia (art and antiques), Via dei Cappellari (furniture), Via dei Sediari (religious ephemera), and Via del Governo Vecchio, Via dei Banchi Nuovi and Via dei Governo (galleries, antiques and second-hand items). Although Trastevere also has its share of small craft, antiques and speciality shops,

it is not a major shopping area; it does, however, have a large general market in Piazza San Cosimato. The other main market in the area covered by this chapter is at Campo de' Fiori (▶ 80–81).

ART AND ANTIQUES

La Sinopia

The artefacts at La Sinopia, one of several antiques shops in this interesting antiques street, are of high quality and though prices are fairly high too, they offer value for money.

🖂 Via dei Banchi Vecchi 21c
☎ 06 687 2869 🕙 Mon–Sat 10–1, 4:30–7:30

BOOKS

Feltrinelli

Part of a large, modern, nationwide chain, Feltrinelli stocks a good range of English-language titles. It also sells a wide selection of attractive cards, magazines and posters, as well as stylish toys and games.

🖂 Largo di Torre Argentina 5a ☎ 06 6680 3248 🕙 Mon–Sat 9–8, Sun 10–1:30, 4–7:30

Libreria del Viaggiatore

This book shop specialises in travel literature, maps and guides, and stocks a selection of English-language titles.

🖂 Via del Pellegrino 78
☎ 06 6880 1048 🕙 Tue–Sat 10–2, 4–8, Mon 4–8

Rinascita

Formerly a serious, high-brow book shop, Rinascita has more recently branched out into "softer" areas such as art books, comics, videos and modern writing. A good selection of English and other foreign-language titles are also available. There is an excellent music shop next door.

🖂 Via delle Botteghe Oscure 1–3
☎ 06 679 7637 🕙 Daily 10–8

CLOTHES

Davide Cenci

You won't be in Rome long before you realise that many of the city's older inhabitants like to adopt a classic English style in clothing and accessories. Davide Cenci is a large, rambling shop near Piazza Navona and this is where Romans have come since 1926 for an Italian take on tweeds, Burberry-type raincoats and crisp double-cuff shirts.

🖂 Via Campo Marzio 1–7 ☎ 06 699 0681 🕙 Tue–Fri 9:30–1:30, 3:30–7:30, Sat 9:30–7:30, Mon 3:30–7:30

COSMETICS AND TOILETRIES

Antica Erboristeria Romana

This fascinating store has been selling herbal remedies and other herbal and natural products since the 18th century.

🖂 Via di Torre Argentina 15 ☎ 06 687 9493 🕙 Mon–Fri 8:30–7:30, Sat 9–7:30

Officina Profumo-Farmaceutico di Santa Maria di Novella

This Roman outlet for a Florence-based shop sells cosmetics, perfumes, and herbal and other natural products, the majority of which are made to traditional methods originally devised by Dominican monks.

✉ Corso del Rinascimento 47 ☎ 06 687 9608 ⓘ Mon–Sat 9:30–7:30

FABRICS

Bassetti

Rows and rows of fabrics fill this store, along with some clothes and home furnishings.

✉ Corso Vittorio Emanuele II 73 ☎ 06 689 2326 ⓘ Jul–Aug Tue–Sat 9–7:30, Mon 3:30–7; rest of year Tue–Sat 9–1, 4–6, Mon 4–6

FOOD

Ai Monasteri

This intriguing shop lies just across

Farmaceutico di Santa Maria di Novella (see above) at the northern end of Piazza Navona. It sells a wide variety of honey, oils, jam, liqueurs and other food products made, grown or gathered at Italian monasteries.

✉ Corso del Rinascimento 72 ☎ 06 6880 2783 ⓘ Mon–Wed, Fri–Sat 9–1, 4:30–7:30; Thu 9–1

Innocenzi

If you're visiting Trastevere's Piazza San Cosimato market, be sure to drop into this wonderful cornucopia of ordinary and extraordinary foods from across the world.

✉ Piazza San Cosimato 66 ☎ 06 581 2725 ⓘ Mon–Wed, Fri–Sat 8–1:30, 4:30–8; Thu 8–1:30

Moriondo e Gariglio

This family-run concern makes and sells delicious and outstanding chocolate in all shapes, sizes and varieties.

✉ Via del Piè di Marmo 21–22 ☎ 06 699 0856 ⓘ Mon–Sat

Valzani

A superb and long-established Trastevere institution celebrated for its cakes, chocolate, pastries and other delicious treats for those with a sweet tooth.

✉ Via del Moro 37b ☎ 06 580 3792 ⓘ Wed–Sat 10–8. Closed Jun–Aug

HOUSEHOLD

House & Kitchen

Unlike Spazio Sette (see below), this is a traditional shop that sells a full range of kitchen utensils – basic and exotic – and other household goods.

✉ Via del Plebiscito 103 ☎ 06 679 4208 ⓘ Mon–Sat 9:30–8, Sun 10:30–2:30. Closed Sun, Jul and Aug

Ceramica Musa

A host of ceramic tiles are available at this colourful shop to the north of the Pantheon.

✉ Via Campo Marzio 39 ☎ 06 687 1242 ⓘ Tue–Fri 9–1, 3:45–7:30, Sat 9–1, Mon 4–7:30. Closed Aug, and Sat

Ornamentum

Rome has several shops offering a beautiful range of furnishing and other fabrics, but none perhaps quite as sumptuous as Ornamentum on Via dei Coronari. This is the ultimate emporium for silks, damasks and other fabrics, as well as an enormous range of tassels, brocades and assorted furnishing accessories.

✉ Via dei Coronari 227 ☎ 06 687 6849 ⓘ Tue–Fri 9–1, 4–7:30, Sat 9–1, Mon 4–7.30. Closed Aug

Spazio Sette

Old mixes with new at Spazio Sette, the city's best furniture, household and design store, where a huge range of consumer desirables are spread over three floors of a Renaissance palace complete with frescoed ceilings and pretty court-yard garden.

✉ Via dei Barbieri 7 ☎ 06 6880 4261 ⓘ Tue–Sat 9:30–1, 3:30–7:30,

Where to...
Be Entertained

CLASSICAL MUSIC

One or two classical music organisations have their headquarters in the centre of Rome (even if they stage their concerts elsewhere). One is the **Associazione Musicale Romana** (AMR) on Via Gregorio VII 268 (tel: 06 3936 6322 or 06 686 8441; www.assmusrom.it), which usually puts on **chamber concerts** in spring and early summer; tickets are obtainable from individual venues. Another organisation is the important **Oratorio del Gonfalone** (tel: 06 687 5952), which has its own orchestra and choir who usually perform at the Oratorio del Gonfalone in Via del Gonfalone, a tiny street between Via Giulia and Lungotevere Sangallo. It specialises in small chamber recitals, but also presents concerts by visiting Italian ensembles.

Many of the city's major **church music** concerts – usually performed by visiting choirs – are staged in the central **Sant'Ignazio,** a large church in Piazza di Sant'Ignazio almost midway between the Pantheon and Via del Corso. Unfortunately, the building has poor acoustics – the best place to sit is as close to the front as possible, so you need to arrive early. Contact visitor centres (▶ 30) for details of forthcoming concerts, or look for posters outside the church. Recitals are usually free.

Several churches in the area offer **organ recitals**, but you need to keep your eyes peeled for posters advertising concerts. A good bet is **San Giovanni de' Fiorentini** in Via Giulia where, after noon Mass on Sunday, you may be treated to the sound of the church's wonderful late 17th-century instrument. The AMR (see above) generally organises an organ festival in the church during September.

NIGHTLIFE

Campo de' Fiori

Campo de' Fiori has become something of a focus for bars that come into their own at nightfall. The place that started the trend is the piazza's gritty **La Vineria** (Campo de' Fiori 15, tel: 06 6880 3268, open Mon–Sat 8:30am–2am, Sun 5pm–1am), also known as Da Giorgio, as authentic a Roman wine bar as you could hope for. It makes few concessions to interior decoration – there is just one plain bar –

and the characters who collect here can be colourful, to say the least. The outside tables are a favourite rendezvous on summer evenings. Almost immediately alongside La Vineria is the **Drunken Ship** (Campo de' Fiori 20–21, tel: 06 6830 0535, open daily 4pm–2am), a boisterous and brash place much favoured by young Romans and foreign visitors alike. It serves mostly beer rather than wine and is further distinguished from its adjacent rival by its bold design and the fact that it has DJs and music most evenings: happy hour usually runs from about 5pm to 8pm.

Around Piazza Navona

For a somewhat calmer alternative to the bars on Campo de' Fiori, try **Cul de Sac** (▶ 108) and **Il Goccetto** (▶ 108) and the perennially hip **Bar della Pace** (▶ 108), the latter perhaps the most popular place to hang out in this part of Rome. For something almost equally trendy but a little less busy, wander round the corner to **Bar del Fico** (Piazza del Fico 26–28, tel: 06 686 5205, open Mon–Sat 9am–2am, Sun 6pm–2am). It is a touch less expensive and in winter has outdoor heating so you can still sit outside.

Jonathan's Angels (Via della Fossa 16, tel: 06 689 3426, open Mon–Fri 8pm–2am, Sat–Sun 2pm–2am), just off Piazza Navona, is an eccentric but delightfully decorated bar, decked out with candles and plenty of kitsch and overpowering paintings.

Also close to Piazza Navona is **Anima** (Via Santa Maria dell' Anima 57, tel: 06 6889 2806, open daily noon–4am), a small and welcoming bar and club with an eclectic music policy. A few minutes from the Pantheon is **Salotto 42** (Piazza di Petra 42, tel: 06 678 5804, Tue–Sun 10am–2am), a cosy place for lunch or, later, cocktails in a stylish setting

Around Piazza Venezia

Irish bars are big in many Italian cities, and Rome is no exception. One of the biggest and best in the city is **Trinity College**, housed near the Palazzo Doria Pamphilj (▶ 104–105) over two floors of a beautiful Renaissance palace at Via del Collegio Romano 6 (tel: 06 678 6472, open daily noon–3am). Good and inexpensive Irish food is served along with the inevitable beers and stouts.

Trastevere

In Trastevere, the best of the night-time bars and pubs is **Della Scala** (Via della Scala 4, tel: 06 580 3610, open daily 5pm–2am), a big and bustling place for beer by the glass, cocktails and light meals and snacks. It is much patronised by the young, and is definitely not the place for a quiet drink. For something quieter, try **Sacchetti** (Piazza San Cosimato 61–2, tel: 06 581 5374, open Tue–Sun 6am–midnight), a family-run bar with

tables outside. It serves delicious ice-cream and home-made cakes and pastries.

Best of the live jazz and blues joints is long-established **Big Mama** (Vicolo San Francesco a Ripa 18, tel: 06 581 2551, www.bigmama.it, open Tue–Sat 9pm–1:30am, Oct–Jun). It describes itself, with some justification, as the "Home of Blues in Rome", staging around 200 concerts a year. Stars of today and yesteryear perform alongside up-and-coming Italian musicians.

Testaccio

Though Trastevere is still lively at night and has many good bars and clubs, it is no longer as trendy as it was a few years ago. The axis of night-time action has now shifted to **Testaccio** and **Ostiense**, traditional working-class districts further south. In summer the district buzzes with clubs, bars and outdoor venues, but it's peripheral to the city centre, so you'll need to take a bus or taxi to get there

Venues of the moment change with some regularity, but you can always be sure to find something to suit your tastes. Two of the more permanent fixtures for live music and dancing are **Akab** (Via di Monte Testaccio 69, tel: 06 5740 4485, www.akabcave.it, open Tue–Sat 11pm–4am) and **Caffè Latino** (Via di Monte Testaccio 96, tel: 06 5728 8556, open Tue–Sun 10:30am–3am or later). **L'Alibi** (Via di Monte Testaccio 40–7, tel: 06 574 3448, open Wed–Sun 11pm– 4:30am), a primarily (though not exclusively) gay club, is one of the most established venues in the city.

CINEMA

Trastevere has one of Rome's few English-language cinemas, the venerable three-screen **Pasquino**, (Piazza Sant'Egidio 10, tel: 06 580 3622), but the auditoria are small and probably only worth a visit if you're desperate to see a movie

Northern
Rome

Getting Your Bearings

This chapter encompasses two contrasting areas of Rome. The first is around Termini, the city's main railway station, an unlovely part of the city you'd avoid were it not for a superb museum and major church; the second is around Piazza di Spagna, an area renowned for the Spanish Steps, full of wonderful streets, fantastic shops, memorable views, and compelling museums and galleries.

The mid 20th-century architecture of Termini railway station has its admirers, but in truth there is little in the area around the station – which is all hustle, traffic, buses and cheap hotels – to tempt you into staying longer than it takes to see the distinguished church of Santa Maria Maggiore and the magnificent collection of Roman statues, mosaics and wall paintings at Palazzo Massimo alle Terme.

Once your sightseeing in this part of the city is finished, you could catch the Metro from Repubblica to Spagna station to visit Piazza di Spagna, a means of avoiding a mostly uninteresting and far from pretty 19th-century part of the city. Alternatively, you could walk from the Palazzo Massimo alle Terme towards Via Vittorio Veneto (often known simply as Via Veneto), famous in the 1950s and 1960s as the focus of Rome's *dolce vita* days of hedonism and high living: today, sadly, it lives largely on its past reputation. You could also take the works of art at Palazzo Barberini, as well as the interior of Santa Maria della Vittoria, home to a notorious Bernini sculpture.

By the time you reach the Trevi Fountain, the most spectacular of the city's many fountains, you have re-entered Rome's old historic core and are close to its most exclusive shopping district, the grid of streets centred on Via Condotti. You could easily spend a couple of hours here window-shopping, perhaps followed by a lazy half-hour people-watching in Piazza di Spagna. Literary pilgrims may want to visit the small museum on the piazza devoted to the poets John Keats and Percy Bysshe Shelley. Then climb the Spanish Steps for views over Rome, and, if the weather's fine, walk northwest from Piazza di Spagna along Viale della Trinità dei Monti. This street offers more fine views and leads into a more open part of the city, allowing you to strike into the Pincian Hill, and from there into the park and gardens of the Villa Borghese. A 1km (half-mile) walk through the park brings you to the Borghese gallery and museum, home to superb sculptures by Bernini and paintings by Caravaggio, Raphael and other major painters. If you don't want to walk, take a cab or bus 116 from Piazza di Spagna.

Previous page: Bernini's *Apollo and Daphne* in the Galleria Borghese
Top left: Apse mosaic depicting Mary and Jesus in Santa Maria Maggiore

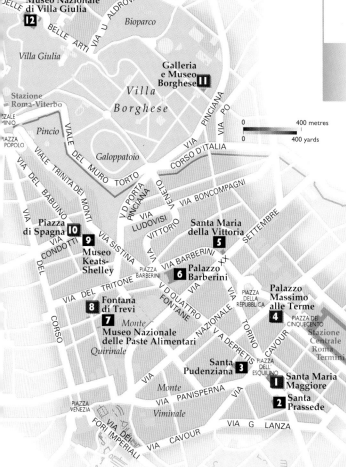

This itinerary, which takes you to some of the most famous sights in Rome's more easterly and northern margi requires you to travel a little further from the city centre th on previous days.

Northern Rome in a Day

8:30am

Make your way to Piazza dei Cinquecento on foot, or by bus, Metro or tax and then walk the short distance to 🚩 **Santa Maria Maggiore** (➤ 118–119 Explore the magnificently decorated church, especially its mosaics, and th visit the small nearby churches of 🟤 **Santa Prassede** (➤ 132) and 🟤 **San Pudenziana** (➤ 132).

9:15am

Walk to the 🟤 **Palazzo Massimo all Terme** (➤ 120–123) and allow a couple of hours to explore the museum's superb collection of classical sculpture and rare Roma. mosaics and wall paintings (left).

11:00am

Walk west towards Piazza di Spagna, perhaps stopping off en route to vis 🟤 **Santa Maria della Vittoria** (➤ 132–133), home to Bernini's erotic sculptu of St Teresa, Santa Maria della Concezione (➤ 16) and the 🟤 **Palazzo Barberini** (➤ 133–134), where works by Raphael, Caravaggio and Titian, among others, are on display.

12:30pm

Make your way to the 🟤 **Trevi Fountain** (right, ➤ 124–125), immortalised in Fellini's film, *La Dolce Vita*, then continue north towards Via Condotti and Piazza di Spagna. If you have time, visit the 🟤 **Museo Nazionale delle Paste Alimentari** (➤ 134).

1:00pm

top for a either a snack lunch or a restaurant meal in the streets around the Trevi Fountain and Piazza di Spagna.

2:00pm

After lunch you might stop for a offee in the historic Antico Caffè Greco (➤ 138). Serious shoppers will want to spend plenty of time in the area around **Via Condotti** (➤ 139) others can visit the **9 Museo Keats-Shelley** (➤ 135). veryone should walk to the top of e **Spanish Steps** (➤ 126–127) to admire the views.

3:00pm

Meander through the parkland of the Villa Borghese to the **11 Galleria Borghese** (➤ 128–131), filled with sculptural masterpieces such as Bernini's *Pluto and Proserpina* (left), as well as magnificent works by Caravaggio and others. If the walk is too far, take a 116 bus or taxi from Piazza di Spagna. Remember you need to reserve in advance for the Galleria.

5:30pm

After seeing the Galleria you'll be far from the city centre. You could walk west through the park to e **12 Villa Giulia** (➤ 135) to see its Etruscan arte- acts or catch the 52, 53, 10 or 116 (from Piazzale Brasile) back to the city centre.

Santa Maria Maggiore

Santa Maria Maggiore is the most important – and possibly the oldest – of some 80 churches in Rome dedicated to the Virgin Mary. Its surroundings are not the prettiest in the city but the ancient basilica's richly decorated interior is one of the most sumptuous in Italy.

According to legend, the church was built after the Virgin appeared to Pope Liberius in a vision on 4 August, 356 and told him to build a church on the spot where snow would fall the following day. Snow duly fell, despite the fact that it was the middle of summer, leading not only to the foundation of a church, but also to the instigation of a feast day – Our Lady of the Snow – on 5 August. In truth, the church was probably founded in the middle of the 5th century, on the ruins of a Roman building dating back to the 1st century, possibly earlier.

This building was probably a temple to Juno Lucina, a mother goddess, much revered by Roman women, and it is probably no accident that a pagan cult was replaced by its Christian equivalent: the new church was dedicated to the mother of Christ as Santa Maria ad Praesepe (St Mary of the Crib). The church's maternal link was further reinforced by relics of Christ's Holy Crib, fragments of which were enshrined beneath the high altar.

Obelisks and pillars stand sentinel outside the church's (usually closed) north and south entrances, one a Roman copy of an Egyptian obelisk (in Piazza dell'Esquilino) removed from the Mausoleo di Augusto, the other a column removed from the Basilica di Massenzio in the Roman Forum. The main south entrance is the usual entry point for visitors.

Much has been added to the church since the 5th century, not least its immense weight of decoration, but the original basilica-shaped plan survives, a design probably adapted directly from the site's earlier Roman structure. Almost the first thing to strike you inside is the magnificent coffered **ceiling**, reputedly gilded with the first gold to be shipped from the New World, a gift from Ferdinand and Isabella of Spain to Pope Alexander VI. A small museum details the basilica's history.

The colossal columns supporting the ceiling lead the eye upwards to a superb 36-panel sequence of **mosaics**, 5th-century works portraying episodes from the lives of Moses, Isaac, Jacob and Abraham. A later, but equally magnificent mosaic (1295) depicting the Coronation of the Virgin swathes the apse, the area behind the high altar, the work of Jacopo Torriti. Complementary swirls of colour adorn parts of the church floor, examples of Cosmati inlaid marble work dating

Mass has be celebrated in Santa Maria Maggiore for more than 1,500 years

ncient marbles
om the
alatine Hill
ere used
decorate
e Cappella
istina,
anta Maria
aggiore's most
nate chapel

from the middle of the 12th century. More 13th-century mosaics can be seen on guided tours to the basilica's loggia.

Among the interior's most impressive additions are a pair of large facing chapels: the **Cappella Sistina** (on the right as you face the altar) and the **Cappella Paolina** (on the left), completed for popes Sixtus V and Paul V in 1587 and 1611 respectively. Little in either is individually outstanding, but the overall decorative effect is overwhelming.

TAKING A BREAK

If you want a leisurely drink, the best advice is to continue on towards Piazza di Spagna. **Monti DOC** (➤ 142), however, is a good local choice.

🖪 199 E1 🖂 Piazza di Santa Maria Maggiore and Piazza dell'Esquilino ☎ 06 483 195 ◷ Apr– p daily 7–7; Oct–Mar 7–6:30 🚇 Termini or Cavour 🚌 5, 14, 16, 70, 71, 75, 84, 105 📋 Free

SANTA MARIA MAGGIORE: INSIDE INFO

Top tip Santa Maria Maggiore is in a relatively unappealing part of the city close to the Termini railway station, but can be easily combined with a visit to the nearby Palazzo Massimo alle Terme. Unlike many churches in the city, it remains open all day.

Hidden gem Look out for the **tomb of Cardinal Consalvo Rodriguez** in the chapel to the rear right (south) of the high altar as you face it. The cardinal died in 1299, and the tomb was completed soon after. Its sculptor is not known, but the beautiful inlaid marble is the work of Giovanni di Cosma, one of the family first responsible for this distinctive "Cosmati" decorative style.

Palazzo Massimo alle Terme

The Palazzo Massimo alle Terme houses part of the Museo Nazionale Romano, one of the world's greatest collections of ancient art. One of the city's newest museum spaces, it provides a magnificent showcase for some of the most beautiful sculptures, paintings and mosaics of the Roman age.

The Palazzo lies close to Rome's unlovely Termini station, but don't be put off, for once inside the superbly restored 19th-century building you're confronted by beauty at every turn. The gallery spreads over three floors: the first two levels (ground and first floor) are devoted largely to sculpture, the top (second floor) mostly to mosaics and a series of frescoed Roman rooms moved from sites around the city. Such painted rooms are extremely rare, most frescoes of this age having long been lost to the elements. They are also surprisingly beautiful, so be certain to leave enough time to do them justice.

These mosaics and paintings distinguish the Palazzo Massimo from its sister museum, the Palazzo Altemps (► 86–89), which is smaller and devoted more to sculpture, and in particular to the outstanding sculptures of the Ludovisi collection.

The wall paintings from the Villa di Livia are part of the rare collection of frescoes and mosaics on the second floor

Beyond the ticket hall and vestibule, bear to your right for the first of the ground floor's eight rooms, which are arranged around the palace's interior central courtyard. Ahead of you, along the courtyard's right-hand side, runs a gallery – one of three – filled with portrait busts and statues that served as funerary or honorary monuments in the last years of the Republican era (the end of the 2nd and beginning of the 1st century BC). Room I opens to the right, where the high-light among several busts and statues of upper-class Roman figures is the **General of Tivoli**. It was probably the work of a Greek sculptor and is thought to have been executed between 90 and 70 BC, at a time when the Romans were conducting numerous military campaigns in Asia.

Room III contains a collection of Roman coins, while the highlight of Room V is a virtuoso statue of **Emperor Augustus** – note the exquisite detail of the emperor's toga. Different in style, but no less compelling, is Room VII's statue of **Niobede**, one of the mythical daughters of Niobe murdered by Apollo and Artemis: the statue shows Niobede trying to remove an arrow shot by Artemis. Other rooms and galleries on this floor contain many more similarly outstanding sculptures, as well as small areas of wall painting that whet the appetite for the exhibits on the museum's top floor (➤ 122).

Sculptures on the next (first) floor move chronologically through the Roman era, picking up the thread of the floor below in Room I with work from the era of the Flavian emperors (after AD 69) – Vespasian, Titus and Domitian. The following 14 rooms contain exhibits spanning the next 400 years.

Interspersed with these are rooms arranged by theme, notably Room VI, which is devoted to the idealised sports and other statues that once adorned ancient Rome's gymnasiums and sporting arenas. Here you'll find the gallery's most famous statue,

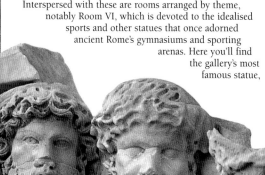

ow right:
e Palazzo
ssimo
ntains a
alth of
e Roman
ulpture

the **Discobolo Lancellotti**, or Lancellotti Discus-Thrower (mid-2nd century AD), the finest of several Roman copies of a celebrated 5th-century BC Greek bronze original. This original was widely celebrated by classical writers as a perfect study of the human body in motion.

A very different, but equally beguiling statue resides in Room VII, devoted to gods and divinities, and shows L'Ermafrodito Addormentato, or **Sleeping Hermaphrodite** (2nd century AD). Like the Discus-Thrower, the sculpture is the best of several known copies made from a popular Greek original created some 400 years earlier. The statue's sensuous appearance made it a popular adornment for gardens and open spaces in the grand houses of private individuals. A far cruder statue, depicting **a masked actor in the guise of Papposileno**, is the most striking figure in Room IX, which is given over to the theatre and performing arts.

Discobolo Lancellotti, a Roman copy of an earlier Greek bronze, dates from the 2nd-century A...

Much of your time in the gallery should be spent on the top (second) floor. Its first highlight is Room II, which is given over to exquisite wall paintings removed from the **Villa di Livia**, a villa belonging to Livia Drusilla, mother of Emperor Augustus (who reigned 27 BC–14 AD). The murals portray a lovely garden scene, rich in greens and blues and

PALAZZO MASSIMO ALLE TERME: INSIDE INFO

Top tips The gallery is not difficult to navigate, but the **gallery guide** (see below) contains a good plan of each floor.
• The gallery shop has many beautiful gifts and books, so bring money and credit cards in case you're tempted.

In more detail The beauty of the Palazzo Massimo – unlike many galleries of antiquities – is that it's not crammed with endless rows of dull statues: quality rather than quantity has been its guiding principle. There are relatively few works, and each is well labelled and well presented. Should you want to know more, it's well worth investing in the excellent guides to the gallery published by Electa-Soprintendenza Archeologico di Roma. Copies in English are generally available from the gallery shop.

filled with finely painted birds, flowers and trees, suggesting the original room was part of a summer house or rest room.

From here, walk back through Room I and along the floor's right-hand (north) gallery to rooms III to V. These contain wall paintings removed from the **Villa Farnesina**, uncovered in 1879. Probably from a villa originally built for the wedding of Augustus' daughter, Julia, these are the most important Roman paintings of their kind, and embrace several distinct styles, from traditional Greek-influenced landscapes and mythological scenes to Egyptian-style friezes and architectural motifs. You rarely see such paintings, making their delicacy, skill and sublime colouring all the more surprising and memorable. Much the same can be said of the many **mosaics** exhibited on this floor, whose beauty and detail are in marked contrast to later – and supposedly more sophisticated – medieval mosaics across the city.

TAKING A BREAK

Places to stop for a drink or snack on the Piazza della Repubblica are somewhat uninspiring, but if you walk a little farther to Via Vittorio Emanuele Orlando 75 you'll find **Dagnino** (Galleria Esedra, tel: 06 481 8660, open daily 7am–10pm), a lovely old-fashioned pastry shop selling Sicilian specialities.

collection
mosaics
housed on
e second
or

🗺 199 E2 ✉ Piazza dei Cinquecento 67 ☎ 06 3996 7700, book online at www.pierreci.it 🕐 Tue–Sun 9–7:45 🍴 No museum café: cafés near by in Piazza della Repubblica 🚇 Termini 🚌 64 and all other services to Piazza dei Cinquecento, Repubblica 💶 Expensive. Combined pass available ➤ 190

Trevi Fountain

The Trevi Fountain (Fontana di Trevi) is the most beautiful of Italy's many fountains. It is perhaps most famous for its tradition – throw a coin in the waters and you will return to Rome – and for actress Anita Ekberg's nocturnal visit in Federico Fellini's classic film, *La Dolce Vita*.

One of the Trevi Fountain's main attractions is that you stumble across it almost by accident. There it is as you turn from one of the three streets that lend the fountain its name (*tre vie* means "three streets") into the small piazza, a sight the writer Charles Dickens memorably described as "silvery to the eye and ear".

The fountain's waters were originally provided by the Acqua Vergine, or Aqua Virgo, an aqueduct begun by Agrippa in 19 BC to bring water to the city from the hills outside Rome. It took its name from the legend that it was a young girl (*vergine*) who showed the original spring to a group of Roman soldiers. Today, the fountain disgorges a colossal 80,000cu m (2.8 million cubic feet) of water daily; in its Roman heyday the aqueduct could carry over 100,000cu m (3.5 million cubic feet) an hour.

The first major fountain to take advantage of this watery bounty was built in 1453 by Pope Niccolò V, who financed the project with a tax on wine. This led irate Romans of the time to sneer that the pontiff had "taken our wine to give us water". The present fountain was begun by another pope, Clement XII, in 1732 – an inscription above the fountain's main arch records the fact – and inaugurated 30 years later by Clement XIII.

The Fontana's designer – probably Nicola Salvi – came up with the novel idea of draping the fountain over the entire wall of the Palazzo Poli, thus adding to its monumental scale and dramatic impact. The fountain's central figure represents Neptune, Oceanus. In front stand two tritons (1759–62) by sculptor Pietro Bracci: the one on the left as you face the fountain represents the stormy sea (symbolised by the agitated horse), while the figure on the right blowing into a conch shell represents the sea in repose.

Anita Ekberg *La Dolce Vita*

Few visitors can resist the temptation to cast a coin into the waters. The tradition echoes the practice of both the ancient Romans, who often threw coins into certain fountains to appease the gods, and early Christians, who would scatter coins onto the tomb of St Peter and other saints and martyrs.

TAKING A BREAK

For superlative ice-cream head to the **Gelateria di San Crispino** (► 138). Alternatively, stop for a coffee at **Antico Caffè Greco** (► 138) – you'll pay a price to drink here as it is one of Rome's most historic cafés.

195 F4 ☒ Piazza di Trevi ◎ Barberini 🚍 52, 53, 61, 62, 63, 71, 80, 95, 116, 119, 175, 492
d 630 to Via del Tritone 🎫 Free

TREVI FOUNTAIN: INSIDE INFO

Top tips Come to admire the fountain **late in the evening**, when the crowds are thinner and the fountain is usually floodlit.
• The fountain area is especially busy on Sunday, when many Romans make it a place to meet for a chat. If you'd rather not share in the boisterous atmosphere, come on another day.

In more detail The **figures in the rectangular niches** either side of Neptune are allegorical figures symbolising "Health" (with a relief above it of the young girl showing soldiers the source of the Acqua Vergine's spring) and "Abundance" (with a relief depicting Agrippa approving the aqueduct's design).

Piazza di Spagna

The Piazza di Spagna is one of Rome's great outdoor salons, a beautiful square that dominates the city's most elegant shopping district and whose famous Spanish Steps provide magnet for visitors at all hours of the day and night.

The Spanish Steps and the church of Trinità dei Monti

The steps are the piazza's most celebrated sight. More properly known as the Scalinata della Trinità dei Monti, they comprise a majestic double staircase that cascades down the slopes of the Pincian Hill from the church of **Trinità dei Monti**. Built between 1723 and 1726, they provide not only one of Rome's most celebrated scenic set-pieces – especially in spring, when huge pots of azaleas adorn the steps – but also a forum that has proved a favoured meeting place for Romans and visitors alike for several centuries.

Both the square and the steps take their name from the Palazzo di Spagna, built in the 17th century as the Spanish Embassy to the Holy See. Before that, part of the piazza was known as the Platea Trinitatis, after the Trinità church. Many foreign visitors made the area their home during the 18th-century heyday of the Grand Tour. The English, in particular, were passionate admirers, so much so that the district became known as the "English ghetto" and boasted a famous café, the Caffè degli Inglesi, a favourite drinking den for expatriates. That particular establishment is no more, but there are two other historic cafés on or near the square: Babington's Tea Rooms (to the left of the steps as you face them), founded in the late 19th century by two English spinsters, and the Antico Caffè Greco in Via Condotti (► 138), founded in 1760 and patronised by the likes of Goethe, Casanova, Shelley, Byron, Baudelaire, Wagner and Liszt.

Another visitor to the area's cafés would probably have been the English poet John Keats, who lodged – and died – in a house to the right of the Spanish Steps. Today, the building is given over to a **museum** (► 135) devoted to the poet and other literary exiles, including Shelley.

At the foot of the Spanish Steps is the tiny **Fontana della Barcaccia**, literally the "Fountain of the Rotten (or Worthless) Boat". Its name derives from the centrepiece, a half-sunken boat with water spilling lazily from its sides; the fountain's low level and less than spectacular display are the result of the low pressure of the Acqua Vergine aqueduct (► 124) which feeds it. The baroque design – possibly based on an earlier Roman model – was probably a joint effort on the part of Pietro Bernini and his more famous son, Gian Lorenzo Bernini. It was commissioned in 1629 by Pope Urban VIII, a member of the Barberini family, whose sun and bee emblems adorn the stonework.

TAKING A BREAK

Both **Babington's** (► 138) and the **Antico Caffè Greco** (► 138) are pretty but expensive, and only worthwhile if you want to savour their historic ambience. Better choices of cafés and bars can be found close by: try **Ciampini al Café du Jardin** (► 138) or the pretty **Antica Enoteca** (► 138). You could also walk to Piazza del Popolo for **Rosati** (► 138).

zza di gna is a eting place Romans and tors alike

➕ 195 F5 ✉ Piazza di Spagna 🚌 119

PIAZZA DI SPAGNA: INSIDE INFO

Top tips Climb to the top of the Spanish Steps from Piazza di Spagna for **good views**. Watch for pickpockets if the square is crowded.

• The Trinità church, begun in 1502, has immense scenic appeal, but nothing inside that really merits a visit.

Galleria e Museo Borghese

The Borghese gallery and museum may be relatively small, but the quality of its paintings and sculptures – notably works by Bernini, Canova, Raphael and Caravaggio – make it one of the jewels of Rome's rich artistic crown.

Wealthy Roman prelates and aristocrats over the centuries often amassed huge private art collections, many of which were later sold, broken up or passed to the city or Italian state. The finest of all such collections was accumulated by Cardinal Scipione Borghese (1579–1633), a nephew of Camillo Borghese, later Pope Paul V. Many works were sold to the Louvre in Paris in 1807, mostly under pressure from Napoleon, whose sister, the infamous Paolina, was married to Prince Camillo Borghese. Nevertheless, the surviving exhibits – which were bequeathed to the state in 1902 – make this the finest gallery of its kind in Rome, its appeal enhanced by a lovely setting, the beautifully restored Casino (1613–15), or summer house, of the Villa Borghese.

The collection is simply arranged over two floors and around some 20 gloriously decorated rooms, the lower floor being devoted mainly to sculpture, the upper floor to paintings. One of the gallery's most famous works greets you in the first room, Antonio Canova's erotic statue of **Paolina Borghese**, in the guise of Venus. This is one of the most sensual sculptures of the Borghese or any other gallery; so sensual, in fact, that Paolina's husband, Camillo Borghese, forbade anyone to see it after its completion – even Canova. Paolina was a willing and knowing model, who when asked how she could possibly have posed naked for the work is said to have replied "the studio was heated". The next room introduces the work of Gian Lorenzo Bernini, the presiding genius – with chief rival Borromini – of the baroque in Rome. The room's principal sculpture is a statue of **David** (1623–4) in the process of hurling his slingshot stone at Goliath, the

Antonio Canova's erotic reclining statue of Paolina Borghese scandalised her husband

17th-
tury Casino
ghese
vides a
gnificent
ting for the
ghese
ery's works
rt

face of which is said to be a self-portrait of the sculptor. It was commissioned by Scipione – the cardinal became one of Bernini's principal patrons – who is said to have held a mirror for Bernini while he worked on the self-portrait.

Room III contains what many consider Bernini's masterpiece, **Apollo and Daphne** (1622–5), which portrays the flight of Daphne from Apollo, capturing the moment Daphne turns herself into a laurel tree to escape the god. An equally bewitching work awaits you in Room IV, **Pluto and Proserpina** (1622), renowned for the detail of Pluto's hand grasping Proserphine's thigh – rarely has the softness of flesh been so convincingly portrayed in stone. The following room contains a statue of a Hermaphrodite, a Roman copy of a Greek original – you may already have seen a similar work in the Palazzo Massimo alle Terme (▶ 120–123). Room VI has more works by Bernini: a statue of Aeneas and Anchises (1613), probably carved by Bernini in collaboration with his

father when he was just 15, and the much later allegorical work *Truth* (1652), which remains unfinished.

In Room VIII you find another Roman original, a celebrated 2nd-century statue of a **Dancing Satyr**. The room is better known, however, for the first of the gallery's important paintings, namely several major works by Caravaggio, many of which were shrewdly snapped up by Scipione when they had been turned down by others as too shocking. Caravaggio is said to have painted self-portraits in at least two of the pictures – as the *Sick Bacchus* (c1593) and as Goliath in *David with the Head of Goliath* (1609–10). His best works here, though, are the **Madonna dei Palafrenieri** (1605–6) and the **Boy with a Basket of Fruit** (1593–5), both notable for their superb sense of realism. The former picture shows the Virgin crushing a serpent, a symbol of evil and also of heresy, an allusion to the confrontation of the time between the Catholic and Protestant Churches.

All manner of other exceptional paintings are collected on the gallery's upper floor. Among the finest is Raphael's **Deposition** (1507), just one of several in the first main room. Other fine paintings include works by Perugino, Andrea del Sarto, Correggio – an outstanding

The lavish interior of the Galleria, onc the Casino, o summer hous of the Villa Borghese, has been beautifully restored

Bernini's sta of David, one the gallery's principal wo

Danaë (1530–1) – Lorenzo Lotto, Bronzino, and Giovanni Bellini. One of the best pictures is kept for the gallery's last room: Antonello da Messina's **Portrait of a Man** (*c*1475), the prototype of this genre of portrait painting.

position by
phael is one
the high-
^ts of the
lleria
rghese

🚩 199 D4 ✉ Piazzale del Museo Borghese 5 ☎ 06 841 7645 (recorded information) ⏰ Tue–Sun 9–7, last entry 5pm 🍴 Gallery café Ⓜ Spagna or Flaminio 🚌 52, 53 and 910 to Via Pinciana or 116 to Viale del Museo Borghese 💶 Expensive

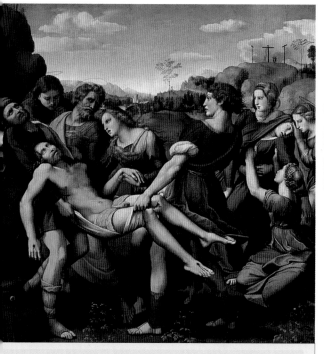

GALLERIA E MUSEO BORGHESE: INSIDE INFO

Top tip Numbers of visitors to the Galleria Borghese are limited, so it's obligatory to reserve your entry ticket. Call 06 32810 or visit www.ticketeria.it to make reservations. The reservation service is open Monday to Friday 9–7, Saturday 9–1. Call well in advance, especially in high season (Easter–Sep).

In more detail One of the Galleria Borghese's most mysterious and outstanding paintings is Titian's beautiful and little-understood **Sacred and Profane Love** (1514). Some claim its subject is actually Venus and Medea or Heavenly and Earthly Love: most critics, though, think it is an allegory of spring, and was inspired by the same strange dream romance, *Hypnerotomachia di Polifilo*, which provided Bernini with the idea for his eccentric elephant statue outside Santa Maria sopra Minerva (▶ 94).

At Your Leisure

2 Santa Prassede

This tiny church, in a side street immediately south of Santa Maria Maggiore, is celebrated for its mosaics, in particular those of the Cappella di San Zeno, situated on the left near the church's entrance. The gold-encrusted chapel was commissioned in 822 by Pope Paschal I as his mother's mausoleum. The square halo of Theodora, Paschal's mother, in the mosaic left of the altar, indicates that she was still alive when the work was commissioned. Other mosaics on the church's triumphal arch portray Christ flanked by angels in a heavenly Jerusalem, while those in the apse depict saints Prassede and Pudenziana. Prassede is said to have witnessed the martyrdom of 24 Christians who were then hurled into a well (marked by a marble slab on the church's floor): the saint then miraculously soaked up their blood with a single sponge.

🚩 202 A5 ⊠ Via Santa Prassede 9a ☎ 06 488 2456 🕐 Daily 7:30–noon, 4–6:30 (but hours may vary) 🚇 Termini 🚌 5, 14, 16, 70, 71, 75 and other services to Piazza dell'Esquilino 🎟 Free

3 Santa Pudenziana

Santa Pudenziana lies just a short walk from Santa Prassede to the northwest of Santa Maria Maggiore. It is said to have been founded between 384 and 399 over the spot where St Peter converted Prassede and Pudenziana, daughters of the Christian senator Pudes. One of the church's treasures is a reliquary containing part of the table on which the saint is believed to have said Mass.

The church's tiny facade dates from the 12th century, but has been much restored since – only the pretty frieze around the door is original. Inside, the highlight is an extraordinary mosaic from the early 4th-century church depicting Christ, the Apostles, and two women thought t represent Pudenziana and her sister

🚩 199 D1 ⊠ Via Urbana 160 ☎ 06 481 4622 🕐 Mon–Sat 8–noon, 3–6, Sun 9–noon, 3–6 (but hours may vary) 🚇 Termini or Cavour 🚌 5, 14, 16, 70, 71, 75 and other services to Piazza dell'Esquilino 🎟 Free

5 Santa Maria della Vittoria

Santa Maria della Vittoria seems like any other modest baroque church (1608–20) but inside its decoration some of the richest in the city, and the last chapel on the left as you fac the high altar contains one of Bernini's most celebrated sculptures the **Ecstasy of St Teresa** (1646). The work portrays the saintly Spanish writer, mystic and nun (1515–82) as she is "pierced" by the love of god –

For Kids

The lively atmosphere at the **Trevi Fountain** (▶ 124–125) appeals to children, and they will also enjoy the **Museo Nazionale delle Paste Alimentari** (▶ 134), dedicated to Italy's favourite food. Further afield, the **Villa Borghese** has lots for youngsters: near the Viale delle Belle Arti entrance to the park are swings, paddleboats, pony rides and train, while the old Villa Borghese zoo has been transformed into the **Bioparco** (Via del Giardino Zoologico 1, tel: 06 360 8211, open daily 9:30–5, expensive), which has specia activities for children. The **Museo Civico di Zoologia** (Via Ulisse Aldovandri 18, tel: 06 6710 9270, open Tue–Sun 9–5, moderate), alongside the zoo, has animal and insect collections. North of Piazza del Popol is the **Explora il Museo dei Bambini** (Vi Flaminia 82–6, tel: 06 361 3776, www.mdbr.it, open Tue–Sun 10–6:45, expensive), aimed at the under-12s and full of good educational and hands-on exhibits.

Bernini's controversial *Ecstasy of St Teresa* is one of the masterpieces of high baroque sculpture

leading patrician families. A magnificent baroque building in its own right, it is a major museum, housing the lion's share of the collection of the Galleria Nazionale d'Arte Antica (the rest resides across the Tiber in the Palazzo Corsini). Long-term restoration keeps much of the huge palace complex closed, but you can see the palace's superb centrepiece, the **Gran Salone**, a vast and fantastically decorated room dominated

mbolised here by an angel with an ow. The statue's erotic overtones – saint is said to be shown transrted by an earthly rather than divine ssion – have caused much controrsy over the centuries. The surround-, chapel, the **Cappella Cornaro**, was mmissioned from Bernini by rdinal Cornaro, hence the eight stats of the cardinal's family admiring statue as if from a theatre box.

🔝 199 D2 ✉ Via XX Settembre 17
☎ 06 482 6190 ◷ Mon–Sat
8:30–noon, 3:30–6, Sun 3:30–6 (but
hours may vary) ◻ Repubblica 🚌 36,
60, 61, 62, 84, 86, 90 to Via XX
Settembre 🎫 Free

Palazzo Barberini

le Palazzo Barberini was begun in
25 for Cardinal Francesco
rberini, a member of one of Rome's

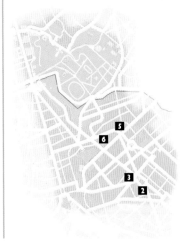

La Fornarina by Raphael, a painting which many believed to be a portrait of his lover

by Pietro da Cortona's allegorical ceiling frescoes depicting *The Triumph of Divine Providence* (1633–9).

Other paintings are displayed chronologically in a series of beautiful rooms, and include major works by Caravaggio, El Greco, Tintoretto, Titian and many more. The single most famous picture is **La Fornarina**, attributed to Raphael, a work long considered, probably erroneously, to portray the artist's mistress, the daughter of a baker (*fornaio* in Italian). Gossips of the time suggest Raphael's premature death 1520) was brought on by his lover's voracious sexual appetite.

✚ 199 D2 ✉ Via Barberini 18 ☎ 06 482 4184, book online at www.ticketeria.it ⏱ Tue–Sat 9–7 Ⓜ Barberini 🚌 52, 53, 56, 61, 62, 63, 80, 95, 116, 119 and 492 to Via del Tritone 💷 Moderate

🟦 Museo Nazionale del Paste Alimentari

This modest but well-organised museum close to the Trevi Fountain is one of Rome's more unusual (but over-priced), thanks to its unique theme – pasta. The displays in its 15 rooms co every aspect of the food, fr its history, cooking techniques and place in art to a collection of pasta-making equipment, model dietary tips and photographs of famous people such as actress Sop Loren enjoying Italy's national dish Visitors are given a portable CD player with multilingual commenta to guide them around the exhibits.

✚ 198 C1 ✉ Piazza Scanderberg 117 ☎ 06 699 1119 ⏱ Daily 9:30–5:30 Ⓜ Barberini 🚌 52, 53, 56, 60, 61, 62, 71, 80, 81, 95, 116 and 119 to Via del Tritone or Via del Corso 💷 Expensive

Off the Beaten Track

Much of the area surrounding Stazione Termini is given over to government ministries or the buildings of the main city university, and holds little visitor appeal. **San Lorenzo**, a traditional residential and student district with a sprinkling of inexpensive restaurants and pizzerias, east of Termini, is an exception (though probably not worth a separate trip unless you are on an extended visit). More worthwhile is the trip along Via Nomentana to the northeast to visit the **catacombs and churches of Santa Costanza** and **Sant'Agnese fuori le Mura** (➤ 17).

Around Piazza di Spagna, you can escape the crowds on **Via Margutta**, a pretty street filled with commercial art galleries, or in the web of **old streets** between Piazza del Parlamento and the ruins of the Mausoleo di Augusto, the circular mausoleum of the Emperor Augustus.

⑫ Museo Nazionale Etrusco di Villa Giulia

The Villa Giulia, tucked away in the northern reaches of the Villa Borghese, is worth the journey if you have a passion for the Etruscans, for a large part of the huge building is given over to the art and artefacts of that mysterious civilisation. The collection is the greatest of its type in the world, but for too long has been neglected and left to gather dust. Many of the rooms contain unexciting rows of urns and other funerary sculpture. Rather more inspiring are the museum's many exquisite pieces of gold and other jewellery, some of the larger sculptures, and the reconstructed Etruscan temple in the villa's extensive gardens.

➕ 198 A5 ✉ Piazzale di Villa Giulia 9 ☎ 06 322 6571; reservations 06 824 620 or www.ticketeria.com ⏰ Tue–Sun 8:30–7:30 🚇 Flaminio 🚌 3, 19, 231, 926 ✋ Moderate

Museo Keats-Shelley

…erary pilgrims will enjoy this lovely …l house to the right of the Spanish …ps, where the 25-year-old English …et John Keats died in 1821 having …me to Rome to seek a cure … consumption.

Since 1909, the house has …en lovingly restored and …eserved as a small literary …useum and working library …r scholars of Keats and his …low English poet, Percy …sshe Shelley, who also died … Italy, drowned off the …scan coast.

The fusty rooms are filled …th old books, pamphlets …d manuscripts, as well as …erary mementoes such as …ats' death mask, a lock of …e poet's hair, part of …elley's cheekbone, and a …iquary containing strands … John Milton's and Elizabeth …rrett Browning's hair.

➕ 195 F5 ✉ Piazza di Spagna 26 ☎ 06 678 4235 ⏰ Mon–Fri 9–1, 3–6; Sat 11–2, 3–6 🚇 Spagna 🚌 117 and 119 to Piazza di Spagna ✋ Inexpensive

…e house in which English poet …n Keats died is now a museum

Where to...
Eat and Drink

Prices
Expect to pay per person for a meal, excluding drinks and service

€ under €20   €€ €20–40   €€€ over €40

Neither of the two main areas covered in this chapter – in and around Termini and Piazza di Spagna – are known for their restaurants: Termini is too downbeat, Piazza di Spagna too full of shops. Yet both have good places to eat in all price brackets, and offer an excellent selection of bars for coffee and snacks, including some of Rome's most historic cafés. Both areas also have small places from another age – the discreet Beltramme, for example – and more modern establishments such as 'Gusto,

a restaurant that wouldn't be out of place in London, Sydney or New York.

Agata e Romeo €€€
The environs of Termini railway station are an unlikely location for this excellent restaurant. The cooking is modern Roman mixed with pan-Italian and international dishes, and gives the lie to the notion that creative cuisine, especially in Italy, is invariably pretentious or unsuccessful. Thus you might eat a traditional dish such as *baccalà* (salt cod), but salt cod that has been smoked and cooked in

an orange sauce; or be tempted by a flan of pecorino (sheep's cheese) with honey. The setting is simple but comfortable – brick arches and plain walls with the occasional painting. The wine list contains an interesting selection of regional Italian and other wines. Reservations are essential.

✚ 202 B5 ☒ Via Carlo Alberto 45
☎ 06 446 6115; www.agataeromeo.it
🕑 Mon–Fri 12:30–2:30, 7:30–10.
Closed 2 weeks in Aug and 1–2 weeks in Jan

Est Est Est €
This pizzeria is a good place for an early and inexpensive supper if you have been shopping on the nearby Via Nazionale, are staying near Termini, or don't mind the walk up from Piazza Venezia. It is one of Rome's oldest pizzerias, having retained its old-fashioned appeal despite several attempted makeovers. Pizzas, a selection of pasta dishes and the cheap wine make this a reli-

incidentally, is taken from a celebrated central Italian wine.

✚ 199 D1 ☒ Via Genova 32 ☎ 06 488 1107 🕑 Tue–Sun 7–11:30pm.
Closed 3 weeks in Aug

Fiaschetteria Beltramme €–€€
You could easily miss this historic but humble-looking trattoria, incongruously located on one of the smart streets near Via Condotti. That may be the idea, for this is a deliberately understated place frequented by locals, artists, shopkeepers, society ladies and – on one famous occasion – by the pop star Madonna. The interior is little more than a long single room whose walls are topped with wicker-covered wine bottles and almost completely covered in paintings left, bought or donated by locals over the years. Food is simple, well cooked and thoroughly Roman. You can't reserve a table, so turn up and hope. No credit cards.

✚ 195 E5 ☒ Via della Croce 39
☎ No phone 🕑 Mon–Sat noon–3,
7:30–10:30

'Gusto €-€€

'Gusto follows the trend of large, modern eateries that began to appear in London and Paris in the 1990s, and the Romans seem to love the result. The atmosphere is chic, sophisticated but also informal, and the decor a mix of designer neutrals, wicker, steel and wood. Downstairs in the busy split-level eatery you can sample pizzas, generous salads and other light meals (be prepared for lunchtime crowds of local office and other workers), while upstairs in the restaurant there is a more ambitious and eclectic menu, combining Italian traditions and stir-fry Eastern cooking. Quality is good (rarely more), but you're here for the atmosphere as much as the food.

🚩 195 D5 ⊠ Piazza Augusto Imperatore 9 ☎ 06 322 6273; www.gusto.it 🕖 Daily 1–3, 7:30–1

Margutta €-€€

Margutta has been in business for many years, which is no small achievement given that it is a vegetarian restaurant, something that until recently was barely known in Italy. The stylish dining area is airy and filled with modern art, a nod to the restaurant's position on Via Margutta, home to many of the city's leading commercial art galleries. The food is always imaginative, never worthy and dull, and the wines, beers and ciders served are all organically produced. At lunch there's a good set-price all-you-can-eat buffet menu. You can also drop by most of the day for a tea or snack in the bar area.

🚩 198 B3 ⊠ Via Margutta 118 ☎ 06 3265 0577 🕖 Daily 12:30–3:30, 7:30–11

Otello alla Concordia €€

In summer, you need to reserve well in advance to secure a table outside in the courtyard-garden of this attractive restaurant. If you are unsuccessful, don't worry, because the interior is almost as pleasant: a long plain room with a wonderful old wooden ceiling. The lively restaurant was one of the favourites of film director Federico Fellini, who lived close by on Via Margutta. The cooking is thoroughbred Roman – ask for house special *spaghetti all'Otello* to sample one of the classic Italian tomato and basil sauces.

🚩 195 E5 ⊠ Via della Croce 81 ☎ 06 679 1178 🕖 Mon–Sat 12:30–3, 7:30–11

PizzaRe €

If the slick 'Gusto (see left) is not for you, this nearby pizzeria (one of a chain) makes a cheerful and more traditional alternative. Not entirely traditional, however, for the pizzas here are Neapolitan – fatter and fluffier than their thinner-crusted Roman rivals. You can choose from around 40 different pizza toppings, as well as a variety of *antipasti* (starters) and tasty salads.

🚩 195 D5 ⊠ Via di Ripetta 14 ☎ 06 321 1468 🕖 Daily 12:30–3:30, 7:30–midnight. Closed 1 week in Aug

La Terrazza €€€

La Terrazza is the restaurant of the exclusive Eden hotel (▶ 35), and combines modern Mediterranean cooking with a magnificent view over the city from its terrace dining-room. The food here is always excellent, sometimes exceptional, but you should be prepared for the occasional culinary experiment that doesn't quite come off. Typical simpler dishes might include smoked scallops with a salad of wild leaves and asparagus, or sea bass with black olives and oregano.

Service at La Terrazza is far more formal than at Agata e Romeo (▶ 136), its rival in this price bracket, so to feel comfortable dress up for the occasion. The prices here are also rather higher, although the special lunch and set-price menus help to keep a brake on spending.

🚩 198 C3 ⊠ Via Ludovisi 49 ☎ 06 478 121 or 06 4781 2752 🕖 Daily 12:30–2:30, 7:45–10:30

Antica Enoteca €

This wine bar opened in 1842 and has been restored in order to retain its pretty old-world appearance. You can order wine by the glass or bottle – or buy fine wines to take away – and choose nibbles from a cold buffet or eat in the restaurant to the rear.

195 E5 ⊠ Via della Croce 76b
☎ 06 679 0896 Wine bar: daily
11:30am–midnight. Restaurant: daily
12:30–3, 7–10:30

Antico Caffè Greco €

The long-established Caffè Greco is Rome's most famous café, and since it was founded in 1740 has played host to the likes of Casanova, Wagner, Lord Byron, Shelley, Stendhal and Baudelaire. Though it has had its ups and downs in recent years (and may no longer be the city's best café), it is still worth the price of a cappuccino to enjoy the historic atmosphere. Locals stand; tourist tend to crowd the sofas. Expect to pay slightly over the odds.

195 E5 ⊠ Via Condotti 86
☎ 06 679 1700 Sun–Mon
10:30–7:30, Tue–Sat 9–7:30

Babington's €–€€

Babington's was founded by two British women at the end of the 19th century and has affected the look and feel of a British tea room ever since. You can sip fine teas (reputedly the best in the city) and nibble dainty cakes here, but the high prices for such simple offerings reflect its smart Piazza di Spagna location.

195 F5 ⊠ Piazza di Spagna 23
☎ 06 678 6027 Daily 9–8:15

Ciampini al Café du Jardin €

You will escape the crowds in Piazza di Spagna at this lovely café near the Villa Medici, but you won't escape the area's relatively high prices. However, it's worth paying a little more to sit in this lovely spot – a calm outdoor area with pond and creeper-covered walls – and the superlative views. The café serves sandwiches, light pasta meals, snack lunches, breakfast, ice-cream and cocktails.

195 F5 ⊠ Piazza Trinità dei Monti
☎ 06 678 5678 Thu–Tue 8–1
(closes earlier in spring and autumn).
Closed Nov–Mar

Dolci e Doni €

Take a cake break just a few steps from Piazza di Spagna in this chic pastry shop and tea room. Alternatively, indulge in a breakfast, brunch or light lunch.

195 E5 ⊠ Via delle Carrozze 85b
☎ 06 6992 5001 Daily 11–9/10.
Closed 2 weeks in Aug

Gelateria di San Crispino €

Walk just a few paces from the Fontana di Trevi and you arrive at this temple to the *gelato*. Most Romans consider it sells the city's best ice-cream and sorbets; some is close to saying the best in the world. There are no cones here, just cups: San Crispino's perfectionist owners, brothers Giuseppe and Pasquale Alongi, claim that cones, with their artificial additives, interfere with the purity and flavour of their fresh fruit and myriad other iced delights. Flavours change with what is seasonally available. Not to be missed.

195 F4 ⊠ Via della Panetteria 42
☎ 06 679 3924 Wed–Mon
noon–midnight or later. Closed mid-
Jan to mid-Feb

Rosati €

Rosati is one of Rome's great cafés – not as old as Caffè Greco (see left), but equally beloved over the years by artists, politicians and writers such as Alberto Moravia and Italo Calvino. Its location is superb, its position having long put it in competition with Canova, the piazza's other historic café.

198 A4 ⊠ Piazza del Popolo 5

Where to...
Shop

The grid of streets at the foot of the Spanish Steps is the epicentre of the Roman chic and the only area that matters for shoppers in search of designer labels and luxury goods. Although Via Condotti is the best-known street, the parallel streets of Via Frattina and Via Borgognona are almost equally full of familiar designer names. Smaller side streets in the vicinity also increasingly have smart boutiques selling shoes, exclusive lingerie, leather goods and other accessories. Some streets specialise in particular items: Via della Croce, for example, has a scattering of good food shops, while Via Margutta is home to many commercial art galleries and antiques shops. Via del Corso and Via del Tritone are lined with mid-market clothes,

shoes and accessory shops, providing an excellent alternative to the Via Condotti designer stores.

The area around Piazza Vittorio Emanuele south of Termini is a different world. It is home to many of Rome's most recent immigrants, and as a result is full of specialist food and other stores selling Chinese, Korean, Somalian and other Asian and African goods. The piazza is also the site of central Rome's main food and general market (Mon–Sat 6–2). Both the square and the surrounding streets are filled with colourful stalls selling fruit, vegetables, cheap shoes, clothing and household goods.

DESIGNER STORES

The outlets of principal Italian and international designers are listed below by street. Note, however, that new outlets open regularly in these streets, and stores often change their locations. Opening hours for the designer stores are generally

Tuesday to Saturday 10–7:30 or 8, some may close Monday morning.

Via Condotti

Battistoni

☒ Via Condotti 61a ☎ 06 697 6111

Giorgio Armani

☒ Via Condotti 77 ☎ 06 699 1460

Gucci

☒ Via Condotti 8 ☎ 06 679 0405

Max & Co

☒ Via Condotti 46a ☎ 06 678 7946

Max Mara

☒ Via Condotti 67–69 ☎ 06 6992 2104

Prada

☒ Via Condotti 92–5 ☎ 06 679 0897

Salvatore Ferragamo

☒ Via Condotti 65 (men) ☎ 06 678 1130 or 06 679 1565

☒ Via Condotti 73 (women) ☎ 06 678 0280

Trussardi

☒ Via Condotti 49–50 ☎ 06 678 0280

Valentino

☒ Via Condotti 13 ☎ 06 678 5862

Via Frattina

Marella

☒ Via Frattina 129–31 ☎ 06 6992 3800

Via Borgognona

Laura Biagiotti

☒ Via Borgognona 43–44 ☎ 06 679 1205

Ermenegildo Zegna

☒ Via Borgognona 7e ☎ 06 678 9143

Fendi

☒ Via Borgognona 36–40 ☎ 06 679 7641

Fratelli Rossetti

☒ Via Borgognona 5a ☎ 06 678 2676

Other designers with outlets in and around Via Condotti and Piazza di Spagna include **Missoni** (Piazza di Spagna 78, tel: 06 679 2555); **Krizia** (Piazza di Spagna 87, tel: 06 679 3772); **Valentino Donna** (Via del Babuino 61, tel: 06 3600 1906); **Emporio Armani** (Via del Babuino 140, tel: 06 3600 2197); and **Armani Jeans** (Via del Babuino 70a, tel: 06 3600 1848).

ANTIQUES

Antichità

Serious antiques hunters prepared to pay for quality will have a field day in Via del Babuino and Via Margutta northwest of Piazza di Spagna. Antichità is one of several tempting shops on these streets, specialising in old fabrics and furnishings.

☒ Via del Babuino 83　☎ 06 320 7585　◷ Tue–Sat 9–1, 3.30–7.30

Bottega del Marmorato

Here you'll find all manner of ornaments in marble, including copies of ancient busts and other antiquities.

☒ Via Margutta 53b　☎ 06 320 7660　◷ Mon–Sat 9–1, 3.30–7.30

Valerio Turchi

This is the place to come if you want to pick up genuine pieces of Roman statues, sarcophaghi or other remnants of the ancient city.

☒ Via Margutta 91a　☎ 06 323 5047

BOOKS

The Lion Bookshop

A great range of English-language books, this shop has a pleasant reading room where you can browse through books over a coffee.

☒ Via dei Greci 33　☎ 06 3265 4007　◷ May–Sep Tue–Sat 10–7.30, Mon 3–7.30, Oct–Apr Tue–Sun 10–7.30, Mon 3–7.30

DEPARTMENT STORES

Energie

Not a department store in the accepted sense, but if you're travelling with teenagers, or wish to buy what the fashion-conscious young Roman is wearing, then this large, loud and buzzy shop has a selection of mid-range contemporary clothes.

☒ Via del Corso 486　☎ 06 322 7046　◷ Mon–Sat 9.30–8, Sun 10.30–8

La Rinascente

This is the only department store in it's a good one. It sells a mainly high-quality selection of clothes, accessories, lingerie and general household and fashion items.

☒ Largo Chigi 20, near the corner of Via del Tritone and Via del Corso　☎ 06 679 7691　◷ Mon–Sat 10–10, Sun 10.30–8

FOOD AND WINE

Buccone

This is one of the biggest and best places in Rome to buy wine – thousands of bottles line the shelves – and a range of other alcoholic drinks such as *grappa* and *amaro*. Wine is available by the glass, and there is a small but excellent selection of hot and cold snacks and fine foods.

☒ Via di Ripetta 19　☎ 06 361 2154　◷ Mon–Thu 12.30–2.30, 9–10.30, Fri–Sat 8–midnight

Pasta all'Uova

Via della Croce does not have as but there are still shops such as this, a little place that sells a variety of fresh and dried pasta. Many of the novelty pastas – unusual colours and designs – make inexpensive gifts.

☒ Via della Croce 8　☎ 06 679 3102　◷ Mon–Wed, Fri–Sat 7.30–7.30, Thu 8–3.30 (8–7.30, in summer)

Salumeria Focacci

Like Pasta all'Uova (see above), this is one of Rome's landmark food stores. There is an excellent selection of cheeses, meats and other gastronomic treats.

☒ Via della Croce 43　☎ 06 679 1228　◷ Mon–Sat 8–8

HATS AND GLOVES

Sermoneta

Giorgio Sermoneta's intimate shop has been selling just about every size, colour and style of Italian glove for over 35 years.

☒ Piazza di Spagna 61　☎ 06 679 1960　◷ Mon–Sat 9.30–7.30, Sun

Borsalino

Hats, hats and more hats: the only place in Rome you need to visit if you are looking for something to wear up top.

📧 Piazza del Popolo 20 ☎ 06 323 3353 🕲 Mon–Sat 10–7:30, Sun 10:30–7:30

CHILDREN'S CLOTHES

La Cicogna

This chain of shops selling excellent clothes for babies and toddlers has several outlets in Rome.

📧 Via Frattina 138 ☎ 06 679 1912 🕲 Mon–Sat 10:30–7:30, Sun 11–7

LINGERIE

La Perla

Many small shops in the Piazza di Spagna district and along Via del Corso sell only lingerie, but none quite offers the quality or sheer style of the garments you'll find here.

📧 Via Condotti 79 ☎ 06 6994 1933 🕲 Tue–Sat 10–7, Mon 3–7

JEWELLERY AND WATCHES

Bulgari

Whether or not you are going to buy anything – and you'll need an enormous credit card limit to do so – it is well worth looking at what is on offer at Bulgari, easily Rome's most expensive and exclusive jewellers.

📧 Via Condotti 10 ☎ 06 696 261 🕲 Mon–Sat 10:30–7:30, Sun 11–7

Swatch Store

This store is about as far removed as is possible from Bulgari in style and content, and sells a wide range of the familiar Swatch brand watches and straps.

📧 Via Condotti 33a ☎ 06 679 1253 🕲 Daily 10–7:30

LINENS

Frette

Hotels or Italian households who have any pretensions to style would not use anything but Frette bed or table linens. Goods are expensive, but of outstanding quality.

📧 Via del Corso 381 ☎ 06 678 6862
📧 Via Nazionale 80 ☎ 06 488 2641 🕲 Mon–Sat 10–7:30

COSMETICS

Materozzoli

This refined shop dates from 1870 and sells an enticing variety of top-of-the-range toiletries, perfumes, cosmetics and bathroom items.

📧 Piazza San Lorenzo in Lucina 5 ☎ 06 6889 2686 🕲 Tue–Sat 10–1:30, 3–7:30, Mon 3:30–7:30

SHOES

Fausto Santini

For something a little different, visit the shop of the city's foremost shoe designer. Some of the designs may seem far-fetched, but none can be called boring, and the quality is good.

📧 Via Frattina 120 ☎ 06 678 4114 🕲 Mon–Sat 10–7:30, Sun noon–7:30

Tod's

For years, no one took much notice of Tod's in Italy. But since they became coveted by the rest of the world – and the US in particular – the locals are as keen as everyone else on the distinctive footwear.

📧 Via Fontanella Borghese 56a ☎ 06 6821 0066 🕲 Daily 10–7:30

STATIONERY

Pineider

The pens and stationery here are the finest and most exclusive in the city.

📧 Via dei Due Macelli 68 ☎ 06 678 9013 🕲 Mon–Sat 10–7, Sun 10–2, 3–7

Vertecchi

This pretty shop crammed with pens, paints, stationery and all manner of items covered in marbled paper is a good place for gifts to take home.

📧 Via della Croce 70 ☎ 06 679 0155 🕲 Mon–Sat 9:30–7:30

Where to...
Be Entertained

CLASSICAL MUSIC

The **opera** season in Rome runs from November to May at the 19th-century auditorium, the **Teatro dell'Opera**, which lies just a few steps from Piazza dei Cinquecento at Via Firenze 72–Piazza Beniamino Gigli 8 (tel: 06 481 601 or 06 481 7003; www.opera roma.it). The reputation of Rome's opera house lags a long way behind that of La Scala in Milan, La Fenice in Venice and San Carlo in Naples, its lowly status not helped by years of mismanagement, union problems and enormous budget deficits. However, while performances may not be exceptional, it is often easier to obtain tickets here than in Milan or elsewhere. The box office is

generally open Tuesday to Saturday 9–5, Sunday 9–1:30 on days when there is no performance or 10:45am to half an hour before the start of any performance. Free phone in Italy for information (tel: 800 016 665) between 10am and 1:30pm. Making a reservation by phone is all but impossible, so it is best to visit the box office in person. In the past, summer productions were held at a variety of outdoor venues, but these have changed repeatedly in the last few years. Contact the visitor centre or the opera house direct for latest information.

The Associazione Musicale Romana (▶ 111) presents a **harpsichord festival** during May in the Villa Medici above the Spanish Steps (▶ 116).

NIGHTLIFE

If you are looking for places to drink in the evening, close to Santa Maria Maggiore lie two of Rome's oldest and best **Irish pubs**: the **Druid's Den** (Via San Martino ai Monti 28, tel: 06 4890 4781, open daily 5pm–2am), and the **Fiddler's Elbow** (Via dell'Olmata 43, tel: 06 487 2110, open daily 5pm–1:30am or later). They lie about a minute or so apart if you want to compare and contrast. If the thought of an Irish establishment doesn't appeal, try the more Italian **Monti DOC** (Via Giovanni Lanza 93, tel: 06 487 2696, open Tue–Sun 7pm–1am, Mon–Fri 1pm–3:30pm), just to the south of Santa Prassede and Santa Maria Maggiore. This easy-going wine bar has a good selection of wines and a range of snacks and light meals.

In a similar vein is **Trimani** wine bar (Via Cernaia 37b, tel: 06 446 9630, open Mon–Sat 11:30–3, 6–12:30am), close to Piazza della Repubblica.

At the other end of the city, near Piazza del Popolo, you can drink and nibble snacks at **Lowenhaus** (Via della Fontanella 16d, tel: 06 323 0410, open Fri–Mon 11am–2am, Tue–Thu 4pm–2am). If pubs or pub-like bars are not for you, don't forget the various alternatives offered by wine bars in the area covered by this chapter, notably the Antica Enoteca (▶ 138) or Ciampini (▶ 138).

If you want to dance or listen to live music you've something of a problem. The only central club is the busy **Gregory's** (Via Gregoriana 54a, tel: 06 679 6386, open Tue–Sun 8pm–3:30am), a live jazz venue with drinks and snack food near Piazza di Spagna, one of the main clubs locally is **Piper**, one of the longest-running clubs in Rome – frequent revamps have allowed it to ride out changes of fashion. It lies some way from the centre to the northwest of Termini at Via Tagliamento 9 (tel: 06 841 4459, open Thu–Sat 11pm–4am)

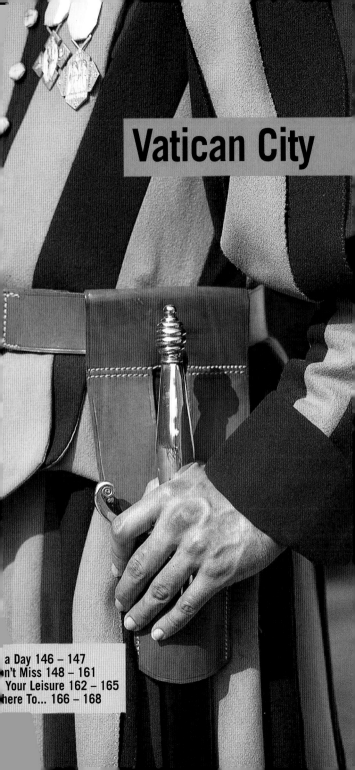

Vatican City

Getting Your Bearings

The Vatican – the world's smallest independent state – contains two of the highlights of any visit to Rome: the immense Basilica di San Pietro, or St Peter's, and the vast Musei Vaticani, or Vatican Museums, home to one of the world's richest and largest collection of paintings, sculptures and other works of art accumulated by the papacy over the centuries.

The Vatican has a long history. Once, the hilly area of Rome west of the Tiber was a place of execution, and later the site of imperial gardens and a circus, or race track, built for the emperors Caligula and Nero in the 1st century AD. In the 4th century, part of the area became the site for a huge basilica – the first St Peter's

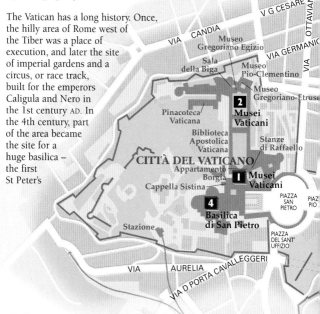

V G CESARE
VIA CANDIA
VIA OTTAVIANO
VIA GERMANIC
Museo Gregoriano Egizio
Sala della Biga
Museo Pio-Clementino
Museo Gregoriano-Etrus
Pinacoteca Vaticana
2 **Musei Vaticani**
Biblioteca Apostolica Vaticana
Stanze di Raffaello
CITTÀ DEL VATICANO
Appartamento Borgia
1 **Musei Vaticani**
Cappella Sistina
4 **Basilica di San Pietro**
PIAZZA SAN PIETRO
PIAZ PIO
Stazione
PIAZZA DEL SANT' UFFIZIO
VIA AURELIA
VIA D PORTA CAVALLEGGERI

– built over or close to the tomb of St Peter, who was crucified in the area sometime between AD 64 and 67.

By the 10th century, attacks by Lombards and Saracens had led to the building of a defensive wall around part of the district, and later to the u of the Castel Sant'Angelo – previously the mausoleum of Emperor Hadrian – as a papal fortress. After the sack of Rome in 1527, the area lost its strategic importance, and the popes moved their residential palace and offices to the Lateran (San Giovanni in Laterano) and then the Quirinale (now government buildings).

By the 19th century, the papacy had controlled vast areas of central Italy, including Rome, for more than 1,000 years. Much of its domain, known as the Papal States, was gifted to the popes in the 8th century by the Frankish king Pepin the Shor and his son Charlemagne. Following Italian unification in 1870, it was stripped of its territories and remained in a stat

★ Don't Miss

❶ The Vatican Museums

Museo Pio-Clementino ➤ 148

Stanze di Raffaello ➤ 150

The Sistine Chapel ➤ 152

❹ St Peter's ➤ 156

At Your Leisure

❷ The Vatican Museums

Museo Gregoriano Egizio ➤ 162

Museo Gregoriano-Etrusco ➤ 162

Sala della Biga ➤ 163

Appartamento Borgia ➤ 163

Biblioteca Apostolica Vaticana ➤ 164

Pinacoteca Vaticana ➤ 164

❸ Castel Sant'Angelo ➤ 165

0 ————— 250 metres

0 ————— 250 yards

of limbo until the Lateran Treaty of 1927, signed with Mussolini, formalised state and papal relations, awarding the papacy full sovereignty of the Vatican State.

Today, the area has its own shops, banks, newspaper, helicopter pad and radio station. Most is out of bounds to the general public, with the important exceptions of St Peter's, the Vatican Museums and – if you reserve a visit in advance – parts of the Vatican Gardens. No documents are needed to enter these, and no barriers exist between them and the city at large.

It should take just a couple of hours to see Peter's, though you may be tempted to linger in the me, which offers the best views in Rome. Just before (or er) seeing St Peter's you might spend an hour in the Castel nt'Angelo – these days outside the Vatican – a fascinating Roman ilding overlaid with later fortifications and papal apartments. Though you could see the highlights of the Vatican Museums – otably the Sistine Chapel and Raphael Rooms – in half a day, if e museums appeal, or you have particular interests, you could st as easily spend several days in the complex, whose 12 museums ntain Egyptian, Etruscan, Greek, Roman, medieval and enaissance treasures. There are also countless beautifully decorated ons and corridors, plus a Pinacoteca, or art gallery, crammed with asterpieces by Raphael, Leonardo da Vinci and others.

Spend the morning at the Vatican Museums, concentrating
the Sistine Chapel, Stanze di Raffaello and Museo Pio-
Clementino, and the afternoon exploring St Peter's.

Vatican City in a Day

9:00am

The Vatican Museums are often crowded, so get there early and aim to see
Michelangelo's superb frescoes (below) in the **①** **Sistine Chapel** (▶ 152– 15
as soon as you arrive. Then consider following one of the museums' itinerari

10:00am

Spend an hour or so visiting the **②** **Museo Gregoriano Egizio** (▶ 162), whic
houses the Vatican's Egyptian collection, and the **①** **Museo Pio-Clementino**
(▶ 148): devote more time to the latter, which contains the best of the
Vatican's immense collection of classical sculpture.

11:00am

Move on to the Etruscan
antiquities of the
② **Museo Gregoriano-
Etrusco** (▶ 162–163) and
the **②** **Sala della Biga**
(▶ 163), which houses a
rare Roman chariot. Then
visit the first-floor **Galleria
dei Candelabri, Galleria
degli Arazzi** and the
memorable **Galleria delle
Carte Geografiche** (▶ 149)

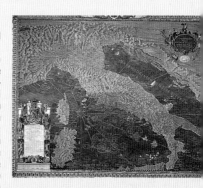

– the galleries occupy a series of long corridors adorned with statues, tap
tries and beautiful painted maps (abov

Noon

t the **1 Stanze di Raffaello**
ght, ➤ 150–151), a suite
rooms covered in paintings
y Raphael, followed by the
Cappella di Niccolò V
➤ 151) and **Appartamento**
Borgia (➤ 163–164).

2:45pm

Vatican Museums have a
eteria, or you could try
imposio or Taverna
gelica (➤ 167) or its
go alternatives, which
uld leave you in the
ximity of Castel
nt'Angelo for the after-
n. Alternatively, buy
nic provisions in the food
ps of Via Cola di Rienzo –
sure to arrive before

n, when most shops close – and walk south to eat lunch by the river or on
ramparts inside Castel Sant'Angelo.

2:00pm

Explore **3 Castel Sant'Angelo** (➤ 165) and the nearby Ponte Sant'Angelo.

3:00pm

Walk down Via della Conciliazione to
iazza San Pietro. Stroll around the
piazza to admire its columns and
the facade of **4 St Peter's**
(➤ 156–161), then explore the
terior. Note that queues for the
me (right) may be long at peak
times of the year.

5:00pm

Catch a 40 or 64 bus back to the
heart of Rome, or walk back via the
Ponte Vittorio Emanuele II.

The Vatican Museums

Start a visit to the Vatican Museums by concentrating on the main highlights – the Museo Pio-Clementino, which contains the best of the Vatican's many classical sculptures; the frescoes in the Stanze di Raffaello (Raphael Rooms); and the Cappella Sistina (Sistine Chapel), celebrated for Michelangelo's famous ceiling paintings.

Visiting the museums can pose something of a challenge, and not just because they are so large: opening hours vary from year to year, as does the order in which you are able to walk around. One-way systems introduced at the busiest times of year can also make it difficult to retrace your steps. The most popular sights – the Sistine Chapel and Raphael Rooms – are also the ones that are farthest from the museum entrance. Try to see these first if you arrive early – you'll avoid the queues – otherwise head first for the Museo Pio-Clementino.

Museo Pio-Clementino and Galleries

Founded by Pope Clement XIV in 1771 and augmented by his successor, Pius VI, this museum made use of the papacy's already immense collection of Greek and Roman antiquities. Here, as elsewhere, the order in which you move through the museum may vary: the highlights, however, are easily seen.

These start with the Vestibolo Rotundo, a hall which leads to the Gabinetto dell'Apoxyomenos, dominated by the **Apoxyomenos**, the only known Roman copy of a 4th-century BC Greek masterpiece. It shows an athlete scraping the sweat, dust and oil from his body in the wake of victory. Returning to the Vestibolo, you move left to the Cortile Ottagono, a small courtyard that contains some of the greatest of all classical statues. The most famous is the **Laocoön**, an intricately carved sculptural group dating from around 50 BC. Created by sculptors from Rhodes, it was found near the Domus Aurea (▶ 69) in 1506 and had a huge influence on Renaissance sculptors, especially Michelangelo. The sculpture shows a Trojan priest, Laocoön, and his two sons fighting with sea serpents.

Other works in the Cortile include the **Apollo del Belvedere**, a Roman copy of a 4th-century BC Greek bronze original, a masterpiece of classical sculpture which, like the Laocoön, greatly influenced Renaissance and other sculptors. The statue of the young god Apollo originally held a bow in one hand, and is thought to have held an arrow in the other. Also here is a statue of **Hermes**, another Roman copy of a Greek original, and the figure of **Perseus** by Antonio Canova, a 19th-century sculptor hugely influenced by the sculpture of

Galleria
e Carte
grafiche
ve) is lined
beautiful
-century
s (detail,
w)

ЭMA
OEM CA

the classical world – his statue here, for example, shows the clear influence of the nearby Apollo del Belvedere.

Beyond the Cortile lies the **Sala degli Animali**, a charming collection of ancient and 18th-century sculpted animals. Moving on, you come to the Galleria delle Statue, where the highlights are the ***Apollo Sauroktonos***, a Roman copy of a 4th-century BC original showing Apollo about to kill a lizard, and the famed **Candelabri Barberini**, a pair of 2nd-century lamps discovered at the Villa Adriana in Tivoli (▶ 172). Close to the Sala degli Animali is the Sala delle Muse, which is dominated by the ***Torso del Belvedere***, probably a 1st-century BC Greek work. The gigantic torso was much admired by Michelangelo, whose famous nudes, or "*ignudi*" in the Sistine Chapel frescoes were directly influenced by the figure.

Other statues worth hunting out include the ***Venere di Cnido*** (Venus of Cnidus) in the Gabinetto delle Maschere, a copy of a famous Greek nude rejected by the islanders of Kos because it was too erotic and eagerly purchased by the Cnidians. Also visit the **Sala a Croce Greca** to see the Sarcofago di Sant'Elena and Sarcofago di Constantina, the sarcophagi – respectively – of the mother and daughter of Emperor Constantine.

Moving on from this museum, you should at some stage walk along the long galleries on the upper of the complex's two floors: one is the Galleria dei Candelabri e degli Arazzi, which is adorned with splendid tapestries, candelabra and other works. This leads on into the highly memorable **Galleria delle Carte Geografiche**, a long corridor decorated with beautiful painted maps (1580–3) of the Papal States, much of Italy, and many of the main cities of each region.

✠ 196 B4 ✉ Viale Vaticano ☎ 06 6988 3322, www.vatican.va ⏰ Mon–Sat 10–1:45, Jan–Feb and Nov–Dec; Mon–Fri 10–4:45, Sat 10–1:45, Mar–Oct. Last Sun of month 10–1:45. Last ticket 1 hour and 20 minutes before closing. Closed on religious and public holidays 🚇 Ottaviano-San Pietro or Cipro-Musei Vaticani 🚌 19, 23, 32, 49, 492, 990 to Piazza del Risorgimento 💶 Expensive. Free last Sun of the month (▶ 155)

Stanze di Raffaello

Raphael was an artist who died aged just 37 and painted relatively little. This makes the Stanze di Raffaello, or Raphael Rooms, which are almost entirely covered in frescoes by the painter, one of Italy's most treasured artistic ensembles. The four rooms were commissioned from Raphael by Pope Julius II in 1508 and completed after the painter's death in 1520 by his pupils: they include scenes inspired by Leo X, who became pope while work was in progress.

The order in which you're allowed to see the rooms varies from month to month, but if possible try to see them in the order in which they were painted. This means beginning with the **Stanza della Segnatura** (1508–11), which served as Julius's library and was the place where he applied his signature (*segnatura*) to papal bulls (edicts). The frescoes here are the rooms' finest – many critics call them an even greater achievement than the Sistine Chapel. The four main pictures provide a celebration of the triumph of Theology, Philosophy, Poetry and Justice, fusing classical, religious, artistic and philosophical themes in a complicated allegorical mixture; it is well worth buying a guide to help decipher the paintings.

The next room to be painted was the **Stanza di Eliodoro** (1512–14), a private antechamber or waiting room. Here the paintings are a form of visual propaganda for Julius and Leo,

A love of a starts at ar early age

Left: The Stanza del Segnatura contains th finest fresc in the Stan Raffaello

Above: Many frescoes in the Stanza di Costantino were completed by Raphael's assistants

Below: Works by Fra Angelico adorn the Cappella di Niccolò V, close to the Stanze di Raffaello

although their professed theme is the timely intervention of Divine Providence in the defence of an endangered faith. Thus the battle scenes in *The Expulsion of Heliodorus from the Temple* – a reworking of a Biblical story – are an allusion to Julius' skill in defending the Papal States from foreign interference. Similarly, the panel ostensibly showing Attila the Hun turning back from Rome actually contains a portrait of the new pope, Leo X (the figure on a donkey). Note the three-part fresco showing *The Deliverance of St Peter from Prison*, the first time Raphael attempted to portray a scene set at night.

The third room chronologically is the **Stanza dell' Incendio** (1514–17), designed as a dining-room for Leo X, who asked Raphael to paint a series of scenes that celebrated the achievements of two of his papal namesakes, Leo III and Leo IV. Thus the main frescoes portray the Coronation of Charlemagne (a ceremony conducted by Leo III in 800); the Oath of Leo III (when Leo denied accusations levelled at him by rivals); the Battle of Ostia (where Leo IV showed mercy to a defeated Saracen navy in 848, an allusion to Leo X's attempts to forge a crusade against the Turks); and the Fire in the Borgo (in which Leo IV – painted here as Leo X – extinguished a fire near St Peter's by making the sign of the Cross).

Much of the Stanza dell'Incendio was painted by pupils working to designs by Raphael, as were the four principal frescoes on the life of the Emperor Constantine in the last room, the **Stanza di Costantino** (1517–24).

Before moving on from the Raphael Rooms, be sure to see the nearby **Cappella di Niccolò V**, a small chapel covered in beautiful frescoes by Fra Angelico showing scenes from the *Lives of St Stephen and St Lawrence* (1447–51).

TAKING A BREAK

If you need a respite from sightseeing, visit the Vatican Museums' café or try **Non Solo Pizza** (➤ 166), a few blocks north of Piazza del Risorgimento.

The Sistine Chapel

You will not want to miss the Cappella Sistina (Sistine Chapel), but expect substantial crowds, a busy atmosphere, and considerable pressure to move on to make way for visitors behind you. This can make for a rather unsatisfactory visit, but detracts little from the majesty of Michelangelo's breathtaking frescoes.

The chapel was built for Sixtus IV between 1477 and 1481, and received its first pictorial decoration between 1480 and 1483, when the lower walls were frescoed by several of the leading artists of their day, notably Perugino, Domenico Ghirlandaio and Sandro Botticelli. A quarter of a century elapsed before Michelangelo was commissioned to fresco the chapel's ceiling, which up to that point had been adorned with a simple wash of blue covered in gold and silver stars.

Michelangelo supposedly proved reluctant to accept the commission, partly because he viewed painting as a lesser art than sculpture, and partly because he was more passionately concerned with creating a tomb for Julius (a project that was never completed). In the event the ceiling would occupy him for four years, work being completed in 1512. The frescoes – controversially restored between 1979 and 1994 – consist of nine main panels, beginning with the five principal events in the Book of Genesis: *The Separation of Light from Darkness; The Creation of the Heavenly Bodies; The Separation of Land and Sea; The Creation of Adam;* and *The Creation of Eve.* These are followed by *The Fall* and *Expulsion from Paradise; The Sacrifice of Noah, The Flood* and *The Drunkenness of Noah.* Scattered around the ceiling are various painted Prophets, Sibyls, Old Testament characters, and 20 *ignudi,* or nude youths. In all, the painting covers an area of 930sq m (1,110 square yards) and contains over 300 individual figures.

The ceiling on its own is a masterpiece, but the chapel contains a second, and probably greater fresco by Michelangelo, the huge **Last Judgement** (1536–41) that covers the entire wall behind the altar. Bear in mind while you admire the painting that it was painted a full 22 years after the ceiling frescoes, during which time Rome had been sacked by the forces of Emperor Charles V in 1527, an event which apparently deeply affected Michelangelo and effectively brought to an end the period of optimism of the Renaissance years.

Something of the darker forces affecting the city and the painter can be glimpsed in Michelangelo's uncompromising vision of a pitiless God venting his judgement on a cowering humanity. Those spared in this judgement are portrayed in the fresco rising to Paradise on the left, while those doomed by it are shown sinking to hell on the right. The dead rise from their graves along the lower part of the painting, while Christ stands at its centre, surrounded by the Virgin, Apostles and assorted saints. Of the 391 figures in the picture, only one is painted gazing directly at the onlooker – the famous damned soul hugging himself as he awaits his doom.

Michelangelo's celebrated ceiling frescoes are the most famous of the many fine paintings in the Sistine Chapel

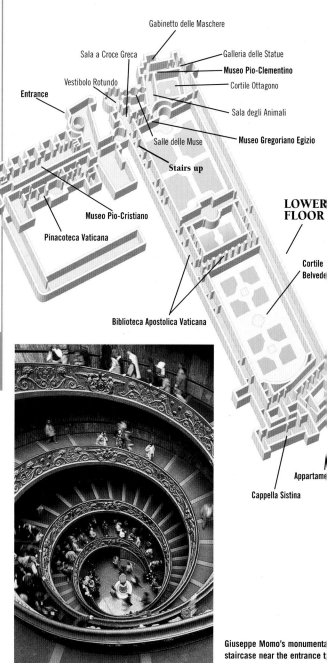

Gabinetto delle Maschere

Sala a Croce Greca

Galleria delle Statue

Museo Pio-Clementino

Vestibolo Rotundo

Cortile Ottagono

Entrance

Sala degli Animali

Museo Gregoriano Egizio

Salle delle Muse

Stairs up

Museo Pio-Cristiano

Pinacoteca Vaticana

LOWER FLOOR

Cortile Belvedere

Biblioteca Apostolica Vaticana

Appartame

Cappella Sistina

Giuseppe Momo's monumenta staircase near the entrance t the Vatican Museums

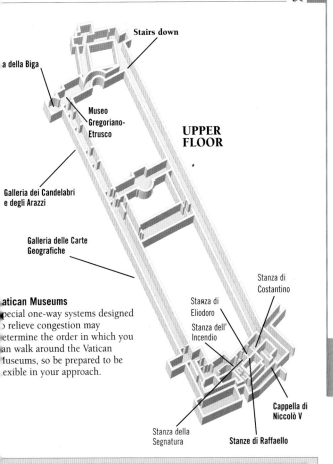

Stairs down

a della Biga

Museo
Gregoriano-
Etrusco

**UPPER
FLOOR**

Galleria dei Candelabri
e degli Arazzi

Galleria delle Carte
Geografiche

atican Museums

pecial one-way systems designed
o relieve congestion may
etermine the order in which you
an walk around the Vatican
1useums, so be prepared to be
exible in your approach.

Stanza di
Costantino

Stanza di
Eliodoro

Stanza dell'
Incendio

Cappella di
Niccolò V

Stanza della
Segnatura

Stanze di Raffaello

THE VATICAN MUSEUMS: INSIDE INFO

Top tips If you're coming from St Peter's note that it's a ten-minute walk to
the Vatican Museums' entrance: if you don't want to walk, take a bus or taxi to
Piazza del Risorgimento, not Piazza San Pietro.
• The Vatican Museums are **closed on Sunday except for the last Sunday of the
month**, when admission is free. Free admission, however, means that the
museums are at their busiest on this day. The museums are open on Mondays,
when most of Rome's state museums are closed.
• If you wish to visit the **Vatican Gardens** (Giardini Vaticani) you need to reserve
your visit three or four days in advance. For more information call the Vatican
Museums (tel: 06 6988 4676 or 06 6988 3322).

In more detail It's well worth buying additional guides to the Raphael Rooms
and Sistine Chapel to help understand the wealth of allusion and meaning in
their paintings.

St Peter's

The Basilica di San Pietro (St Peter's) is the world's most famous church, an important place of Catholic pilgrimage, and the one sight in Rome that you simply must see, even though there are few important works of art inside.

History of the Basilica

The church is built over the shrine of St Peter, one of the Apostles and the fi pope. The huge basilica you see today is not the original St Peter's. St Peter

himself was crucified during the persecutions of Emperor Nero somewhere between AD 64 and 76, probably on the hilly slopes above the present church and his followers then buried him in a cemetery near by. The position of his tomb is reputedly marked by the present-day high altar, a notion supported b extensive archaeological work that has taken place around the site since 1939 Some sort of shrine to the saint probably existed by 200, but the first church for which records survive was raised in 326 by Pope Sylvester I during the reign of Constantine the Great, the first Christian emperor.

This church survived for well over 1,000 years. By 1452, however, its main fabric was in a parlous state, leading Nicholas V, pope at the time, to suggest the construction of a new basilica, funds for which would be collected from across the Christian world. Nicholas had 2,500 wagonloads of stone removed from the Colosseum and carried across the Tiber to prepare for construction. In the event, building only began in 1506, and would proceed – with many false starts and alterations to the original plans – for the best part of 300 year

The architect charged with designing the new church and pulling down the old one – a task that required some 3,000 labourers – was Bramante. He died in 1516, and it was 1539 before Giuliano da Sangallo won a commission to complete the building. His plans proved ill fated, however, and in 1546 Pope Paul III called in Michelangelo to salvage the increasingly troubled project. The artist, then aged 72, demolished Sangallo's additions and advanced an ambitious plan for a colossal dome. Much work on this dome was accomplished by the time of Michelangelo's death in 1564, only for it to be amended in 1590 by another architect, Giacomo della Porta.

o: St Peter
throned. The
tue's right
t has been
rn smooth by
kiss of
grims

ove: Piazza
n Pietro
ovides a
ajestic
tting for
Peter's
silica

In 1605, Carlo Maderno was asked to redesign the church yet again, a scheme that involved, among other things, the construction of the present facade in 1612. Finishing touches were added by the great baroque architect, Gian Lorenzo Bernini. The new church – a monument to architectural compromise – was eventually consecrated on 18 November, 1626, precisely 1,300 years after the consecration of the original basilica.

The Piazza and Basilica

Bernini was responsible not only for last-minute refinements to the church, but also for **Piazza San Pietro** (1656–67), the enormous square (340m by 240m/370 by 260 yards) that provides St Peter's grand setting. The piazza's vast colonnades reach out in two half-circles, symbolising arms stretching out to embrace visiting pilgrims. The colonnades are four columns deep and contain 284 columns – be sure to hunt out the famous pair of **stone discs**, one near each of the square's fountains. These mark the focus of each colonnade's ellipse, and the point at which the four sets of columns appear to line up as a single pillar. The statues surmounting the colonnades represent 140 saints, while the colossal 350-tonne obelisk at the centre of the piazza was brought to Rome from Egypt by Caligula in AD 37. The orb at the top contains a fragment of the Holy Cross (it was thought at one time to contain the ashes of Julius Caesar).

Turning to the **facade**, note the central balcony, from which a new pope is proclaimed and where the pope proclaims new sainthoods and delivers his "Urbi et Orbi" blessing on various holy days. Note, too, the statues across the top of the facade, which depict Christ, John the Baptist and 11 of the Apostles – the missing disciple is St Peter. The most celebrated of the five portals ranged across the facade is the one on the extreme right, the **Porta Santa**, which is opened only during Holy Years, the most recent of which was the year 2000. The central doors (1433–45), cast to commemorate the Council of Florence in 1439, survive from the original St Peter's. They are among only a handful of treasures from the old basilica, most of which were destroyed by Bramante, who earned the nickname "ruinante" (the destroyer) as a result. On either side of the portico stand statues of Constantine (1670) and Charlemagne (1735), to the right and left respectively.

Inside, the first overwhelming impression is one of immense size: the church measures 185m (200 yards) long, 119m (390 feet) high at the dome, and can accommodate upwards of 60,000 people. For many years it was the largest church in the world, losing the title only when a copy of St Peter's was built in Yamoussoukro, in the Ivory Coast. Just inside the entrance, look out for the series of brass line inscriptions on the marble floor which set out the world's next 14 largest churches. Look out, too, for the red porphyry disc a few metres from the entrance which marks the spot where Charlemagne was crowned Holy Roman Emperor in 800.

Below: Two colonnades flank Piazza San Pietro

t: Piazza
Pietro and
nd from
ome of
eter's

The items of genuine artistic merit found among the swathes of marble and decorative artifice are actually few in number, and take less time to see than you might imagine. The first of these is also the greatest: Michelangelo's statue of the **Pietà** (1498–9), which shows Mary cradling the dead Christ. Created when the sculptor was 23, it is Michelangelo's only signed work, the sculptor having reputedly added his name when he heard onlookers disputing the statue's authorship. The work is behind glass after being vandalised in 1972.

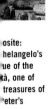

osite:
helangelo's
ue of the
tà, one of
treasures of
eter's

Further down the church, the crossing is marked by the high altar – used only by the pope on special occasions – and a vast altar canopy, or **baldacchino** (1624–33), created by Bernini using bronze removed from the roof of the Pantheon. It was created for Urban VIII, a member of the Barberini family, hence the repeated appearance on the work of the Barberini symbol – the bee. Behind you on your right as you face the canopy is a 13th-century statue of **St Peter Enthroned**, unmissable by virtue of its right foot, which has been caressed to smoothness following a 50-day indulgence granted by Pius IX in 1857 to anyone kissing the statue after confession. The statue's authorship is disputed: it was long thought to be a 5th-century work, but was later attributed to the 13th-century Florentine sculptor Arnolfo di Cambio.

In the apse beyond the high altar stands Bernini's elaborate **Cattedra di San Pietro** (1656–65), a bronze canopy built to encase a throne reputedly used by St Peter (although probably dating from the 9th century). To its left and right lie two

Left: The she
scale of
Bernini's orr
baldacchino
altar canopy
impresses
many visitor

Right: Part
of the congre
gation at an
outdoor Mas
in Piazza Sa
Pietro

Above:
St Peter's is
renowned for
its many tom
and monume

important papal tombs: Bernini's **Monument to Urban VIII** (1627–47) on the right, which became the model for baroque tombs across Europe, and Guglielmo della Porta's **Monument to Paul III** (1551–75) on the left. The latter's female figures of Justice and Prudence are said to be modelled on the Pope's sister and mother. Look also for Antonio Benci detto il Pollaiolo's **Monument to Pope Innocent VIII** (1498) – by the second main pillar of the nave on the right as you walk back towards the entrance. One of the artefacts saved from the old basilica, it shows Innocent twice – once sitting and once recumbent.

All else in the basilica, however, pales into insignificance when set alongside the views from the **dome**. The entrance is at the end of the right-hand nave as you face the altar, from where you can take the lift or climb the steps to the first stage. From here, more steps lead to the higher drum and gallery, and then continue up to a steeper and narrower one-way staircase to the topmost lantern.

TAKING A BREAK

Taverna Angelica (➤ 167) is a good choice for a simple meal within easy striking distance of St Peter's.

✚ 196 B4 ✉ Piazza San Pietro, Città del Vaticano ☎ 06 6988 1662 or 06 6988 3462 🕐 Basilica: Apr–Sep daily 7–7; rest of year 7–6. Dome: Apr–Sep daily 8–5:45; rest of year 8–4:45. Grotte: as for Basilica. Treasury: Apr–Sep daily 9–6; rest of year 9–5 🚇 Ottaviano-San Pietro 🚌 40 or 62 to Via della Conciliazione, 64 to close to Piazza San Pietro or 19, 23, 32, 49, 492, 990 to Piazza del Risorgimento 💶 Basilica: free. Dome, Grotte & Treasury: moderate

ST PETER'S: INSIDE INFO

Top tips A **rigid dress code** is enforced in St Peter's, which is, of course, primarily a place of worship. Women should not wear shorts, short skirts or skimpy tops; they should also avoid displaying bare shoulders. Men should also avoid shorts and dress with decorum.

• The one thing you should definitely do when you visit St Peter's is **climb the dome**, as the view of the city and surrounding countryside from the top is one of the finest in the city. Try to arrive early, as long queues develop; and pick a day when visibility is good.

In more detail There is plenty to see beneath St Peter's, where you'll find the **Sacre Grotte Vaticane**, a crypt which contains the tombs of numerous popes. The entrance is by the pillar in the church's crossing with the statues of St Peter and St Andreas.

One to miss The Treasury contains gifts made to St Peter's over the centuries, but its best artefacts have all been moved to the Vatican Museums.

At Your Leisure

2 Vatican Museums

The following museums and rooms within the Vatican Museums are some you might see on a longer or second visit. Entry details are the same as for the main museum complex (▶ 149). There are still more museums not discussed below: these include the **Museo Sacro** (sacred art from catacombs and early Christian churches in Rome); **Museo Storico** (coaches and weapons); **Museo Missionario Etnologico** (anthropological artefacts brought to Rome by missionary and other expeditions); **Museo Chiaramonti** (a huge quantity of Greek and Roman sculpture); and **Museo Gregoriano Profano** (a collection of secular or "profane" art – mostly more Greek and Roman sculpture).

Museo Gregoriano Egizio

The Vatican's Egyptian collection was founded by Pope Pius VII and collected in this nine-room museum by Pope Gregory XVI in 1839. It

The Museo Gregoriano-Etrusco exhibits some of the finest Etruscan artefacts

contains a wide range of mummies, monumental statues, headstones, papyri and sarcophagi from the 3rd millennium BC to the time of Christ. Many were found in and around Rome itself, having been brought to the city from Egypt, which formed part of the Roman Empire for sever[...] centuries. Highlights include the 6[...] century BC statue of Udya-horres-n[...] in Room I, the head of a statue of Pharaoh Monthuhotep II (2100– 2040 BC) in Room V and the bronz[...] incense burners in Room VI.

Museo Gregoriano-Etrusco

This 18-room museum is excellent [...] your interest in the Etruscans – wh[...] dominated central Italy before the rise of Rome – is not enough to tak[...] you all the way to the much larger Etruscan collection of the Villa Giu[...] (▶ 135). Like the Villa Giulia, this museum has its fair share of dull u[...] and vases, but it also contains som[...] of the greatest of all Etruscan arte[...] facts. The most celebrated of these [...] the **Mars of Todi** (Room III), a larg[...] bronze statue named after the Umbrian town in which it was fou[...]

The Museo Gregoriano-Egizio houses the Vatican's Egyptian collection

disparate and unconnected 1st-century elements. Part of it may once have formed a votive offering, but for years was used as an episcopal throne in the church of San Marco. Niches around the walls contain accomplished Greek and Roman statues: some date back as far as the 5th century BC.

Appartamento Borgia

This suite of apartments was built for Pope Alexander VI, a member of the notorious Borgia family, during his papacy (1492–1503). Almost a palace within a palace, it proved so sumptuous that subsequent popes chose to use it as their principal lodgings for the next hundred years. Room I, the Sala delle Sibille, is where the infamous Cesare Borgia is said to have had Alfonso of Aragon, the husband of his sister, Lucretia Borgia, murdered. Today, the room is more remarkable for its frescoes, part of a fine series of paintings in the suite executed between 1492 and 1495 by the Umbrian artist Pinturicchio. The pictures cover a wide variety of themes, embracing religious, humanist and mythical subjects – the best are in Room V, the Sala dei Santi. Other rooms in this

worth special attention are the bits of Room II, most of which e taken from the **Regolini-assi Tomb** (c650 BC) uncovered 836 at Cerveteri just north of e. The Etruscans, like the ptians, buried the deceased with manner of everyday items they ht need in the afterlife, thereby viding archaeologists with a hic picture of their domestic artistic habits.

a della Biga
single marble-decked
n features a Roman
, or two-horsed
iot recon-
cted in
from

complex are given over to the Collezione d'Arte Religiosa Moderna, a collection of modern religious art.

Biblioteca Apostolica Vaticana

The Vatican Library easily rates as the world's most valuable collection of books and manuscripts. Books were accumulated by the popes for centuries, but only found a perma- nent home in 1474 during the papacy of Sixtus IV. Material has been systematically added to the library ever since, amounting to some 100,000 manuscripts, 70,000 archive volumes, 800,000 printed works, 100,000 prints and maps, and around 75,000 handwritten and illustrated books. Only a fraction of the collec- tion is displayed here, but all the items are beautiful, and some – such as handwritten material by Michelangelo, Martin Luther, Petrarch and others – of immense historical importance.

Pinacoteca Vaticana

Even on its own, the Vatican's Pinacoteca, or art gallery, would b considered one of Rome's major collections of medieval, Renaissar and other paintings. Its 16 rooms offer a chronological insight into development of religious art, and would be richer still had Napoleo not pilfered many of their treasur the beginning of the 19th century.

Room I opens with 11th-, 12th and 13th-century Tuscan and Umbrian works, followed by one the gallery's highlights – Giotto's **Stefaneschi Triptych** (*c*1315). Commissioned by Cardinal Stefaneschi, it was originally inter for one of the principal altars in t old St Peter's. Among the gallery's other star attractions are two majestic paintings by Raphael in Room VIII, a ***Transfigurat*** (1517–20) and the ***Madonna of Foligno*** (1512–13), as well

The sculpted angel that line the Ponte Sant'Angelo, close Castel Sant'Angelo, known as the "Bree Maniacs"

For Kids

Children should relish the view from the top of the dome of **St Peter's** (► 161), though they may find the climb to the top hard work (only the fittest adults sho even contemplate carrying small children up the steps). **Castel Sant'Angelo** (► 165), which not only looks like a "real" castle, but also has lots of spooky corridors and hidden corners, is almost guaranteed to intrigue youngsters.

In the Vatican Museums you need to be very selective if you have children w you: try them with the **Sala degli Animali** (► 149), the gallery of maps (► 149) the mummies of the Egyptian museum (► 162).

Italian painters: Fra Angelico, Titian, Caravaggio, Veronese and many others.

3 Castel Sant'Angelo

There is no mistaking the Castel Sant'Angelo, whose dramatic round bulwarks rise on the banks of the Tiber just to the east of St Peter's. Today, the castle is a museum, but it started life in AD 130 as a mausoleum for Emperor Hadrian. Its circular design – which formed the basis for all subsequent structures on the site – was copied from the Mausoleo di Augusto near the Capitoline Hill, which in turn was probably based on the design of Etruscan tombs. The mausoleum was used as a resting place for emperors until AD 271, when it was incorporated into the city's defences. It then remained Rome's principal fortress for over 1,000 years.

On entering the castle, you walk along deep, subterranean passages, part of the original Roman-era mausoleum, and then climb up to the ramparts, which offer excellent views across the city. Immediately below, look out for the Ponte Sant'Angelo, a bridge adorned with statues of angels sculpted to a design by Bernini. The castle's various military and other exhibits are fairly dull, unlike the variety of beautifully decorated papal apartments and libraries woven into the fortress's labyrinth of rooms and passageways.

f the Beaten Track

or a glimpse of the inner sanctum of tican City (most of which is served for those working or living in 's tiny state), book on to one of the urs of the **Vatican Gardens** (▶ 155). Outside Vatican City, the small grid streets known as the Borgo – tween Borgo Sant'Angelo and Via escenzio – is the least-visited clave near St Peter's.

nardo da Vinci's unfinished *erome* in Room IX. These are just r highlights among many, for gallery possesses rks by most ling

🚩 194 A5
✉ Lungotevere Castello 50 ☎ 06 681 9111 🕑 Tue–Sun 9–7:30 🚌 30, 49, 70, 87, 130, 186 and other services to Piazza Cavour and Lungotevere 💶 Expensive

Where to...
Eat and Drink

Prices
Expect to pay per person for a meal, excluding drinks and service
€ under €20 €€ €20–40 €€€ over €40

The area around St Peter's and the Vatican suffers from a shortage of good restaurants compared to other parts of the city. Once, the grid of streets between Via della Conciliazione and Via Crescenzio, an area known as the Borgo, was filled with artisans' workshops and traditional little eating places. Most of these have gone now, or have been replaced by restaurants aimed specifically at the tourist market. A few old places remain, however, along with one restaurant – Les Étoiles –

that ranks among Rome's finest. There's a fair amount of choice if all you want is a quick snack, and an abundance of places on Via Cola di Rienzo – a street renowned for its food shops – to buy picnic supplies.

Dal Toscano €€
This lively restaurant is convenient for the Vatican Museums, being just east of the entrance on Via Germanico between Via Ottaviano and Via Vespasiano. It's also popular with locals and families, so reservations are recommended, at least in the

evenings. As the name suggests, this is not a place for Roman specialities, but rather the thick *bistecca alla fiorentina* (T-bone steaks), *ribollita* soups, and other staples of Tuscany.

➕ 196 C5 ✉ Via Germanico 58–60
☎ 06 3972 5717 ⏰ Tue–Sun
12:30–2:30, 7:30–11. Closed 1 week in Dec and 2 weeks in Aug

Les Étoiles €€€
This is one of the great Roman restaurants for a treat or celebration. From the moment you enter the stylish dining-room and see the view of St Peter's you know you're in for something special. The Italian food and courteous service are as good as the view, and the menu changes from day to day, depending on the availability of produce and the mood of the chef. The restaurant forms part of the Atlante Star hotel, and has a roof garden and terrace for dining out in summer.

➕ 197 D4 ✉ Via dei Bastioni 1
☎ 06 687 3233 or 06 689 3434
⏰ Daily noon–2:30, 7:30–midnight

Non Solo Pizza €
Non Solo Pizza (Not Only Pizza) serves pizza by the slice (and full pizzas after 7pm) and a selection of Roman-style deep-fried delicacies: stuffed olives, rice and cheese balls, courgette flowers and the like. It also serves a limited daily selection of inexpensive hot dishes, a good option for lunch after a visit to the Vatican Museums. The restaurant is in a side street a couple of blocks north of Piazza Risorgimento.

➕ 196 C5 ✉ Via degli Scipioni 95–97 ☎ 06 372 5820 ⏰ Tue–Sun 8:30am–9:30pm

Osteria dell' Angelo €€
You need to reserve a table at this popular restaurant on a side street just north of the busy Viale delle Milizie. The sophisticated cooking goes beyond the usual local and Italian staples, while the decoration is dominated by sporting photographs, a nod to the rugby-playing past of the owner, the eponymous Angelo. On balmy

summer evenings, you can eat outdoors.

➕ 196 C5 ▢ Via Giovanni Bettolo 24 ☎ 06 372 9470 ⏰ Tue–Fri 12:45–2:30, 8–11; Mon, Sat 8–11

Osteria Croce €

This is a reasonably convenient option for the Vatican Museums: just walk north up Via Leone IV and turn right after six blocks to find this very popular and traditional trattoria patronised mostly by Romans rather than foreign visitors.

➕ 196 C5 ▢ Via Giovanni Bettoio 24 ☎ 06 372 9470 ⏰ Tue–Fri 12:30–2:30, 7:30–10:30, Mon, Sat 7:30–10:30, Sun 12:30–2:30

Pellachia €

If you're shopping for food or other goods on Via Cola di Rienzo, treat yourself to an ice-cream at Pellachia, one of the best ice-cream parlours in this part of Rome.

➕ 197 D/E5 ▢ Via Cola di Rienzo 103 ☎ 06 321 0807 ⏰ Tue–Sun 6am–1am. Closed 1 week in Aug

Il Simposio €–€€

Walk to the northwest corner of Piazza Cavour just east of the Castel Sant'Angelo for this striking wine bar, wine shop (downstairs) and restaurant. Decoration in the wine bar consists of some spectacular wrought ironwork featuring grape and vine motifs. The restaurant just beyond the bar offers first-class Italian food but at higher prices than in more basic wine bars. The choice of wines is excellent – over 2,000 Italian vintages by the bottle and a selection by the glass.

➕ 194 B5 ▢ Piazza Cavour 16 (corner of Via Tacito) ☎ 06 321 1502 ⏰ Mon–Fri 12:30–2:30, 7:30–11, Sat 7:30–11. Wine shop: Tue–Sat 8:30–1:30, 7:30–11, Mon 4:40–8

Taberna de' Gracchi €–€€

The Taberna de' Gracchi is a reliable restaurant for lunch if you have

visited the Castel Sant'Angelo, for it lies just north of the Castel, close to Piazza Cola di Rienzo.

➕ 197 E5 ▢ Via dei Gracchi 266–8 ☎ 06 321 3126; www.tabernagracchi.com ⏰ Tue–Sat 12:30–2:30, 7:30–10:30, Mon 7:30–10:30

Taverna Angelica €€

This, the best mid-range restaurant within easy reach of St Peter's, lies on the south side of a tiny piazza on Borgo Vittorio in the heart of the Borgo. Despite its location, it is not a typical Roman trattoria, for the modern interior is minimalist, and the cooking light, innovative and biased towards fish and seafood. The wine list is good, and includes some by the glass. Covers are limited, so be sure to make a reservation.

➕ 197 D4 ▢ Piazza delle Vaschette 14a ☎ 06 687 4514; www.tavernaangelica.it ⏰ Dinner only: daily 7:30–midnight, plus lunch on Sun. Closed 3 weeks in Aug

Tre Pupazzi €–€€

If you can't get into Taverna Angelica (see left), try this 400-year-old place just around the corner to the east. It is far more traditional in appearance and cuisine, and serves good fish, pizzas and pasta dishes.

➕ 197 D4 ▢ Via dei Tre Pupazzi 1 ☎ 06 686 8371 ⏰ Mon–Sat 12:30–2:30, 7:30–11

Veranda €€–€€€

The Veranda forms part of the Hotel Columbus, close to St Peter's and traditionally favoured by visiting cardinals and other clergy. What sets this restaurant apart is not the food, which can sometimes be a little over adventurous, but its lovely terrace garden. This provides a tranquil and pleasant setting for eating outdoors when the weather is suitable.

➕ 196 C4 ▢ Hotel Columbus, Via della Conciliazione 33 ☎ 06 687 2973 ⏰ Daily 12:30–3, 7:30–11

Where to... Shop

The area surrounding the Vatican and St Peter's is not the place to go for shops. More or less the only things that you'll find for sale here are religious souvenirs and postcards. The Borgo's grid of streets still contains the occasional **artisan's workshop**, but nothing to compare with the number or variety of similar workshops on Via dei Cappellari and the other streets around Campo de' Fiori (▶ 109–110). One exception is **Italia Garipoli** (Borgo Vittorio 91a, tel: 06 6880 2196, closed Sun), which specialises in linens, curtains and other fabrics.

Where you will find a variety of shops is in the mainly modern in particular Via Cola di Rienzo, one of the busiest shopping streets in northwest Rome. The street has a wide variety of shops selling mid-range clothes, shoes and other commodities, but is especially known for its *alimentari* – **food shops**. One of the best known is **Castroni** (Via Cola di Rienzo 196, tel: 06 687 4383, www.castroni.com, closed Sun), which combines Italian staples (cheese, hams, olive oils and so on) with food specialities from around the world. Alternatively, visit **Franchi** (Via Cola di Rienzo 200–204, tel: 06 686 4576, closed Sun), one of Rome's most mouth-watering delicatessens; where you can buy picnic provisions or the counter staff will make up delicious take-out sandwiches and snack lunches to order.

Via Cola di Rienzo also has some surprises. Look out for **Costantini** (tel: 06 321 3210, closed Sun, Mon morning, and Aug), a good wine shop to the south at Piazza

Where to... Be Entertained

Since 1958 the **Pio auditorium** (Via della Conciliazione 4), close to St Peter's, has staged a variety of classical music concerts. Rome's foremost classical musical association, the **Accademia Nazionale di Santa Cecilia** (tel: 06 8024 2501; www.santacecilia.it) has its own orchestra, and also organises concerts by visiting choirs, orchestras and other ensembles. Choral and organ music can be heard in St Peter's. The Accademia is among many organisations that perform at Rome's spectacular **Parco della Musica** auditorium (Viale Pietro de Coubertin 34, tel: 06 8609 2492; www.musicaperroma.it or www.auditorium.com (box office

Music of a different sort can be heard two blocks north of the entrance to the Vatican Museums at **Alexanderplatz** (Via Ostia 9, off Via Leone, tel: 06 3974 2171, open Mon–Sat 9pm–2:30am). This is probably Rome's best venue for live jazz; you can also eat in the adjoining restaurant (reservations recommended). Another good pub-club for live jazz, blues and rock is the long-running **Fonclea** (Via Crescenzio 82a, tel: 06 689 6302, open daily 7 or 8pm–2am, admission usually free except Sat). Similar music can be heard farther north at the **Four Green Fields** pub (Via C Morin 38, off Via della Giuliana, tel: 06 372 5091, open daily 6pm–2am, admis-

Excursions

Rome is so filled with museums, ancient monuments and other sightseeing temptations that many people on a short visit prefer to stay in the city, rather than visiting the variety of towns and sights within the vicinity. However, there are two interesting excursions, which are easily made and offer an excellent counterpoint to the city and – should you need it – an escape from its often busy streets. The most popular is Tivoli, a town to the east of Rome, known for its gardens and the Villa Adriana, the ruins of Emperor Hadrian's vast private villa. The second is Frascati, a town nestled on the slopes of the Alban Hills, the volcanic peaks that rise just south of the city. Easily reached by train from Termini, the town is best known for its white wine, cooling summer breezes and lofty views over Rome.

Those with more time to spend exploring the area might also want to investigate Ostia Antica, Rome's old sea port, and today an extensive archaeological park to the west of the city. Further up the coast to the north are Cerveteri and Tarquinia, two major Etruscan towns with large ancient necropolises, or tombs, while inland to the south lies Palestrina, known for its great pre-Roman temple. If you want a complete change, consider Orvieto, a fascinating Umbrian hill town with an outstanding cathedral around 80 minutes from Rome by train. Contact the visitor centre (▶ 30) for further details or for information on companies offering guided coach tours to these sights.

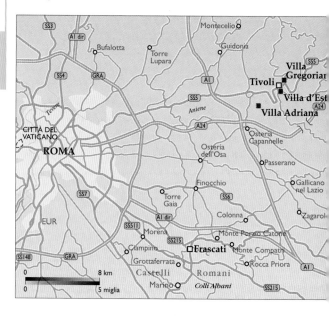

Tivoli

e ancient town of Tivoli – Roman *Tibur* – is the most
pular one-day excursion from Rome. Some 36km (22
es) from the city, it's known for two principal sights: the
la d'Este, a Renaissance villa celebrated for its gardens,
l the Villa Adriano, a vast Roman-era villa and grounds
ated by Emperor Hadrian. Also worth seeing are the more
ent and more rugged grounds of the Villa Gregoriana.

la d'Este

e Villa d'Este began life as a Benedictine convent, but was
verted into a country villa in 1550 for Cardinal Ippolito II
ste, a wealthy collector and patron of the arts and a scion
 one of Italy's premier noble families – he was the son of
rezia Borgia. These days, the villa contains a lacklustre
ection of faded rooms, and takes second place to its extra-
inary, stylised – but extremely beautiful – gardens.
ome of the gardens' most eye-catching features are their
ntains, of which the most impressive is the **Viale delle
to Fontane**, or Avenue of One Hundred Fountains, with
countless jets of water. Also look out for Bernini's elegant
tana del Bicchierone and the so-called Owl and Organ
ntains, which – when they worked – could reproduce the
nd of an organ and the screeching of an owl. The Fontana
Roma, or Rometta, is also worth seeking out – it features
dels of the Tiber, Tiber Island (► 178) and several of
ne's major ancient monuments.

The Viale
delle Centro
Fontane at the
Villa d'Este

✉ Largo Garibaldi ☎ 0424 600 460 or toll-free in Italy 199 766 166,
ww.villadestetivoli.info ⏰ Tue–Sun 8:30–6:15/6:45, Apr–Sep;
:30–4/5:15, rest of year 🎫 Gardens: moderate/expensive

Villa Gregoriana

The Villa Gregoriana is generally less crowded than the Villa d'Este and – although not particularly well maintained – is perhaps more interesting and beautiful. Centred on a pair of waterfalls and a 60m (200-foot) gorge cut by the River Aniene, it lies in the town's northeast corner about 300m (330 yard from the Villa d'Este. The park was created in 1831 when Pope Gregory XVI built tunnels to divert the waters of the Aniene to protect Tivoli from floodin From the ticket office follow the path signposted to the Grande Cascata, or Large Waterfall, which brings you to steps and a terrace overlooking the waterfall. Other paths near by meander around the lush and often overgrowr park, passing through the ruins of a Roman villa, among other things, and dropping down to the valley floor past ancient shrines and grottoes before a long climb up the other side of the gorge past the ruined Temple of Vesta.

✉ Largo Sant'Angelo at the junction of Viale Mazzini & Via Quintilio Varo
☎ 0774 3996 7701, www.villasgregoriana.it ⏱ Tue–Sun 10–6:30, Apr–mid-Oct; 10–2:30
Mar, mid-Oct–Nov; Dec–Feb by appointment only 💷 Moderate

Villa Adriana

Leave plenty of time for the Villa Adriana as its site covers an area equal to that of ancient Rome – making it probably the largest villa ever created in the Roman world. It was begun in AD 125 and completed ten years later by Emperor Hadrian. Many of its treasures, statues and stone have long gone, bu the site remains a wonderfully pretty and romantic place, and enough surviv of the villa's many buildings to evoke their original grandeur.

Hadrian reproduced or adapted the designs of many of the great buildings he had visited during his travels around the empire: the "Pecile" colonnade through which you enter, for example, reproduces the Stoa Poikile of Athens in Greece. A small museum collects finds made in the ongoing excavations, but you will get most pleasure by simply wandering the site at random. Be

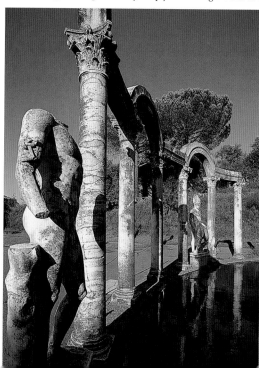

The columns and statues that line the Canopus at th Villa Adriana are copies fro the Temple of Serapis near Alexandria

TIVOLI: INSIDE INFO

Getting there It is possible to take a **train** from Termini to Tivoli, but as most trains stop frequently, this is a particularly slow, albeit painless, way of getting to the town. Tivoli's station is in Viale Mazzini, approximately 400m (0.25 miles) southeast of the Villa Gregoriana.
• **Buses** to Tivoli depart approximately every 10 to 20 minutes from the Ponte Mammolo Metro station on Line B; journey time is 50 minutes.

Top tips Tivoli's **visitor centre** lies close to the entrance to the Villa d'Este on the north side of Largo Garibaldi (tel: 0774 311 249).
• The Villa d'Este is extremely popular, so be prepared for lots of visitors: **arrive early** to see the gardens at their least crowded. Avoid the heat of the afternoon in high summer. Allow time to explore Tivoli's attractive tangle of streets.

Hidden gem In the Villa Adriano look out for the **Teatro Marittimo**, or Maritime Theatre, a small colonnaded palace built by Hadrian on an island in an artificial lagoon. It is thought that this was the emperor's private retreat, the place to which he would retire for a siesta or to indulge his love of poetry, music and art.

fountains one of the highlights of gardens at a d'Este

sure to walk along the sunken stone passageway (known as a *cryptoporticus*) while exploring the Villa Adriana. Past artists have burned their names on the ceiling with candle smoke.

To reach the Villa Adriana from Tivoli, take a taxi or catch the local No 4 or 4x CAT bus from the bus station in Piazza Massimo or from the stop outside the tourist office on Largo Garibaldi.

✉ Via di Villa Adriana-Via Tiburtina ☎ 0774 530 203 🕐 Daily 9–7, Apr–Sep; 9–7:30 May–Aug, 9–6:30 Oct, 9–5 Nov–Jan; last ticket sold 1 hour earlier 💶 Moderate

TAKING A BREAK

A good restaurant choice in Tivoli is the **Antica Osteria dei Carrettieri** (Via Domenico Giuliani 55, tel: 0774 330 159, closed Wed). Out of town, on the road to the Villa Adriana, the best option is **Adriano** (Via di Villa Adriana 194, tel: 0774 382 235, open daily); you can eat outside in summer. Alternatively, buy food and drink from shops in Tivoli and take them to the Villa Adriana for a picnic.

Frascati

Frascati offers a cool, calm retreat from Rome's heat and hustle on hot summer days, providing a pleasant combination of good food, local wine and sweeping views of the city.

If you have time to spare, Frascati is the place to go. Trains depart from Termini approximately hourly and the journey takes about 30 minutes. You are treated to an ever-more attractive rural outlook as the train wends its way into the Colli Albani (Alban Hills), to the south of Rome. Steps from Frascati's small station lead through gardens to Piazzale (or Piazza) Marconi, the town's principal square, home to the visitor centre at No 1 (tel: 06 942 0331). Above the square stands the **Villa Aldobrandini**, one of the few old buildings to survive the bombing during 1943 and 1944 that destroyed 80 per cent of old Frascati.

Vineyards in the hills above Rome produce Fascati's famous white wine

The villa was built for Cardinal Pietro Aldobrandini between 1598 and 1603 and is still owned by the Aldobrandini family. Though the villa itself is closed to the public, some of the grounds, which are noted for the excellent views over Rome in the hazy distance, can be visited. Look out for the garden's Teatro dell'Acqua, a semicircular array of fountains and statues in which the central figure of Atlas is said to be a represention of Pietro Aldobrandini's uncle, Pope Clement VIII.

Frascati's other major public park is the less appealing **Villa Torlonia**, entered from close to the town hall building (the Municipio) near Piazzale Marconi. In the rest of the town, leave a short time for the rebuilt Duomo in Piazza San Pietro and the church of the Gesù (Piazza del Gesù), known for its late 17th-century paintings by Andrea dal Pozzo.

TAKING A BREAK

Cacciani (Via Armando Diaz 13, tel: 06 942 0378, closed Mon, also Sun pm in winter), which has an outdoor terrace for dining in summer, is the best restaurant in Frascati. For something simpler and less expensive, try **Zarazà** (Viale Regina Margherita 45, tel: 06 942 2053, closed Mon, also Sun pm, Sep–May).

Villa Aldobrandini gardens

🕓 Mon–Fri 9–1, 3–6, Apr–Sep; 9–1, 3–5, rest of year 🎫 Free, though passes must be obtained from Visitor Centre at Piazza G. Marconi 1 (tel: 06 942 0331). Note that the visitor centre is closed on Saturday afternoon and all day Sunday

Walks

1 GHETTO TO TRASTEVERE

Walk

This walk takes you to three of the city's smaller and prettier enclaves: the old Jewish Ghetto area, a lovely labyrinth of quiet streets; the Isola Tiberina, an island on the River Tiber; and the larger Trastevere district, an equally appealing but better-known collection of cobbled lanes, tiny squares, and interesting shops, cafés and restaurants.

DISTANCE 4.25km (2.6 miles) **TIME** Allow 3–4 hours
START POINT Piazza del Campidoglio ✚ 195 F1
END POINT Campo de' Fiori ✚ 194 C2

1–2

Start in **Piazza del Campidoglio** (▶ 48–49) just off Piazza Venezia. With the church of Santa Maria in Aracoeli on your left, walk to the rear of the piazza and take the lane to the right of Palazzo Senatorio, the palace ahead of you. Follow the lane as it winds downhill, admiring the views of the **Roman Forum** (▶ 50–55) on your left. Turn right at the bottom on Via della Consolazione and cross Piazza della Consolazione. Bear left off the piazza down Via San Giovanni Decollato. At the end of this street on the left stands **San Giorgio in Velabro**. The church takes its name from the marshy area (the Velabro) by the Tiber where – according to legend – the shepherd Faustulus found Romulus and Remus, Rome's founding twins (▲ 7). The church's simple Romanesque interior – almost bare save for an apse fresco – is one of the city's finest. There are two ancient arches near by: the one adjoining the church is **Arco**

Trastevere's quiet streets and piazzas are wonderful places to explore

degli Argentari (Arch of the Moneychangers) erected in AD 204 in honour of Emperor Septimius Severus; the other, in the short Via del Velabro in front of the church, is the **Arco di Giano**, and dates from the time of Constantine (4th century).

2–3

Continue down Via del Velabro and Passaggio di San Giovanni Decollato, which open into the large **Piazza della Bocca della Verità**. On the right, in an area of grass and trees, stand two almost perfectly preserved Roman temples: the circular Tempio di Vesta and rectangular Tempio di Fortuna Virilis (both 2nd century BC). Beyond them, on the piazza's left (south) flank stands

Santa Maria in Aracoeli

Palazzo Senatorio

Foro Romano

Arco degli Argentari

San Giorgio in Velabro

Arco di Giano

Santa Maria in Cosmedin

VIA DELLA CONSOLAZIONE

PIAZZA DELLA CONSOLAZIONE

PIAZZA VENEZIA

PIAZZA DEL CAMPIDOGLIO

VIA SAN G

VIA DI VELABRO

DECOLLATO

PIAZZA BOCCA DELLA VERITA

① ② ③

Tempio di Vesta

Tempio di Fortuna Virilis

LUNGOTEVERE DEI PIERLEONI

Fontana delle Tartarughe

Portico d'Ottavia

VIA DEL PORTICO D'OTTAVIA

VIA D FUNARI

VIA DEL SANT'ANGELO IN PESCHERIA

PIAZZA MONTE SAVELLO

PIAZZA MATTEI

Sinagoga

LUNG DEI CENCI

GHETTO

VIA DELLA REGINELLA

PIAZZA D CINQUE SCOLE

Isola Tiberina

PONTE FABRICIO

PONTE CESTIO

San Bartolomeo

⑤

LUNGOTEVERE DELL'ANGUILLARA

LUNGOTEVERE DELLA LUNGARETTA

PIAZZA IN PISCINULA

④

PIAZZA S SONNINO

T R A S T E V E R E

Tevere

⑥

PONTE SISTO

PIAZZA TRILUSSA

PIAZZA SANT'EGIDIO

VIA DI SAN DOROTEA

Santa Maria in Trastevere

PIAZZA DI SANTA MARIA IN TRASTEVERE

VIA DELLA SCALA

VIA GARIBALDI

⑧

CAMPO DEI FIORI

PIAZZA FARNESE

VIA DEI CAPPELLARI

VIA D FARNESI

⑦

ELLEGRINO

VIA GIULIA

Santa Maria dell'Orazione e Morte

MORETTA

0 200 metres

0 200 yards

Verità at Santa Maria in Cosmedin

face the church, look for the round stone relief (an old Roman drain cover) known as the Bocca della Verità (Mouth of Truth). Legend claims that the mouth will clamp shut on the hands of dissemblers. The church, one of the few in the city to have escaped a baroque makeover, vies with San Clemente for the title of Rome's loveliest medieval interior.

healing. Walk around the island's perimeter and look into the 10th-century church of San Bartolomeo in the square in front of the piazza before crossing the Ponte Cestio on the island's south. This brings you to the **Trastevere district** (▶ 95–98).

Like the Ghetto, this is an area you may want to explore in more depth; this walk simply takes you through Trastevere's heart, but almost any random route through the web of streets is rewarding.

La Fontana delle Tartarughe in Piazza Mattei

building begun in 146 BC, now partly enmeshed in the 8th-century church of Sant'Angelo in Pescheria. Turn right (north) here on Via del Sant' Angelo in Pescheria and then left at the top of the street on Via dei Funari. This takes you to **Piazza Mattei** and the heart of Rome's old Jewish Ghetto, where Jews were segregated after 1556; the walls were torn down in 1848, but many Jewish families and businesses are still based in the area. Piazza Mattei is known for one of the city's most charming fountains, the **Fontana delle Tartarughe**, or Fountain of the Tortoises (designed 1581); it takes its name from the little bronze tortoises drinking from the fountain's upper basin.

3–4

From the area in front of the church walk northwest following the line of the Tiber on Lungotevere dei Pierleoni. Continue past Piazza Monte Savello on your right until Lungotevere dei Pierleoni becomes Lungotevere dei Cenci and you see Rome's distinctive **synagogue** (Sinagoga) ahead of you on the right. Turn right, before you pass the synagogue, on Via del Portico d'Ottavia. This takes you to the **Portico d'Ottavia**, a tiny fragment of a great Roman

The Isola Tiberina and the ruined Ponte Rotto

4–5

From Piazza Mattei you should explore some of the surrounding side streets and piazzas at random for a flavour of the area. Then take Via della Reginella left (south) off the piazza, and on reaching Via Portico d'Ottavia turn right then left through Piazza delle Cinque Scole to rejoin Lungotevere dei Cenci. Turn left and then first right on the Ponte Fabricio which crosses the Tiber to the **Isola Tiberina (Tiber Island)**. Much of the island is given over to a hospital, continuing a tradition begun in 291 BC, when a temple here

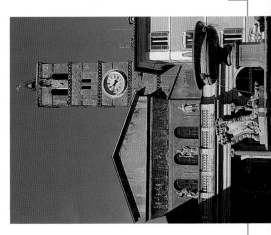

Places to Visit

Santa Maria in Cosmedin

➕ 201 D4 ☒ Piazza della Bocca della Verità 18 ☏ 06 678 1419 ⏰ Apr–Sep daily 9–1, 2–7; rest of year 9–1, 2–6

5–6

Beyond the Ponte Cestio cross the main, busy Lungotevere dell'Anguillara and continue straight into Piazza in Piscinula. Turn right out of the piazza on Via della Lungaretta. Cross Piazza Sonnino–Viale di Trastevere and pick up the continuation of Via della Lungaretta and follow it to Piazza di Santa Maria in Trastevere and the church of **Santa Maria in Trastevere** (▶ 96–97). Walk out of the piazza to the right of the church as you face it, then bear right at the rear of the church into Piazza Sant'Egidio. From the piazza follow Via della Scala until you reach Via Garibaldi. Turn right here on Via di San Dorotea, which leads to Piazza Trilussa, a small square almost on the Tiber. From here cross the Tiber on the pedestrians-only Ponte Sisto, turn left, then take the right fork into **Via Giulia**, framed by a pretty vine-draped archway.

6–7

Walk down Via Giulia, one of Rome's most elegant streets, noting the stone skulls on the facade of **Santa Maria dell'Orazione e Morte** (▶ 100) on the left at the junction with Via dei Farnesi. Via Giulia was laid out in 1508 for Pope Julius II (hence Giulia), providing what, at the time, was the city's main approach to

St Peter's. In 1655 a major city prison was established at the present-day No 52.

Where Via Giulia opens out into a piazza, turn right onto Vicolo della Moretta, a short street that takes you to a junction of several streets. If you have time, turn left and walk a little way down Via dei Banchi Vecchi, which, like Via Giulia, is dotted with interesting shops. Otherwise, turn right on Via del Pellegrino and then first right on Via dei Cappellari.

7–8

Via dei Cappellari is one of the most distinctive streets in this part of Rome, chiefly because it is still lined with traditional artisans' workshops, most of which are given over to furniture-making and restoration. It has a long history of artisanship, taking its name from the *cappellari*, or hatters, who were once based here. Other streets in the vicinity are named after similar trades (Via dei Baullari – the street of the trunkmakers; Via dei Chiavari – the street of the locksmiths; and Via dei Giubbonari – the street of the tailors). Continue down Via dei Cappellari, passing under the dark arch midway down and you emerge into **Campo de' Fiori** (▶ 80–81).

Santa Maria in Trastevere, noted for its facade mosaics

2 PIAZZA VENEZIA TO PIAZZA NAVONA

Walk

This walk meanders through the heart of the medieval and Renaissance city, taking you to several key sights – notably the Trevi Fountain (Fontana di Trevi) – but also to a succession of lesser churches, streets and monuments that you might not otherwise discover on a tour of the area's major attractions.

DISTANCE 3km (1.9 miles) **TIME** Allow 2–3 hours
START POINT Piazza Venezia ✚ 195 F2
END POINT Piazza Navona ✚ 194 C3

1–2

Start on the northern flank of **Piazza Venezia** facing the Monumento a Vittorio Emanuele II. Walk out of the piazza to your left (east) along Via Cesare Battisti and turn left into Piazza dei SS Apostoli. On your right in the piazza stands the 15th-century Palazzo Colonna, home to the **Galleria Colonna**, an art gallery filled with first-rank paintings by mostly Italian masters. Alongside to the left lies the church of **SS Apostoli**. Behind a palace-like facade, the baroque interior is known for its huge altarpiece by Domenico Muratori, and Antonio Canova's 1789 *Tomb of Clement XIV*, in the north (left) aisle by the sacristy door. Continue to the end of Piazza dei SS Apostoli.

2–3

Turn right at the junction with Via del Vaccaro and first left on Via dell'Archetto. Cross Via dell'Umiltà and carry on down Via delle Vergini. Turn right on Via delle Muratte to emerge in the square containing the **Fontana di Trevi** (▶ 124–125). Take Via dei Crociferi from the piazza's northwest corner (to the rear left as you face the fountain) and continue straight on along Via dei Sabini to emerge on Via del Corso. Across the Corso to the right lies the open area

Marco Aurelio at its heart. The column was raised between AD 180 and 196 to celebrate the military victories of Marcus Aurelius in northern Europe. The sculpted reliefs portray episodes from the Emperor's campaigns.

3–4

Walk across Piazza Colonna and through either of the small streets off its western flank – Via della Colonna Antonina is the one on the left. Either one brings you to Piazza di Montecitorio, another large piazza, dominated by Bernini's 1650 Palazzo di Montecitorio, seat of the lower house of Italy's parliament, the Camera dei Deputati. Take Via Uffici di Vicario west off the piazza, passing the historic Giolitti café on the left, then turn right up Via di Campo Marzio. Take the third left, Via dei Prefetti, and then turn right on Via della Lupa to emerge in **Piazza Borghese**, which takes its name from the Palazzo Borghese (closed to the public), the large palace across the street. This was the

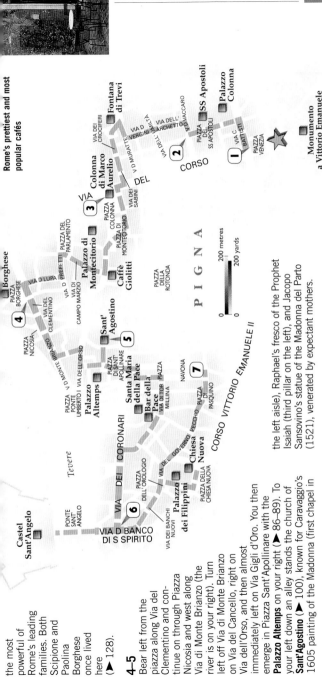

Rome's prettiest and most popular cafés

Fontana di Trevi

Colonna di Marco Aurelio **3**

Palazzo di Montecitorio

Caffè Giolitti

Palazzo Borghese **4**

Sant' Agostino **5**

Palazzo Altemps

Santa Maria della Pace

Bar della Pace

Chiesa Nuova **7**

Castel Sant'Angelo

Palazzo dei Filippini **6**

SS Apostoli

Palazzo Colonna

Monumento a Vittorio Emanuele II

PIAZZA VENEZIA

CORSO **2**

1

PIGNA

CORSO VITTORIO EMANUELE II

Tevere

0   200 metres
0   200 yards

the most powerful of Rome's leading families. Both Scipione and Paolina Borghese once lived here (▶ 128).

4–5
Bear left from the piazza along Via del Clementino and continue on through Piazza Nicosia and west along Via di Monte Brianzo (the river is on your right). Turn left off Via di Monte Brianzo on Via del Cancello, right on Via dell'Orso, and then almost immediately left on Via Gigli d'Oro. You then emerge in Piazza Sant'Apollinare with the Palazzo Altemps on your right (▶ 86–89). To your left down an alley stands the church of Sant'Agostino (▶ 100), known for Caravaggio's 1605 painting of the Madonna (first chapel in

the left aisle), Raphael's fresco of the Prophet Isaiah (third pillar on the left), and Jacopo Sansovino's statue of the Madonna del Parto (1521), venerated by expectant mothers.

5–6

Return to Piazza Sant'Apollinare and walk south to the adjoining Piazza Cinque Lune and into **Piazza Navona** (▶ 82–85). Take Via di Sant'Agnese in Agone (which becomes Via di Tor Millina) midway down the piazza on its west side. You might pause for a drink at Bar della Pace (▶ 108) on the corner of Via della Pace. As you face the bar, a short distance away to its right stands **Santa Maria della Pace**, a charming (if rarely open) church begun in 1482. It contains frescoes of the Sibyls by Raphael and a cloister added in 1504 by Bramante, one of the architects of St Peter's. Return to the bar and turn right down Via della Pace and then straight on down Vicolo delle Vacche and Via della Vetrina. Turn left on **Via dei Coronari**, renowned for its antiques shops. At the end of the street continue straight down the short Vicolo del Curato to emerge on Via del Banco di Santo Spirito. You may wish to turn right here to look at the **Ponte Sant'Angelo** and **Castel Sant'Angelo** (▶ 165).

6–7

If not, turn left and then first left on Via dei Banchi Nuovi. This leads eventually to **Piazza dell'Orologio**, named after the delightful clock

the piazza's far right. This forms part of the **Palazzo and Oratorio dei Filippini**, a complex largely rebuilt by Francesco Borromini after 1637. For a closer look at the Oratorio's facade, turn right (south) off the piazza down Via dei Filippini. You emerge on the busy Corso Vittorio Emanuele II in front of the 16th-century **Chiesa Nuova** ("new church"); the Oratorio is squeezed between the palace on the left and the church facade on the right. Look inside the Chiesa Nuova to admire Pietro da Cortona's ornate frescoes and the decoration (1664) of the vault, apse and dome, and three majestic paintings by Peter Paul Rubens (1608) in the presbytery around the high altar. Return to Piazza dell'Orologio and turn right to follow Via del Governo Vecchio – a more interesting walk than following Corso Vittorio Emanuele II – to Piazza del Pasquino and back to Piazza Navona.

One of many antiques shops on Via dei Coronari

Taking a Break

Try the trendy, ever-popular **Bar della Pace** (▶ 108) or the equally hip, but quieter **Bar del Fico** (▶ 112). Alternatively, there are plenty of cafés from which to choose in Piazza Navona.

Places to Visit

Galleria Colonna
✚ 195 F3 ⊠ Via della Pilotta 17 ☎ 06 678 4350 ⊙ Sat 9–1. Closed Aug ⚫ Moderate

Sant'Agostino
✚ 194 C4 ⊠ Via di Sant'Agostino ☎ 06 6880 1962 ⊙ Daily 8–noon, 4:30–7:30

Santa Maria della Pace
✚ 194 C4 ⊠ Vicolo dell'Arco della Pace 5 ☎ 06 686 1156 ⊙ Tue–Fri 10–12:45 (but hours may vary)

Chiesa Nuova
✚ 194 B3 ⊠ Piazza della Chiesa Nuova

3 PIAZZA DEL POPOLO

Walk

This short walk offers memorable views over the city from above Piazza di Spagna and concludes in Piazza del Popolo, the northernmost square of the "old" Rome. It also gives you the chance to explore the Pincio Gardens (Giardino del Pincio), on the fringes of the Villa Borghese, the city's principal park. The walk can easily be extended to take in the park.

1–2

Start in Piazza di Spagna (▶ 126–127), allowing time to look at the shops here and in the surrounding grid of streets. Admire the **Fontana della Barcaccia** at the foot of the Spanish Steps, and decide if you wish to visit the **Keats-Shelley museum** (▶ 135). Then climb to the top of the Spanish Steps. Turn to admire the view over the piazza below and spend a few moments inside the church of **Trinità dei Monti** at the top of the steps. It is best known for its frescoed chapels and for two faded 16th-century paintings by

Daniele da Volterra. The obelisk in front of the church was raised here in 1788, but was brought to Rome in the 2nd or 3rd century AD, when its hieroglyphics were carved in emulation of those on a similar obelisk in Piazza del Popolo.

2–3

From the piazza in front of Trinità dei Monti turn left as you face the church. This takes you into **Viale Trinità dei Monti**, a street that hugs the side of the hill and offers fine views over the city's roof-tops towards the dome of St Peter's in the middle distance. After the street kinks slightly to the left, you pass the **Villa Medici** on your right, bought by Napoleon in 1801 and home to the French Academy since 1803. It was built in about 1540 for a Tuscan cardinal, and purchased in 1576 by Ferdinando de' Medici, a member of the famous Florentine family. Much of the family's

sculpture collection was kept here before being returned to Florence. The scientist Galileo was a famous if reluctant occupant of the villa, having been kept here by the Inquisition between 1630 and 1633. The villa is open only rarely, but hosts occasional exhibitions. The magnificent gardens also open intermittently – currently Sunday morning – but are well worth seeing.

3–4

Viale Trinità dei Monti ends at the junction with Viale Mickiewicz (or Viale Mickiew) and Viale Gabriele d'Annunzio. Turn right on the former to climb to the **Pincio**, a series of gardens laid out between 1809 and 1814 on the Pincian Hill. The area has a long history as an open space, having formed ancient Rome's *Collis Hortulorum*, a series of gardens belonging to the emperors and several of the city's most

The water clock in the Pincio Gardens

An ancient Egyptian obelisk dominates Piazza del Popolo

important Roman roads, the Via Cassia and Via Flaminia, entered the city at this point, following the line of the present Via del Corso to the Capitoline Hill and Roman and Imperial fora (▶ 48–49 and 50–55). Today, the square is dominated by the obelisk of Pharaoh Rameses II, brought from Egypt by Emperor Augustus in the 1st century and raised here in 1589. On the square's northern flank stands the important church of **Santa Maria del Popolo** (▶ 103–104), while on its southern edge rise the two almost identical 17th-century churches of **Santa Maria dei Miracoli** and **Santa Maria di Montesanto**. From the piazza you can return to central Rome either down Via del Corso – which is lined with clothes and other shops – or the quieter Via di Ripetta, the latter route allows you to

prominent aristocratic families. Turn left where the Viale doglegs right to become Viale Belvedere and make for Piazzale Napoleone I, the best of several good viewpoints, before exploring the garden. If you wish to push on to the Villa Borghese for a longer walk, follow Viale dell'Obelisco east from Piazza Bucarest and its obelisk. Otherwise retrace your steps and return to Viale Gabriele d'Annunzio and turn right to follow this street down to **Piazza del Popolo.**

4–5

Piazza del Popolo's present appearance dates largely from the 16th century, but it formed the old city's northern focus long before that. Two

Taking a Break

Canova (Piazza del Popolo 16, tel: 06 361 2231, open daily 7:30–10:30 or later) in the Piazza del Popolo is a lively place for a drink

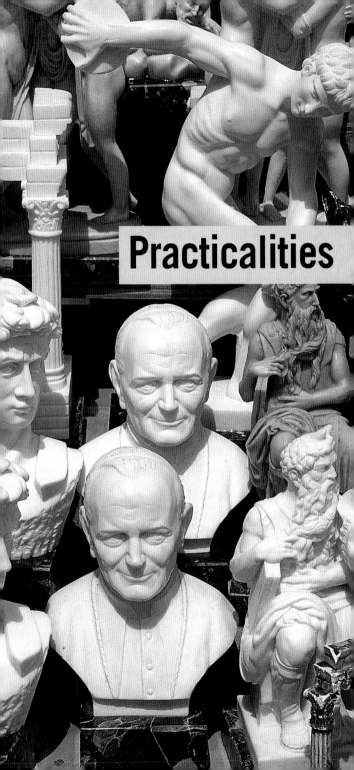

Practicalities

GETTING ADVANCE INFORMATION

Websites
- Official tourism site of the City of Rome: www.romaturismo.it
- Rome City Council: www.comune.roma.it
- Museum on-line reservations: www.ticketeria.it
- Official Vatican site for all aspects of the Holy See: www.vatican.va

In Italy
Ente Provinciale per II Turismo di Roma (ENIT)
Via Parigi 5, Roma
☎ 06 3600 4399
   06 488 991

BEFORE YOU GO

WHAT YOU NEED

		UK	Germany	USA	Canada	Australia	Ireland	Netherlands
● Required ○ Suggested ▲ Not required △ Not applicable	Some countries require a passport to remain valid for a minimum period (usually at least six months) beyond the date of entry – check before you travel.							
Passport/National Identity Card		●	●	●	●	●	●	●
Visa (regulations can change – check before you travel)		▲	▲	▲	▲	▲	▲	▲
Onward or Return Ticket		○	○	●	●	●	○	○
Health Inoculations (tetanus and polio)		▲	▲	▲	▲	▲	▲	▲
Health Documentation		○	○	▲	▲	▲	○	○
Travel Insurance		○	○	○	○	○	○	○
Driver's Licence (national)		●	●	●	●	●	●	●
Car Insurance Certificate		●	●	●	●	●	●	●
Car Registration Document		●	●	●	●	●	●	●

WHEN TO GO

Rome

☐ High season   ☐ Low season

JAN	FEB	MAR	APR	MAY	JUN	JUL	AUG	SEP	OCT	NOV	DE
7°C	8°C	12°C	14°C	18°C	25°C	28°C	32°C	23°C	18°C	13°C	9°
45°F	46°F	54°F	57°F	64°F	77°F	82°F	90°F	73°F	64°F	55°F	48

☀ Sun   ☁ Cloud   🌧 Wet   ⛅ Sun/Showers

Temperatures are the **average daily maximum** for each month, although temperatures of over 35°C (95°F) are likely in July and August, making the city extremely hot and uncomfortable. Average daily minimum temperatures are approximately 6 to 10°C (10–18°F) lower.

The best times of the year for good weather are May, June, July, August and September. Thunderstorms are possible in summer and through September and October. Winters (January and February) are short and cold, but snow is extremely rare. Spring starts in March, but March and April can be humid and sometimes very rainy. Autumn weather is mixed, but often produces crisp or warm days with clear skies.

the UK	In the US	In Australia
T	ENIT	Italian Consulate
rinces Street	630 Fifth Avenue	Level 26,
don W1R 8AY	Suite 1565	44 Market Square
020 7408-1254	New York NY 10111	Sydney NSW 2000
	☎ 212/245-4822	☎ (02) 9262 1666

TTING THERE

Air Rome has two main airports: Leonardo da Vinci (better known as Fiumicino) and mpino. Most UK and other European and international carriers fly to Fiumicino. Low-cost d charter airlines usually fly to Ciampino. There are many non-stop flights to Rome from ndon (Heathrow, Gatwick and Stansted) as well as regional airports in the UK, most major ropean cities and many US and Canadian cities. Flights from Melbourne and Sydney ke one stop, usually in Bangkok; from other cities in Australia and New Zealand, the best nnections are in Hong Kong or Singapore.

ket prices tend to be highest at Easter, Christmas and in summer. Best prices are :ained the further you reserve in advance but check airlines, travel agents, newspapers d the internet for special offers. Non-direct flights via hub airports such as Heathrow or ankfurt may offer substantial savings. Short stays are generally expensive unless a turday night stay is included. City-break packages include flights and accommodation. **port taxes** are included in ticket prices and no fee is payable at either Rome airport. **pproximate flying times** to Rome: New Zealand (24 hours), east coast of Australia 1 hours), western US (11 hours), eastern US and Canada (8–10 hours); London (2 hours), ankfurt (1 hour).

Rail Ticket prices are usually the same or more than equivalent air fares. Numerous fast d overnight services operate to Rome from most European capitals, with connections from ajor towns. Rome has several stations, but most international services stop at Stazione rmini or Roma Tiburtina.

ME

Rome is one hour ahead of GMT in winter, one hour ahead of BST in summer, six hours ahead of New York and nine hours ahead of Los Angeles. Clocks are advanced one hour in April and turned back one hour in October.

JRRENCY AND FOREIGN EXCHANGE

urrency Italy is one of the majority of European Union countries to use a single urrency, the euro (€). Coins are issued in denominations of 1, 2, 5, 10, 20 and 50 ents and €1 and €2. Notes are issued in denominations of €5, €10, €20, €50, 00, €200 and €500.

change Most major **travellers' cheques** – the best way to carry money – can be anged at exchange kiosks (*cambio*) at the airports, at Termini railway station and in change offices near major tourist sights. Many banks also have exchange desks, but es can be long.

edit cards Most credit cards (*carta di credito*) are accepted in larger hotels, restaurants d shops, but cash is often preferred in smaller establishments. Credit cards can also e used to obtain cash from ATM cash dispensers, although this can be expensive – ost credit cards charge a fee for this. Contact your card issuer before you leave home find out which machines in Rome accept your card.

WHEN YOU ARE THERE

CLOTHING SIZES

UK	Rest of Europe	USA	
36	46	36	
38	48	38	
40	50	40	
42	52	42	Suits
44	54	44	
46	56	46	
7	41	8	
7.5	42	8.5	
8.5	43	9.5	
9.5	44	10.5	Shoes
10.5	45	11.5	
11	46	12	
14.5	37	14.5	
15	38	15	
15.5	39/40	15.5	
16	41	16	Shirts
16.5	42	16.5	
17	43	17	
8	34	6	
10	36	8	
12	38	10	
14	40	12	Dresses
16	42	14	
18	44	16	
4.5	38	6	
5	38	6.5	
5.5	39	7	
6	39	7.5	Shoes
6.5	40	8	
7	41	8.5	

NATIONAL HOLIDAYS

1 Jan	New Year's Day
6 Jan	Epiphany
Mar/Apr	Easter Monday
25 Apr	Liberation Day
1 May	Labour Day
29 Jun	St Peter and St Paul Day
15 Aug	Assumption of the Virgin
1 Nov	All Saints' Day
8 Dec	Feast of the Immaculate Conception
25 Dec	Christmas Day
26 Dec	St Stephen's Day

OPENING HOURS

○ Shops ● Post Offices
● Offices ◐ Museums/Monument
◐ Banks ◐ Pharmacies

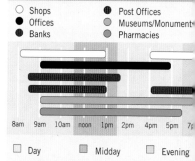

8am 9am 10am noon 1pm 2pm 4pm 5pm 7p

□ Day ▨ Midday □ Evening

Shops Hours vary. Usually Tue–Sat 8–1, 4–8pm; Mon 4–8pm. Many stores now open all day (*orar continuato*) from 9:30 or 10 to 7 or 7:30.

Restaurants Usually 12:30–3, 7:30–10:30pm; many close Sun evening and Mon lunchtime, wit a statutory closing day (*riposo settimanale*)

Museums Hours vary greatly: usually Tue–Sat 9–7 Sun 9–1.

Churches Usually daily 7–noon, 4:30–7pm, but closed during services.

Banks Major branches may also open Sat and hav longer weekday hours.

Post offices Usually Mon–Fri 8:15–2, Sat 8:15–noon or 2.

EMERGENCY	113
POLICE	113 or 112
FIRE	113 or 115
AMBULANCE	113 or 118

RSONAL SAFETY

me is generally safe – pick-
ckets are the main worry –
t take precautions:
Carry money and valuables
in a belt or pouch.
Wear your camera – never
put it down.
Leave valuables and jew-
ellery in the hotel safe.
Avoid gangs of street children. If approached, hang
on to your possessions,
raise your voice and – if
necessary – use force to
push them away.
Guard against pickpockets,
especially in tourist areas.
Avoid parks and the streets
around Termini at night.

ice assistance:
113 from any phone

TELEPHONES

Telecom Italia (TI)
payphones are on
streets and in bars,
tobacconists and
restaurants. Most
take coins or a
phone card (una
scheda telefonica),

bought from post offices, shops
or bars. Tear the corner off the
card before use.
To dial numbers in Rome while
there, dial the 06 code then
the number. Cheap rate is
Mon–Sat 10pm–8am. Hotels
usually add a surcharge to calls
from rooms. Dial 170 to make
reverse charge calls. Dial 12 for
operator or directory enquiries.

International Dialling Codes
Dial 00 followed by

UK:	44
USA / Canada:	1
Irish Republic:	353
Australia:	61
Germany:	49

POST

Rome's central post office
(ufficio postale) is at Piazza
San Silvestro 18–20. Stamps
(francobolli) are bought from
post offices and bars. Mail
boxes are red (slots for city
mail and other destinations),
or blue for the more efficient
posta prioritaria (priority post).

ELECTRICITY

urrent is 220 volts AC, 50
ycles. Plugs are two-round-
n continental types; UK
and North
American visitors
will require an
daptor. North American visi-
rs should check whether
10/120-volt AC appliances
quire a voltage transformer.

TIPS/GRATUITIES

Tipping is not expected for all services and rates are
lower than those elsewhere. As a general guide:

Pizzerias	Nearest €0.50 or €2.50
Trattorias	Nearest €0.50 or €2.50
Smart restaurant	10 per cent or discretion
Bar service	€0.10–€0.25
Tour guides	Discretion
Taxis	Round up to nearest €0.50
Porters	€0.50–€1 per bag
Chambermaids	€0.50–€1 a day

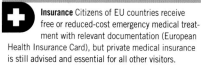

UK
☎ 06 4220 0001

USA
☎ 06 46 741

Ireland
☎ 06 697 9121

Australia
☎ 06 8527 2299

New Zeala
☎ 06 441 7

HEALTH

Insurance Citizens of EU countries receive free or reduced-cost emergency medical treatment with relevant documentation (European Health Insurance Card), but private medical insurance is still advised and essential for all other visitors.

Doctors Ask at your hotel for details of English-speaking doctors.
Dental Services Travel insurance should cover dental treatment, which is expensive.

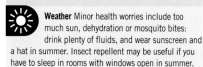

Weather Minor health worries include too much sun, dehydration or mosquito bites: drink plenty of fluids, and wear sunscreen and a hat in summer. Insect repellent may be useful if you have to sleep in rooms with windows open in summer.

Drugs Prescription and other medicines are available from a chemist (*una farmacia*), indicated by a green cross. Hours are usually Mon–Sat 8:30–1 and 4–8pm, but a rota system ensures that some are always open. Two 24-hour pharmacies are: Piram (Via Nazionale 228, tel: 06 488 0754); Farmacia della Stazione (Piazza dei Cinquecento-corner Via Cavour, tel: 06 488 0019).

Safe Water Tap water is safe. So, too, is water from public drinking fountains unless marked "*Acqua Non Potabile*".

CONCESSIONS

Young People/Senior Citizens Young visitors and students aged under 18 from European Union countries are entitled to free entrance or reduced rates to most galleries. Similar concessions are available to senior citizens over 60. A passport will be required as proof of age.

Museums/Galleries The Special Museum Card (€7) gives entry to each of the Palazzo Altemps, Palazzo Massimo alle Terme, Crypta Balbi and Terme di Dioclenziano. The Archeologia card (€20) gives entry to these four sights plus the Colosseum, Palatino, Terme di Caracalla, Villa dei Quintili and Tomba di Cecilia Metella. Both are valid seven days and can be obtained from participating sights.

TRAVELLING WITH A DISABILITY

Rome is a difficult city for those with disabilities, espe cially if you use a wheelcha Streets are narrow, busy, of cobbled and usually filled with badly parked cars. The are few pavements or dropp kerbs. Transport, museums, hotels and other public spaces are improving, but much remains to be done. For information on accessib ity, contact the Consorzio Cooperative Integrate (CO.II Via Enrico Giglioli 54a, tel: 06 712 9011 (www.coinsociale.it) or the "COINtel" phone informatic service 06 2326 9231.

CHILDREN

Most hotels, bars and restau rants welcome children, but few have baby-changing facilities. Be extremely care ful with young children on Rome's busy streets.

TOILETS

Best facilities are in hotels; Rome has few public toilets Bars have toilets, but standards are poor. Ask for *il bagno* or *il gabinetto*.

LOST PROPERTY

Airport 06 6595 3343
Buses 06 581 6040
Metro 06 487 4309 (Line A 06 5753 2264/5 (Line B)

RVIVAL PHRASES

s/no **Sì/non**
ease **Per favore**
ank you **Grazie**
u're welcome **Di niente/prego**
m sorry **Mi dispiace**
oodbye **Arrivederci**
ood morning **Buongiorno**
oodnight **Buona sera**
ow are you? **Come sta?**
ow much? **Quanto costa?**
would like... **Vorrei...**
pen **Aperto**
osed **Chiuso**
day **Oggi**
morrow **Domani**
onday **lunedì**
esday **martedì**
ednesday **mercoledì**
ursday **giovedì**
iday **venerdì**
turday **sabato**
nday **domenica**

RECTIONS

lost **Mi sono perso/a**
ere is...? **Dove si trova...?**
he station **la stazione**
he telephone **il telefono**
he bank **la banca**
he toilet **il bagno**
rn left **Volti a sinistra**
rn right **Volti a destra**
straight on **Vada dritto**
the corner **All'angolo**
e street **la strada**
e building **il edificio**
e traffic light **il semaforo**
e crossroads **l'incrocio**
e signs for...
e indicazione per...

IF YOU NEED HELP

Help! **Aiuto!**
Could you help me, please?
   Mi potrebbe aiutare?
Do you speak English? **Parla inglese?**
I don't understand **Non capisco**
Please could you call a doctor
   quickly? **Mi chiami presto un
   medico, per favore**

RESTAURANT

I'd like to book a table
   Vorrei prenotare un tavolo
A table for two please
   Un tavolo per due, per favore
Could we see the menu, please?
   Ci porta la lista, per favore?
What's this? **Cosa è questo?**
A bottle of/a glass of...
   Un bottiglia di/un bicchiere di...
Could I have the bill?
   Ci porta il conto

ACCOMMODATION

Do you have a single/double room?
   Ha una camera singola / doppia?
with/without bath/toilet/shower
   **con/senza vasca/gabinetto/
   doccia**
Does that include breakfast?
   E'inclusa la prima colazione?
Does that include dinner?
   E'inclusa la cena?
Do you have room service?
   C'è il servizio in camera?
Could I see the room?
   E' possibile vedere la camera?
I'll take this room **Prendo questa**
Thanks for your hospitality
   Grazie per l'ospitalità

MBERS

zero	12	**dodici**	30	**trenta**	200	**duecento**
uno	13	**tredici**	40	**quaranta**	300	**trecento**
due	14	**quattordici**	50	**cinquanta**	400	**quattrocento**
tre	15	**quindici**	60	**sessanta**	500	**cinquecento**
quattro	16	**sedici**	70	**settanta**	600	**seicento**
cinque	17	**diciassette**	80	**ottanta**	700	**settecento**
sei	18	**diciotto**	90	**novanta**	800	**ottocento**
sette	19	**diciannove**	100	**cento**	900	**novecento**
otto	20	**venti**			1000	**mille**
nove			101	**cento uno**	2000	**duemila**
dieci	21	**ventuno**	110	**centodieci**		
undici	22	**ventidue**	120	**centoventi**	10,000	**diecimila**

MENU READER

acciuga anchovy
acqua water
affettati sliced
  cured meats
affumicato
  smoked
aglio garlic
agnello lamb
anatra duck
antipasti
  hors d'oeuvres
arista roast pork
arrosto roast
asparagi
  asparagus
birra beer
bistecca steak
bollito
  boiled meat
braciola
  minute steak
brasato braised
brodo broth
bruschetta
  toasted bread
  with garlic or
  tomato
  topping
budino pudding
burro butter
cacciagione
  game
cacciatore, alla
  rich tomato
  sauce with
  mushrooms
caffè corretto /
  macchiato
  coffee with
  liqueur/spirit,
  or with a drop
  of milk
caffè freddo
  iced coffee
caffè lungo
  weak coffee
caffè latte
  milky coffee
caffè ristretto
  strong coffee
calamaro squid
cappero caper
carciofo
  artichoke
carota carrot
carne meat
carpa carp

casalingo
  home-made
cassata
  Sicilian fruit
  ice-cream
cavolfiore
  cauliflower
cavolo
  cabbage
ceci chickpeas
cervello brains
cervo venison
cetriolino
  gherkin
cetriolo
  cucumber
cicoria chicory
cinghiale boar
cioccolata
  chocolate
cipolla onion
coda di bue
  oxtail
coniglio rabbit
contorni
  vegetables
coperto
  cover charge
coscia
  leg of meat
cotolette cutlets
cozze mussels
crema custard
crostini canapé
  with savoury
  toppings or
  croutons
crudo raw
digestivo after-
  dinner liqueur
dolci cakes /
  desserts
erbe aromatiche
  herbs
fagioli beans
fagiolini
  green beans
faraona
  guinea fowl
farcito stuffed
fegato liver
finocchio fennel
formaggio
  cheese
forno, al baked
frittata omelette
fritto fried
frizzante fizzy
frulatto whisked

frutti di mare
  seafood
frutta fruit
funghi
  mushrooms
gamberetto
  shrimp
gelato ice-cream
ghiaccio ice
gnocchi potato
  dumplings
granchio crab
gran(o)turco
  corn
griglia, alla
  grilled
imbottito
  stuffed
insalata salad
IVA VAT
latte milk
lepre hare
lumache snails
manzo beef
merluzzo cod
miele honey
minestra soup
molluschi
  shellfish
olio oil
oliva olive
ostrica oyster
pancetta bacon
pane bread
panna cream
parmigiano
  Parmesan
passata sieved
  or creamed
pastasciutta
  dried pasta
  with sauce
pasta sfoglia
  puff pastry
patate fritte
  chips
pecora mutton
pecorino
  sheep's milk
  cheese
peperoncino
  chilli
peperone red /
  green pepper
pesce fish
petto breast
piccione
  pigeon
piselli peas

pollame fowl
pollo chicke?
polpetta
  meatball
porto port wi?
prezzemolo
  parsley
primo piatto
  first course
prosciutto
  cured ham
ragù meat sa?
ripieno stuffe?
riso rice
salsa sauce
salsiccia
  sausage
saltimbocca
  veal with
  prosciutto ?
  sage
secco dry
secondo piatt?
  main cours?
senape must?
servizio comp?
  service cha?
  included
sogliola sole
spuntini snac?
succo di frutt?
  fruit juice
sugo sauce
tonno tuna
uova strapazz?
  scambled e?
uovo affogato
  in carnica
  poached eg?
uovo al tegam?
  fritto
  fried egg
uovo alla coq?
  soft-boiled
uovo alla sod?
  hard-boiled?
vino bianco
  white wine
vino rosso
  red wine
vino rosato
  rosé wine
verdure
  vegetables
vitello veal
zucchero sug?
zucchino
  courgette
zuppa soup

Streetplan

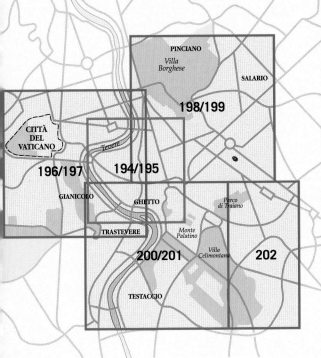

PINCIANO

Villa Borghese

SALARIO

198/199

CITTÀ DEL VATICANO

Tevere

196/197

194/195

GIANICOLO

GHETTO

Parco di Traiano

TRASTEVERE

Monte Palatino

Villa Celimontana

200/201

202

TESTACCIO

Legend

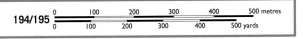

Main road	Park
Other road	Important Building
Steps	Featured place of interest
Rail line	Metro station

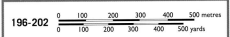

194/195 0 100 200 300 400 500 metres
0 100 200 300 400 500 yards

196-202 0 100 200 300 400 500 metres
0 100 200 300 400 500 yards

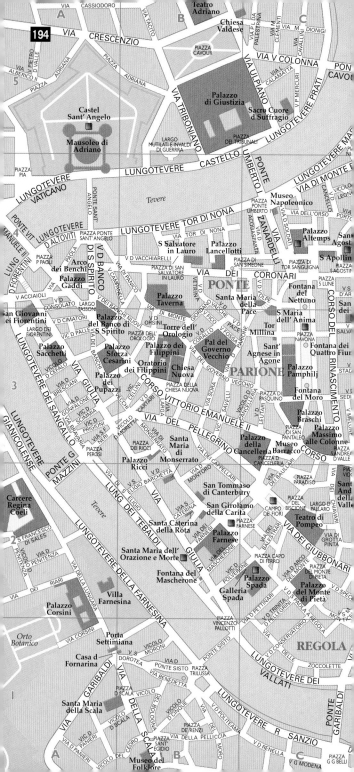

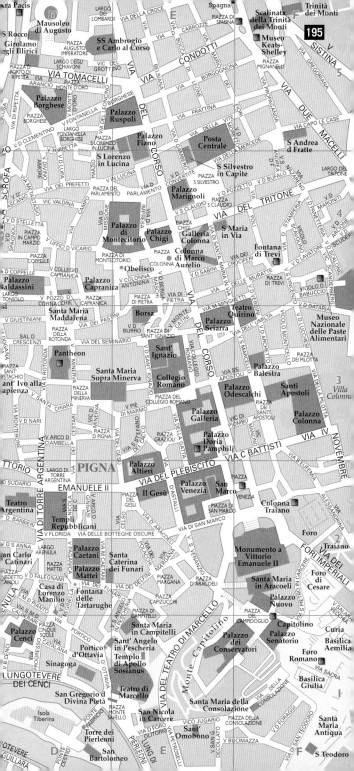

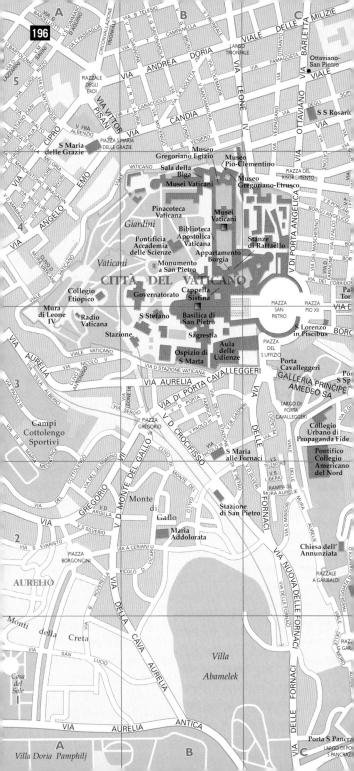

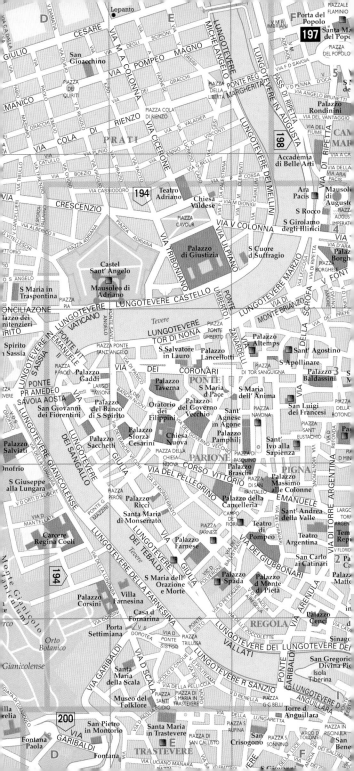

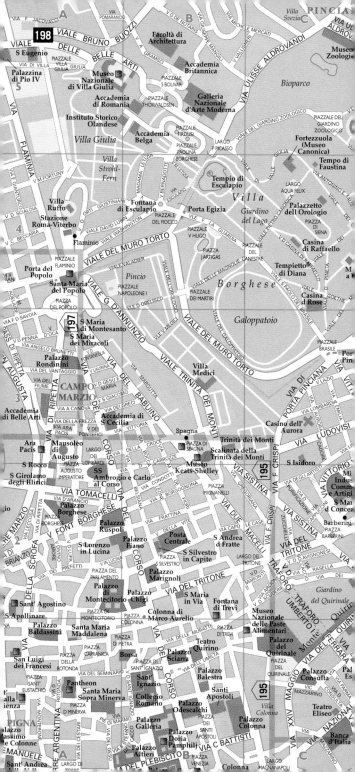

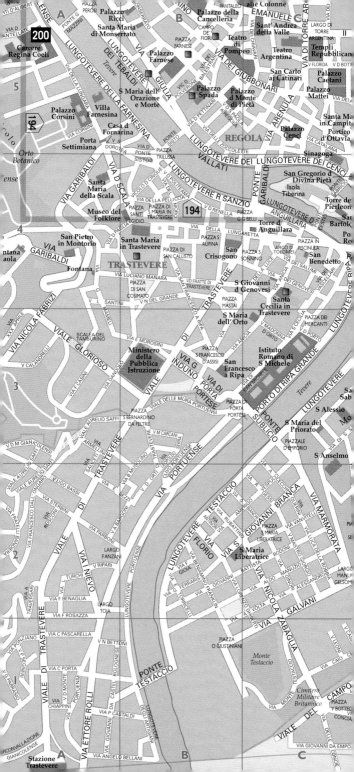

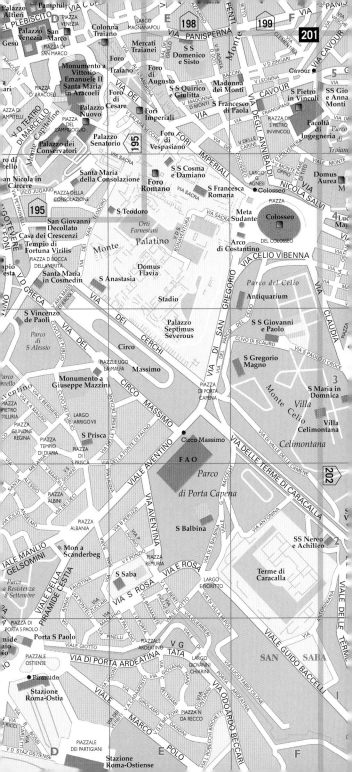

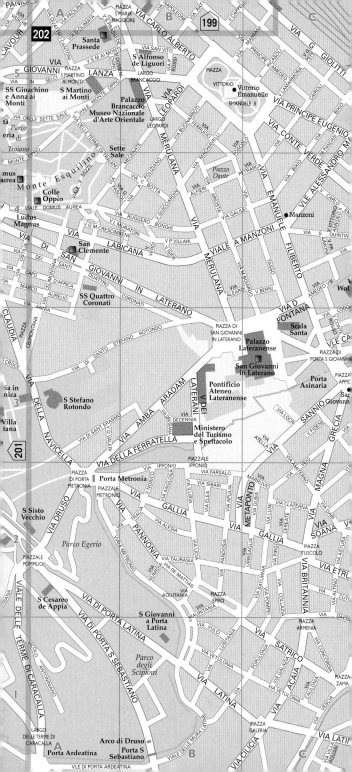

Picture credits

Front and back covers: (t) AA Photo Library/Dario Miterdiri; (ct) AA Photo Library/
Simon McBride; (cb) AA Photo Library/Jim Holmes; (b) AA Photo Library/
Clive Sawyer; Spine AA Photo Library/Simon McBride

The Automobile Association wishes to thank the following photographers and libraries
for their assistance with the preparation of this book.
AKG, LONDON 14b, 17l, 57t, 71; ART DIRECTORS AND TRIP PHOTO LIBRARY 12t
(C Rennie), 47b (C Rennie), 65t (C Rennie), 114t (C Rennie), 118/9 (C Rennie); AXIOM
PHOTOGRAPHIC AGENCY 119 (J Morris); BRIDGEMAN ART LIBRARY, LONDON 6
The Colosseum and Alban Mount (w/c and gouache over pencil, chalk and ink) by
Samuel Palmer (1805-81) Ashmolean Museum, Oxford, UK, 13t David by Gian Lorenzo
Bernini (1598-1680) (marble) (detail) Galleria Borghese, Rome, Italy, 13b View of the
exterior facade, designed by Francesco Borromini (1599-1667) 1638-77(photo) San
Carlo alle Quattro Fontane, Rome, Italy/Joseph Martin, 21bl Ignudo from the Sistine
Ceiling (pre-restoration) by Michelangelo Buonarroti (1475-1564) Vatican Museums and
Galleries, Vatican City, Italy, 104 The Conversation of St Paul, 1601 (oil on canvas) by
Michelangelo Merisi da Caravaggio (1571-1610) Santa Maria del Popolo, Rome, Italy,
131 The Entombment, 1507 by Raphael (Raffaello Sanzio of Urbino) (1483-1520)
Galleria Borghese, Rome, Italy, 134 La Fornarina, c. 1516 (panel) by Raphael (Raffaello
Sanzio of Urbino) (1483-1520) Palazzo Barberini, Rome, Italy, 144 Sistine Chapel ceiling
and lunettes, 1508-12 (fresco) (post restoration) by Michelangelo Buonarroti (1475-
1564) Vatican Museums and Galleries, Vatican City, Italy, 146t Sistine Chapel Ceiling:
Creation of Adam, 1510 (fresco) (post restoration) by Michelangelo Buonarroti (1475-
1564) Vatican Museums and Galleries, Vatican City, Italy, 153 Sistine Chapel Ceiling,
1508-12 (fresco) (post restoration) by Michelangelo Buonarroti (1475-1564) Vatican
Museums and Galleries, Vatican City, Italy; CEPHAS 174 (Mick Rock); MARY EVANS
PICTURE LIBRARY 6-8 b/g, 8t; GETTYONE/STONE 2 (i), 2(iii), 3 (iii), 5, 20-3, 21br,
43, 45, 56, 82/3, 125, 126, 154, 156/7, 169; THE RONALD GRANT ARCHIVE 124;
ROBERT HARDING PICTURE LIBRARY 58b, 60, 90/1; JOHN HESELTINE ARCHIVE
10t, 11b, 12b, 14t, 16tr, 16c, 64/5, 65b, 87, 165, 171; IMAGES COLOUR LIBRARY 3 (ii),
3 (iv), 18/9, 20, 51b, 116b, 143, 145, 161, 175, 177; THE KOBAL COLLECTION 8b
(20th Century Fox); MARKA 81b (M Cristofori), 116t (F Garufi), 121 (F Garufi), 123
(F Garufi); POPPERFOTO 19; SCALA 2 (iv), 3 (i), 15, 17r, 47c, 61, 62, 75, 86, 88, 96,
113, 120, 122, 128, 129, 130b, 146b, 149t, 149b, 150b, 151t, 160t, 162.

The remaining photographs are held in the Association's own photo library (AA
PHOTO LIBRARY) and were taken by ALEX KOUPRIANOFF except for the following:
Jim Holmes 7, 20/1t, 20/1b, 22tr, 22br, 23b, 25t, 44, 57b, 62/3, 66, 77t, 77b, 80b, 81t,
83t, 84, 89, 93, 97b, 106, 117t, 135, 147t, 147b, 150t, 158/9, 159, 160b, 163, 180; Dario
Miterdiri 16tl, 24/5, 48/9, 58t b/g, 69, 100, 101, 103, 117c, 127, 130t, 133, 157; Clive
Sawyer 22cb, 25b, 54/5, 76t, 76b, 85, 164, 173; Peter Wilson 55, 58c, 59, 67, 151b, 158.

SPIRAL GUIDES

Questionnaire

Dear Traveler

Your comments, opinions and recommendations are very important to us. So please help us to improve our travel guides by taking a few minutes to complete this simple questionnaire.

Send to: Spiral Guides, MailStop 66, 1000 AAA Drive, Heathrow, FL 32746–5063

Your recommendations...

We always encourage readers' recommendations for restaurants, nightlife or shopping – if your recommendation is added to the next edition of the guide, we will send you a FREE AAA Spiral Guide of your choice. Please state below the establishment name, location and your reasons for recommending it.

_____

_____

_____

_____

_____

Please send me AAA Spiral_____
(see list of titles inside the back cover)

About this guide...

Which title did you buy?

_____ **AAA Spiral**

Where did you buy it? _____

When? m m / y y

Why did you choose a AAA Spiral Guide? _____

_____

_____

_____

Did this guide meet your expectations?

Exceeded ☐   Met all ☐   Met most ☐   Fell below ☐

Please give your reasons _____

_____

_____

_____

continued on next page...

Were there any aspects of this guide that you particularly liked?

_____

_____

_____

_____

_____

Is there anything we could have done better?

_____

_____

_____

_____

About you...

Name (Mr/Mrs/Ms) _____

Address _____

_____

_____ Zip _____

Daytime tel nos. _____

Which age group are you in?

Under 25 ☐ 25–34 ☐ 35–44 ☐ 45–54 ☐ 55–64 ☐ 65+ ☐

How many trips do you make a year?

Less than one ☐ One ☐ Two ☐ Three or more ☐

Are you a AAA member? Yes ☐ No ☐

Name of AAA club _____

About your trip...

When did you book? m m / y y   When did you travel? m m / y y

How long did you stay? _____

Was it for business or leisure? _____

Did you buy any other travel guides for your trip? ☐ Yes   ☐ No

If yes, which ones? _____

_____

Thank you for taking the time to complete this questionnaire.